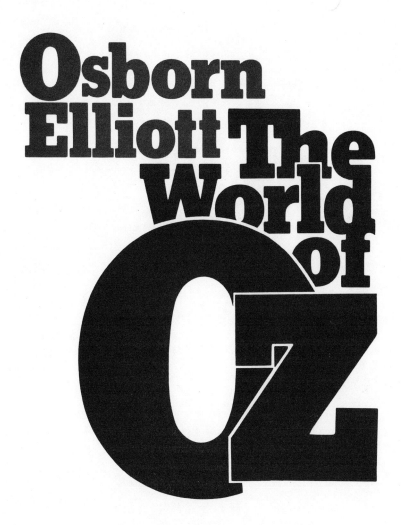

Osborn Elliott The World of Oz

THE VIKING PRESS · NEW YORK

LIBRARY OF CONGRESS CATALOGING IN PUBLICATION DATA
Elliott, Osborn.
The world of Oz.
1. Elliott, Osborn. 2. Journalists—United States
—Biography. I. Title.
PN4874.E6A38   070.4′092′4 [B]   79–20649
ISBN 0–670–78770–1

Printed in the United States of America
Set in Linotype Baskerville

ACKNOWLEDGMENTS

Selection from Stewart Alsop's letter to Osborn Elliott, copyright © 1980
by Joseph Alsop, Trustee, Stewart J. O. Alsop Trust. Used by permission
of the Estate of the Author.

An excerpt from "The Quaker Graveyard in Nantucket" in *Lord
Weary's Castle* by Robert Lowell, copyright 1946, 1974 by Robert Lowell.
Reprinted by permission of Harcourt Brace Jovanovich, Inc., and Faber
and Faber Ltd.

A selection from "When Lilacs Last in the Dooryard Bloom'd" from *The
Complete Poetry of Walt Whitman,* edited by J. E. Miller. Reprinted by
permission of Houghton Mifflin Company.

"Richard Cory" by Edwin Arlington Robinson from *The Children of
the Night* is reprinted by permission of Charles Scribner's Sons.

Selections from letters by John Steinbeck to Yevtushenko, Simonov, and
Tvardovsky, copyright © 1980 by Elaine Steinbeck, John Steinbeck IV,
and Thom Steinbeck. Used by permission of the author's heirs.

Lyrics from "New York, New York" from *On the Town* by Betty
Comden and Adolph Green, copyright 1945, 1949 by Warner Bros. Inc.
Copyright renewed © 1973, 1977 by Warner Bros. Inc. Used by permission
of Warner Bros. Music.

All photographs not credited are from the author's collection.

HONORING MY FATHER AND MY MOTHER
ADMIRING MY BROTHER
LOVING MY WIFE AND OUR CHILDREN

FOR INGER

PREFACE
Who? What? Where?
When? Why? How?

I have always been hooked on journalism—as an eight-year-old pecking out my first "newspaper" on a toy typewriter, as a cub reporter for *The New York Journal of Commerce*, as a young writer for *Time*, as editor of *Newsweek*, and as dean of Columbia University's Graduate School of Journalism. I have long been impressed by journalism's demands for compression and clarity; enchanted—mostly—by its practitioners and their oft-feigned cynicism; flattered by the access it offers to statesmen, artists, and tycoons; infuriated by its imperfections—and as often as not, no doubt, blind to them as well.

In the course of three decades as a professional journalist, I have found the rewards enormous. From a front-row seat in the press box, I have been privileged to witness some of the most heroic, and some of the most horrible events of our times—the conquest of space, the fight for civil rights, the women's movement for equality, the Vietnam war, the campus rebellion, the sexual revolution, the urban crisis, mindless assassinations of public figures—as well as mindless assaults by certain public figures on public institutions. These happenings left their mark on all Americans; where they affected me particularly, I have tried to tell how and why in these pages.

Over the years, I have had interviews with five presidents, audiences with two popes and the emperor of Japan. I traveled to Africa and Australia and Vietnam and the Soviet Union—and spent the most interesting week in my life living, and learning, in the black ghettos of America. I also enjoyed myself. I was nattered at by Nasser, charmed by Giscard, irritated by Indira. I fell in love (unrequited) with the likes of Bacall, Sills, MacLaine, and Ullmann. I called Leonard "Lenny," Henry "Henry," and Teddy "Ted." I ran a big magazine which, I like to think, became something of a force in the journalism of our day. And I was extremely well paid for having all that fun for all those years.

To this day, my friends are mostly journalists. I belong to a happily purposeless lunch club whose other members are Theodore White, the journalist-author; John Chancellor, the journalist-anchorman; Richard Clurman, the journalist-consultant; Irving Kristol, the journalist-professor; A. M. Rosenthal, the executive editor of *The New York Times,* and his associate, Arthur Gelb; and William F. Buckley Jr., the journalist-everything. We swap stories, get one-up on each other, and talk about the world—or at least the world as it is viewed by *The New York Times.* We come to no conclusions that I have yet been able to discern. We can't even reach a decision on a new name for the group, which for some reason has always been called the Rosenthal for President Club. It has been suggested that we rename ourselves the Buckley for Columnist Club, but seven of the eight members think that this would be reaching for the impossible, so we have kept the original title for more than ten years.

It was at a meeting of our group, in the spring of 1978, that I first decided I would write this book. Having dispensed with the important business of the day—in that instance, the perils of being audited by the Internal Revenue Service—we turned to lesser matters, such as the neutron bomb and the normalization of relations with China. Then, suddenly, Buckley leaned across his round-and-shiny-marble dining table, nearly knocking over the Mouton Rothschild, and fixed me with the famous stare that stoppeth one in three.

"What are you up to, Oz?" he asked.

I had recently finished a year or so as a deputy mayor of New York, having before that left *Newsweek* after twenty-one years. I gazed back at the Ancient Mariner.

"I'm writing a book," I said.

· · ·

I offer here no Sermon on the Mount, no solemn exegesis on morality and sin. I hope this notebook of people, places, and events will entertain and even instruct those who have had more than a passing interest in the tumultuous events of the recent past.

The book is dedicated to my wife, whose editorial suggestions were irritatingly correct throughout, and who was able to keep her business going smoothly, and our complicated family life going tenderly, despite the lout who spent the better part of a year typing grouchily in the back room.

To Thomas Guinzburg, go my thanks for his initial faith in the book. To Olga Barbi Aparicio, my longtime colleague at *Newsweek*, my appreciation for her painstaking exactitude in checking facts, filling many potholes in my memory, and undertaking the horrible job of styling and typing the manuscript over and over again. To Robert Silver, a tip of the hat for his good editorial suggestions.

And from one editor to another, a special tribute: Thank you, Elisabeth Sifton, for reminding me that even (or especially) an editor needs an editor; to use your most unfavorite word, which you will find in only one other passage here, you had quite an *impact* on me.

My greatest appreciation, and heartfelt gratitude, go to all my friends at *Newsweek*. They enriched my life. And they made me look pretty good.

CONTENTS

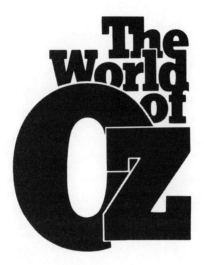

·I·
PHIL

I loved Phil Graham, he was my friend and boss. Phil the witty, Phil the brilliant, Phil the electric—that long and lanky, graceful, handsome, generous, joyous, mean, impossible, tragic, comic, manic-depressive Phil. His smile could light an avenue.

His background was middle-class Floridian, some politics, some cattle, some real estate. At Harvard Law School in the 1930s, he became president of the *Law Review;* when he went to Washington, he clerked for Stanley Reed and Felix Frankfurter. He cut a glittering path. He married big money, and made it bigger—and always wondered if he could have made it on his own. He killed himself when he was forty-seven. He was so intelligent that friends still argue, seventeen years later, whether he was truly mad when he placed that shotgun to his head—or whether he took his life in a moment of rationality, fearing what destruction he might inflict if he allowed himself to live.

Graham was a friend of John Kennedy and a friend of Lyndon Johnson. In hotel-room dealings at the 1960 Democratic National Convention in Los Angeles, he helped persuade Kennedy to offer the vice-presidency to LBJ. Graham was, by then, well established as the publisher of *The Washington Post,* but even without that leverage he would have been a force. He had that lean and hungry look.

He was hungry to be the best, the biggest, the most powerful publisher in America, and late that year opportunity came knocking—with a little bit of help from Phil's friends. *Newsweek,* the poor-second Johnny-come-lately of the newsmagazines, was up for sale. Vincent Astor, who owned most of the magazine's stock, had died, and his holdings now reposed in the Vincent Astor Foundation, whose board wanted no part of so risky a venture as a magazine in its portfolio. Suddenly, prospective buyers were popping out from behind the potted palms of the Plaza Hotel in New York and other watering spots around the country.

One of the aspiring purchasers was Malcolm Muir, who had for years run *Newsweek* for Vincent Astor; Muir and his family were frantically trying to put together a group to buy the magazine that he had bossed for so long. But Muir was on the outs with Astor's widow, Brooke, who now controlled the Astor Foundation, and it seemed a hopeless proposition. Doubleday was interested. So was S. I. Newhouse, owner of twenty-nine newspapers as well as *Vogue, House & Garden,* and *Mademoiselle.* Charles Spalding, a Kennedy friend and deal-maker, made a run, too.

The corridors of *Newsweek* shivered with rumors. The editor, John Denson, left to become editor of the New York *Herald Tribune,* a job he thought would provide more security, greater challenge, and a surer road to riches. Meanwhile, morale was plummeting at *Newsweek.* Gibson McCabe, president of the company, was the senior non-Muir on the business side of the magazine; I, as managing editor, was the senior non-Muir on the editorial side. Almost daily, McCabe and I were being romanced by eager investors seeking support from within the company. We had more surreptitious drinks with more secretive people in more dim bars and restaurants than either of us can now remember. In each and every case, we explained that we could not possibly join forces with outside bidders, so long as the Muirs, our bosses, were actively trying to take control. I paid a call on Brooke Astor, an old friend, and told her that she and her foundation had better hurry up and make a decision before the whole magazine fell apart.

As the months passed, it became clear that the Muirs' cause was lost. One evening Ben Bradlee, then a reporter in *Newsweek*'s Washington bureau, called me at home. Benjamin Crowninshield Bradlee was his full name, but this was not your run-of-the-Ritz Boston Brahmin. "Ozzie baby," he said, "I know where the smart money is. It's in Phil Graham's pocket." We agreed that Bradlee should approach Graham, for whom he had once worked as a reporter on *The Washington Post*. When Ben called, Phil invited him to come right around. They talked until three or four o'clock in the morning, and at the end Graham asked Bradlee to have a memo on his desk by 9:00 a.m. Bradlee stayed up the rest of that night, banging out a fifty-page paper on *Newsweek*, its past, its present, its potential, its people. "It was the best and fastest writing I've ever done," Ben said later. For many nights after that, Bradlee and I were on the phone together, scheming like a couple of anarchists (I still remember his old Washington phone number—FE 8-3864). Phil Graham was interested.

In 1940, Graham had married Katharine Meyer, whose father, Eugene, had bought *The Washington Post* in a bankruptcy auction a few years before. The price had been a minuscule $825,000. Meyer poured additional money into the paper and raised some more by selling stock to employees, a number of whom later became millionaires as a result. But after World War II, the *Post* was still struggling. Meyer, just then moving into the presidency of the International Bank for Reconstruction and Development, made his son-in-law publisher; Phil Graham, a veteran of the Army Air Corps, was thirty-one years old, and raring to go. But it took him some time to make the big move that propelled the *Post* into first place in the capital's morning-newspaper field. In 1955, for $8,500,000, Graham managed to buy the Washington *Times-Herald*. He merged it with the *Post* and started building a radio-television division for diversification.

When *Newsweek* became available in 1960, Graham was once more in an acquisitive mood. But if he bought the magazine, Phil wondered, who the hell would be its editor? Elliott, said Bradlee in his fifty-page memo—and so it was arranged for me to meet Graham in February 1961. I flew to Washington, and we spent an hour together in the cozy library of Phil's spacious Georgetown house. Phil was relaxed, talking smoothly, his long legs stretching halfway to Europe, his infectious smile crinkling his angular face; I played the role of the "old pro" editor, not too tough, not too wise-ass. I was thirty-six years old and for two years had been managing editor of the magazine. That was the No. 3 editorial job, although it sounded like No. 1. Phil and I hit it off from the start.

By early March, Graham was in hot pursuit of *Newsweek*. He called friends who had friends who were members of the conservative Astor Foundation board to get the message to them that he was no wild-eyed radical. He sent an emissary to Rome to meet with Averell Harriman, an important minority stockholder of *Newsweek*. He moved into the Carlyle Hotel in New York, and asked me to bring Gib McCabe, my business-side colleague, up for dinner. Midway through the evening, we were interrupted by Graham's assistant, a legal stenographer with the unlikely name of Charlie Paradise. Bursting into the room, Paradise shouted excitedly: "Uncle Harvey's got the money!" He was speaking in a code worked

out between Graham and his lawyer, Fritz Beebe, a partner
in Cravath, Swaine & Moore. It meant that Beebe—who really
did have an upstate uncle named Harvey—had succeeded in
arranging a loan from Prudential Life to help finance the
purchase of *Newsweek*.

Next morning, McCabe and I were called by Allan Betts, the
man who was running the Astor Foundation for Brooke Astor.
Would we please come right over? He had something important to discuss. We knew, of course, what it was all about. But
we certainly didn't anticipate what followed.

Betts greeted us in his Park Avenue office with a thin,
bankerly smile—as close as he ever came to laughing, so far
as I know—and proceeded to make an astonishingly generous
offer. That afternoon, he said, the board of the Astor Foundation was meeting to decide which of two final bidders would
get the *Newsweek* prize. He wanted to outline the two bids
to us—"and I assure you, gentlemen, that the board will act
as you recommend."

McCabe and I said modestly that we could not possibly
assume the responsibility of deciding for the board, but we'd
be happy to say what we thought of the bids and the bidders.

It turned out that the two finalists were Doubleday and
The Washington Post; in financial terms, said Betts, the bids
were almost identical at about $15 million each, which would
buy *Newsweek* and the $6 million in cash in its till. What
did we think? First McCabe, then I, outlined our reasons for
preferring *The Washington Post*. We bloviated a bit about
the then popular concept of synergy: the *Post* and *Newsweek*
were both in the news business, they had common interests,
each would benefit from the other. But what we really ended
up saying was that we had fallen in love with Phil Graham—I
some weeks before; Gib at dinner the night before. Betts be-
stowed a fiduciary guffaw—no noise, just that thin line of lips—

and said, "I couldn't agree with you more. I've never been so impressed by a man in my life as by Phil Graham. Why, do you realize that he arrived in New York a few days ago and installed a special phone line between his suite in the Carlyle and my office here? And yesterday he came in"—here Betts's eyeballs almost rolled out of their sockets—"he came in and made out a check for two million dollars as a down payment!"

(I later learned from Graham some further details on that. As it happened, all Phil had with him at the time was a personal check, so he simply crossed off his own printed name on the side and wrote in "The Washington Post Company" along with his signature. Then he made out the check, payable to the Vincent Astor Foundation, and handed it to Betts. "I'd never written a check for two million before," Graham said, "and I didn't know whether you should add, at the end, 'and zero zero cents.' Finally, I just went squiggle, squiggle, squiggle. That seemed to do the trick.")

"Gentlemen," said Betts to McCabe and me, "the Astor board will meet at two this afternoon. You can be sure that they will vote to sell *Newsweek* to Phil Graham and *The Washington Post*."

We left Betts's office for a liquid lunch. Downstairs, I stopped in a phone booth to call Graham at the Carlyle. The raspy voice of Ben Bradlee was on the other end of the line; he had come up from Washington that morning—as *Newsweek*'s boss Malcolm Muir was to say, more than a bit tartly, later in the day—"to be in on the kill."

"What's the news?" asked Bradlee.

"The news is that you can tell Phil to start to get ready to commence to get drunk."

Bradlee relayed the word, and in the background I could hear Graham saying, "Drunk happy—or drunk sad?"

That afternoon, Phil Graham arrived at the *Newsweek*

building on Madison Avenue and presented himself to the receptionist on the eleventh floor. "I have an appointment to meet Mr. Betts in Mr. Muir's office," he said, without giving his name. On the interoffice "squawk box" Malcolm Senior asked his son "Mac," then *Newsweek*'s executive editor (and my immediate boss), to peek into the reception room to see who was there. Mac took a look, recognized Phil Graham, and reported back to "the old man" (as even Muir Senior called himself). And that was the way that Malcolm Muir, then seventy-five and head of *Newsweek* for a quarter of a century—the man who had been trying so hard to buy the magazine himself—learned who the successful bidder finally was.

Things can get rough in the executive suite.

Within half an hour, twenty or thirty of the magazine's top business and editorial people were haled into a tiny conference room to get the official word. Muir was crushed, but he handled himself like a gentleman. "As you all know," he said, his white mustache drooping a bit, "my family and associates have been trying to buy *Newsweek*. We have failed. This is, of course, a great disappointment to me. But given that failure, I cannot imagine anyone I would rather have succeed than my old friend Phil Graham." (I think he had met Phil for the first time that very afternoon.) Graham made some appropriate noises about what a fine magazine *Newsweek* was and what potential it had yet to fulfill; he said McCabe would continue as president and head of business operations, and he named me editor. To the press, Phil pronounced prophetically: "It may be fun, and it may be agony."

That evening, there was a celebration. Phil and I left the office together to pick up my wife, Deirdre. By the time she joined us, Phil had been jumping up and down so energetically in the taxi that his gray fedora was squashed down on his head. "We bought it! We bought it!" he cried. We went to the "21" Club. Phil's wife, Katharine, was there. I had met her only briefly once or twice, and remembered her as quiet and shy. None of us knew, of course, how soon she would inherit the top *Washington Post* job from her husband. Kay seemed as happy as everyone else—even though she had learned some time before that she had tuberculosis and had decided to keep the news from Phil until the *Newsweek* deal was made. She was gutsy even then.

Ben and Toni Bradlee and Fritz and Liane Beebe made up the rest of the party—in retrospect, a poignant group: Phil and Fritz long since dead, the Elliotts and Bradlees long since divorced. But the evening was bibulous and full of laughs, as the victors savored their spoils. "Now that Oz is editor," Beebe said to my wife, "what do you want?" "All I want is a Ford station wagon," Deirdre said. With my salary suddenly doubled—that was the way Phil Graham did things —we soon bought that wagon, the first respectable car we ever owned.

The next day, I paid a call on Malcolm Muir. Among other things, I wanted him to know that I had played no part in the undoing of his son, who had hoped to be editor of *Newsweek* but who now was offered some vague executive position on *The Washington Post*. Muir was crestfallen. "Now that you are editor," he said, "the relationship between you and me will change. But there are certain things, Oz, that I would like to continue doing the same old way." Such as? "Such as attending the weekly story and cover conferences." I told Muir I had decided to abolish all those conferences and henceforward would deal with the editors individually. This was, of course, a lie. But I think I probably spared "the old man" a lot of embarrassment—and myself the impossible situation of having Muir looking over one shoulder, and Graham the other, as I set about remaking the magazine.*

Newsweek was a shambles. Not only had the editor left, the whole staff was shot through with drunks, incompetents, and hacks. But as Bradlee had made clear in his memo to Phil Graham, there were also some excellent younger people, recruited in recent years. Two senior editors, in particular, had impressed me for quite different qualities. One was Gordon Manning, a former sportswriter and managing editor of the defunct *Collier's*, who had a razor-edge wit and a keen nose for news. The other was Kermit Lansner, a former philosophy professor at Kenyon, former editor of *ARTnews*, and possessor of a brain as subtle and nuanced as a Calder mobile. I asked them if they would serve as co-equal executive editors under me, and they agreed—Lansner after some hesitation, thinking that the post of Paris bureau chief might be more his *pôt de crème*.

Within a week or so I made a lunch date with Phil Graham to introduce my new top team—and to reintroduce myself. "What are these guys like?" Phil asked. "Do I have to wear shoes?" Normal guys, no shoes needed, I answered as casually as I could. We arrived at his suite in the Carlyle and rang the bell. Graham appeared, wearing no shoes. In fact, he had nothing on but a towel; he'd just taken a shower. "Phil," I said, "I didn't say not to wear *anything*."

Graham put on slacks and a shirt, joined us in the living room for a drink, and a waiter wheeled in a lunch table with shrimp cocktails and lamb chops. Things were a bit tense and awkward. Manning and Lansner had never met Graham, and I knew him only slightly. How would he react to this

---

* Malcolm Muir got a good contract, for ten years, as a kind of publisher emeritus; he died in 1979, at the age of ninety-three.

rather oddly matched triumvirate—a Jewish intellectual, a wise-cracking sportswriter, an Ivy League wasp? At one point during the lunch, my eyes fell upon a little white pill on the floor between Graham and me. I leaned over and picked it up. It was a Miltown. "Is this yours, Phil?" I asked. He reached into his pants pocket and pulled out a vial. "No, mine are right here." The Miltown was my own.

Looking back now, I have the impression of spending a lot of the next weeks in limousines with Phil, as he shuttled from *Newsweek* to Penn Station and the next train to Washington. Lacking dollar bills for a tip one day, he said to me: "Oz, will you please 'bunch' the driver?" (I didn't know how much a limousine chauffeur should be "bunched," and no doubt tipped the man too little or too much.) Then, suddenly, Phil disappeared from the *Newsweek* scene. We thought, God, what a fantastic guy. He's decided to give us free rein and let us run our own show to see what we can do. We didn't know then that he had been suffering from depressions for years, and that he had gone into another slump after his exhilarating purchase of the magazine.

Some weeks later we faced our first big story under the new ownership—the horribly miscalculated Bay of Pigs adventure in Cuba, supported by some of "the best and the brightest" who were later so loyally to advance America's involvement in the swamp of Vietnam. I figured I'd better call the new proprietor of *Newsweek*, this friend of Kennedy's, and make sure that we were at least roughly on the same wavelength concerning this unexpected disaster so early in the Kennedy administration. I put through a call to *The Washington Post* switchboard; I think I eventually reached Graham at home.

"Phil? I'd like to ask you a question. If you cast your mind back over all the Eisenhower years, can you think of a single disaster as great as this one?"

Silence on his end. And then, at last: "The reason for the long silence is that, for the first time in my life, I am trying to think before I speak. I guess the answer is, no, I can't think of anything as bad." Graham went on to suggest that in the long run the Bay of Pigs would probably be viewed as a tiny ripple, and would not merit much more than a footnote in the history books.

Whether he was right or wrong didn't really matter to me then. For what I got from Graham in that first conversation about a specific news story—one of the very few such discussions we ever had—was the freedom to call the shots as we, the editors, saw them. *Newsweek*'s story the next week started this way: "Only 90 days after it took power, the Kennedy Administration suffered a setback as grave as any that befell President Eisenhower during his entire eight years in office."*

At least in part because of the Bay of Pigs disaster, an old American political phenomenon was once more bubbling to the surface in 1961. From the anti-Catholic Know-Nothings of the 1850s to the anti-Semitic rantings of Father Coughlin in the 1930s, America had always had its radical right—and now the far right was beginning to fulminate again. The target was Communism in all its real and imagined guises. A fast-growing group called the National Indignation Convention was out to impeach Chief Justice Earl Warren for his clearly (to them) "pinko" leanings; Captain Eddie Rickenbacker, the World War I hero who was then chairman of Eastern Airlines, was praising the late Senator Joseph McCarthy for having "had the courage to oppose the enemy. . . . Some day the American people will erect a monument to his memory." The

* Somewhat naïvely, as Vietnam was later to prove, the article went on to speculate that the Bay of Pigs fiasco might prove to be a plus in the long run: "In the future, Administration ventures in this realm will be based not on high hopes and dreamy expectations but on solid reality."

John Birch Society's founder, Robert Welch, expressed his "firm opinion that Dwight Eisenhower is a dedicated and conscious agent of the Communist conspiracy." For whatever the reasons—the unsettling Bay of Pigs disaster; a stalemate in Korea almost a decade before; the disintegration and death of Joe McCarthy; the clear and present danger then threatening Berlin—the radical right was on the move, and it was rallying under the banner of the John Birch Society's best-known member, Major General Edwin A. Walker.

With Phil Graham's full concurrence, we decided to do a major *Newsweek* cover story analyzing the phenomenon. "Thunder on the Right," featuring General Walker on the cover, appeared the week after Thanksgiving 1961. It proved to be the most controversial story yet in *Newsweek*'s history. Thousands of letters cascaded in; hundreds of readers angrily canceled their subscriptions or wrote to *Newsweek*'s advertisers urging them to withdraw their ads. "The article," wrote one reader in Annapolis, "is a perfect example of extremism —a viciously unfair and biased type of extremism, very obviously penned by an extremist of the far left, quite probably a member of the Communist Party."* Another reader vented his rage in a telegram: IF YOUR PUBLICATION DOES NOT HAVE THE GOOD SENSE TO BE ANTI-COMMUNIST, THOSE OF MY HOUSEHOLD DO. CANCEL MY SUBSCRIPTION AND SEND MY REFUND TO THE LOCAL NATIONAL INDIGNATION HEADQUARTERS HERE IN DALLAS. A third—who could hardly have known that the daughters

---

* The "cover package," like many major *Newsweek* stories, was a group effort; more than forty correspondents, reporters, photographers, researchers, writers, and editors were involved. But the main part was written over Thanksgiving by Al Leech, a rather conservative newspaperman (and amateur magician) from the Midwest, who later became public-relations manager for that bastion of Communism, the Allis-Chalmers Manufacturing Co. in Milwaukee, Wisconsin.

of *Newsweek*'s editor were even then learning their Roman Catholic catechism—concluded: "Your outrageous slandering of McCarthy proves you're nothing but a bunch of anti-Catholic bigots."

It is hard to realize now that for a national publication like *Newsweek* to print such a story was, in the early sixties, considered by many liberals to be an act of courage. My friend Schuyler Chapin, later to become general manager of the Metropolitan Opera, and after that dean of Columbia University's School of the Arts, was one such admirer. "At last," he wrote—in a letter that I picked to lead off the next week's magazine—"a responsible journal has taken the obviously difficult and desperately important subject of this country's lunatic fringe and devoted care to its presentation. . . ."

"Thunder on the Right" gave a lot of grief to our advertising department. A number of right-wing corporations—particularly in the Midwest and especially in heavy industry—which had threatened to cancel their *Newsweek* advertising when *The Washington Post* took over the magazine, now were only too happy to see their worst fears substantiated. *Newsweek* had indeed sold out to the pinkos, and why should any self-respecting company support such a publication with its precious advertising dollars? Gib McCabe insisted on dealing personally with each such threatened cancellation, and succeeded in turning them all around. On one trip to Milwaukee, after McCabe rolled his big, innocent Irish eyes at a hefty advertiser, the client thrust an envelope into his hand, and told him not to open it until he was on the plane to New York. It turned out to be an application for membership in the John Birch Society.

Phil Graham and the rest of us rejoiced at the ruckus we had stirred up with "Thunder on the Right." We knew that we had done a responsible journalistic job on a touchy and important subject, and that we had gained a lot of attention, to boot. With that cover story, we thought, *Newsweek* had announced to the world that it was under new management, and it was a magazine to watch.

. . .

In those early months—except for his few weeks of depression immediately after buying the magazine—Phil Graham was forever prodding, probing, encouraging, helping. He had a great feeling for people. When *Newsweek*'s advertising director, Charles Kane, dropped dead in 1962, Gib McCabe was devastated at the loss of this close friend. Graham put an arm around McCabe's shoulder and said: "I imagine what's really bothering Louise Kane now is how she'll take care of their children. What's wrong with setting up a foundation?—we're not exactly broke—so you tell Louise that she needn't worry."

Phil loosened the purse strings on every front, enabling both McCabe, on the business side, and me, editorially, to hire competitively. For a number of years, the magazine had been known along Madison Avenue as "Boozeweek" because of the lunchtime habits of some of its advertising salesmen. All that began to change—particularly with McCabe's hiring of L. L. ("Pete") Callaway, a supersalesman from Time Inc. Callaway, poor fellow, had the misfortune of becoming *Newsweek*'s new publisher the very week that Phil Graham first entered a mental institution. But Pete went about his work, and by firing the incompetents and hiring such proven pros as *Time*'s promotional genius Bill Scherman, he quickly turned the magazine's sales and marketing staff into a highly professional organization.

The money that Graham made available prompted us all to think big. One night in 1962, at a dinner party in New York, Mike Cowles, publisher of *Look*, told me that Walter Lippmann's contract with the *Herald Tribune* was about to expire. "If I were you," Cowles whispered into my ear, "I'd get

Lippmann under contract to *Newsweek* and *The Washington Post.*" Cowles figured astutely that, with the *Trib* in trouble, Lippmann could be tempted. While I had known Lippmann as a family friend for years, Graham knew him better, and I thought Phil would be by far the more effective persuader. I passed the word, and within a few months Lippmann was writing for *Newsweek* and the *Post*—with a $100,000-a-year lifetime contract. We let the world know about this major-league acquisition with a four-color cover photograph of JFK and huge type announcing WALTER LIPPMANN ON KENNEDY. From then on, Lippmann wrote a biweekly column. It wasn't always his best stuff, and Lippmann had terrible problems confining himself to the page allotted him, but his very presence added enormously to the specific gravity of the magazine; it told people "out there" that *Newsweek* now counted.

The editorial budget grew rapidly, and with the additional funds we were able to extend our reach around the world and deeper into the workings of our own country. *Newsweek*'s first cover story on Vietnam appeared in 1961; it featured Ngo Dinh Diem, and opened with a prophetic anecdote: "The Vietnamese colonel, in jungle-green uniform and U.S. steel helmet, turned bitterly to his general. 'I know exactly where their command post is,' he said. 'But every time we advance on it, those bastards disappear.'" But our cover stories were not always so perspicacious. Analyzing Richard Nixon's 1961 bid for the governorship of California, we opined: "If Nixon loses to [Pat] Brown, his political career will unquestionably be finished."

· · ·

Phil Graham was not one to deny the pleasures of big-time journalism to his top editors. He sent me on a trip abroad, and arranged a series of meetings for me overseas. In London,

Lady Pamela Berry, owner of *The Daily Telegraph*, threw a
party attended by all of Whitehall plus a good part of Fleet
Street's press establishment. One guest was a bright young
editor named Jocelyn Stevens, who had recently launched a
snippy magazine called *The Queen*. "I'd like you to meet the
man who killed society," said Pam Berry acidly, "and who
has been committing necrophilia with it ever since."

Graham also sent me on a tour of eight American cities, to
wave the *Newsweek* flag and get to know the academic, political, business, and journalistic establishments around the country. Once again, he arranged for friends to receive me and to
help in the education of his new young editor. Walker Cisler, a
utilities tycoon, put together a dinner in Detroit, and I gave
a speech—all about *Newsweek* and its great new future. Publisher Marshall Field III had a lunch for businessmen at the
Chicago Club, and I gave The Speech again. Edward Levi of
the University of Chicago threw an academic dinner, and
again The Speech unfolded. In San Francisco, it was the turn
of Wally Haas, boss of Levi Strauss (and Kay Graham's cousin)
to play host, and to hear The Speech. In Houston, it was the
charming Oveta Culp Hobby, and in Atlanta, publisher Jack
Tarver. All these people had to hear The Speech only once;
not so for my poor wife and *Newsweek*'s Jim Cannon, who
were both along to hold my hand.

In my first year or two as *Newsweek*'s editor, I can remember only one direct order from Phil Graham, and that was to
fire a particular editor who had grown old and stale and was
too much in his cups; (Phil readily agreed that the man should
get a full year's severance pay). But even in those early times
I began to learn that Graham could be impossible. It was in
the midst of my "eight-city tour" of America that I got word
that he had hired Emmet John Hughes as a *Newsweek*
columnist to alternate with Lippmann—with not a word about
it to me. Hughes was a good writer, albeit, as he himself might

put it, with a rather baroque style. He had been a colleague of mine at *Time,* and I was hurt and angry and embarrassed that Graham had not consulted me before taking Hughes on.

Phil himself took a trip to Europe and hopped around the Continent making all sorts of promises to *Newsweek*'s staff in the field without so much as a by-your-leave to me. Did the Bonn bureau chief want a transfer to London? Done. And the London man wanted Rome? Fine. Why not send Rome to Vienna and Vienna to Moscow? When reports of such promises—or promises of promises—filtered back to me in New York, I drafted my first-ever letter of protest to Phil. "Certainly," I began, "I don't expect or want you to be a eunuch proprietor; this place has too much to gain from you, balls and all." I put the letter aside and tried again:

> It used to be fun and vastly stimulating to work *with* you, and *for* the magazine, but it ain't anymore. . . . Under the old arrangement, I felt free to make the decisions that must be made, day after day, to keep things operating. Now I find myself second-guessing. . . .
>
> I find it increasingly impossible to edit *Newsweek* the way it deserves to be edited. I don't have to tell you that creativity is a delicate flower—even within this breast—and it obviously can't blossom if the greenhouse temperature isn't right. . . .
>
> The disintegration is now well under way. How can I retain the respect of the people who work for me if I'm merely a conveyor belt for orders?

I didn't send that letter, either; I telephoned instead. I reached Graham at the Ritz in Paris, and in my mind's eye I could see his lanky frame tipping back on a delicate chair with his feet perched on a Louis XIV desk, a French telephone to his ear. I was angry, and unloaded on him verbally what I had decided not to say in writing. "Look, Phil," I said, "if this is the way you want to run this magazine, you're just going to have to get another editor. I can't do it like this."

Again, a long silence at his end of the line. Finally, he said—pronouncing my name with the accent heavily on the second syllable—"Oz-BORN . . . I love you." I don't know what you do with a man like that. He promised to behave better, and not to meddle, and for months he lived up to that promise as we went about the difficult and often unpleasant business of restaffing the magazine from top to bottom.

Here was one instance of a domino theory working productively. With Kermit Lansner the philosopher and Gordon Manning the sportswriter as my two chief lieutenants, I had a couple of excellent men who attracted a bright and lively new team of writers, editors, and correspondents. For three years or more we worked happily together as a troika. Because of our lofty and somewhat precarious perch, and our dependence on one another, we came to be known to the staff as the Wallendas, after the famous high-wire circus family; our suite of offices was called the Wallendatorium.

For Kermit life ranged between the elegant and the vulgar —two of his favorite words—and he exacted as much elegance as he could from the cultural- and foreign-news staff that worked for him. Gordon could find a story where others would not think to look, and the daily shower of scribbled or badly typed memos that issued from his desk became legendary—and, to the recipients, a pain in the ass. But at the end of every week, Manning would always fire all congratulatory memos to the deserving.

Sometimes, in the cultural area, it would be Manning's sharp news sense that would be called into play. And sometimes, when elegance and style and a sense of history were called for, Lansner would move more directly into "hard news" coverage. A case in point was the Cuban missile crisis of 1962. I asked Lansner to write the lead article for the magazine that week, and he captured the drama in all its terrifying dimensions. His story marched across the page this way:

> Everything that happened on the surface took place in seven short days—seven days in which the world had to face up to the true terrors of its existence as it never has done before. . . .
>
> To call the events of those seven days a crisis dilutes their real meaning, for this week was not only unique in itself; it may turn out to have consequences of incalculable importance for this century.
>
> What happened was that for the first time since thermonuclear weapons and the missile capacity to deliver them became the common property of the U.S. and the Soviet Union, the two nations engaged in direct confrontation. . . .

One of the more pleasant tribal rites of the newsmagazine business is the annual sales conference, usually held in some sunny clime, where the editors are encouraged to boast to the advertising-space salesmen about the journalistic wonders they have performed in the past year, and to unveil the splendors yet to come. At such a meeting, at a resort hotel in Ponte Vedra, Florida, in 1962, Manning, Lansner, Bradlee, and I made for the golf course after our editorial presentation. As Bradlee was addressing his ball for an approach shot to the green, Manning cried out: "Watch out, Bradlee, there's a rattlesnake behind you!" "Goddamn it, Manning, cut the bullshit," said Ben. But just then we all heard the unmistakable buzzing of a rattler. Bradlee jumped a mile. His old caddie took an iron from his golf bag, and with one graceful swoop knocked the head off the snake. "That was a pretty good shot, Sam," said Manning. "What club did you use?"

Years later, long after Bradlee had become top editor of

The Washington Post, Gordon Manning reflected on the incident. "Just think," he said, "if I'd let that rattlesnake bite Ben's ass, the whole course of history would have changed. There would have been no Watergate investigation, and Nixon would be emperor today."

After Manning himself left *Newsweek* to run his own show at CBS News, he called me up one day and said: "You and Kermit have got to take me out and get me drunk at lunch."

"Why?"

"I'll tell you later."

Lansner and I cleared our calendars, and at lunch the awful truth was revealed: that morning Gordon had acquired his first pair of reading glasses. "It's all downhill from here," he moaned. We sent him back to CBS a little drunk and only a little bit happier. By sheer coincidence, a couple of years later, I was to have dinner with Manning on the very day I had been inflicted with my own first pair of reading glasses.

I got to Giambelli's before he did, ordered a martini and, for Gordon's benefit, placed my new spectacles halfway down my nose. When he arrived, I glanced up from the menu, peering at him over my new horn-rims.

"It hasn't happened!" he said in horror.

"Yes, I got them just today."

Never at a loss for words, Manning said: "In two months your penis will fall off."

I am happy to report that in this one instance Gordon Manning, always the stickler for accuracy, was wrong.

While Lansner, Manning, and I were trying to put things into shape in New York, Ben Bradlee was running *Newsweek*'s Washington bureau with his special mix of élan, panache, and toughness (sometimes pretended) that Jason Robards later captured so well in the movie version of *All the President's Men.* We were, to Bradlee, "you fucks in New York"; he never failed to give us the respect he thought we were due. Bradlee was a special friend of Jack Kennedy, and some second-thinkers have since charged that this closeness led *Newsweek* to bend too sympathetically toward the people and policies of the Kennedy regime. I didn't believe so then, and I don't believe so now. On the contrary, we editors in New York were forever challenging Bradlee with just that nasty supposition, and he was constantly pressed to justify stories in ways he would not have been, had his friendship with Kennedy not been so well known to all. At the end of each week, Manning would spend half the night arguing points with Bradlee, to make sure we were not being "had" by the Kennedy administration.

I think *Newsweek* was fair—and tough. In the spring of 1963, we ran a Press story on the administration's attempts at "managing" the news: "Lying. Suppressing facts. Distorting information. Favoring friendly reporters. Harassing unfriendly critics. In recent months, the Kennedy Administration has been accused—and often found guilty—of employing these tactics to project a favorable image of itself in the press, on radio and on television. . . ."

But there was, in fact, a curious "synergy"—that word again—between the new *Newsweek* and the new administration in Washington. It was, to some degree, generational—the World War II generation taking over. Phil Graham was very much a part of it. He was a few years older than we, but he—like Lansner, like Manning, like Bradlee, like Kennedy, like me—had served in the Pacific in World War II (Phil in the Army, the rest of us in the Navy). There was, as Bradlee later suggested in his *Conversations With Kennedy*, a shared language, much of it crude. There was also a shared belief that our generation had earned the right to change the world for the better, and would damn well do so. The philosophical Lansner, I suspect, had his doubts about this, and in the longer run he was perhaps right. But none of us then could anticipate how our high hopes would sour as the sixties tumbled by.

Now I can see, in retrospect, that we were not only naïve about the world but blind to something close to us. We *Newsweek* people did not see, until very late, how sick Phil Graham was. His long absence after he bought the magazine was the first signal we missed. His erratic behavior while traveling abroad was another. His drinking, his swearing, his capricious promises—we put all these down as endearing eccentricities. Then, one evening in late 1962, Lansner called me at home. Kermit had found an old medical text and read a page of it to me. It offered a list of symptoms suggesting manic depression and it included the following: highly erotic behavior; heavy drinking; excessive use of foul language; no apparent lapses in logic.

Lansner read on through the checklist, and then said, "Doesn't this describe Phil?"

Unhappily, it did, and as 1962 faded into 1963, Graham's behavior became even more unpredictable. He took off with an Australian girl, who worked in *Newsweek*'s Paris bureau, and flew all over the world with her. He made a drunken speech, uninvited, at an editors' conference in Phoenix, berating the audience in vulgar terms, and had to be dragged away from the microphone. He made cruel fun of his daughter, Lally, at a lunch with *Newsweek* editors. "Pretty bright for a little Jew girl," he said. Once Phil had a flunky call me from the airport and order me to do a certain story, or not do it, or do it in a particular way—I've forgotten which. "He said to tell you," the aide reported, "that if you don't oblige, you can pick up your final paycheck next week." "Thanks," I said, and hung up. I didn't pay attention, and I didn't pick up that final paycheck until many years later.

In the late winter of 1963, Graham entered Chestnut Lodge, a mental institution outside Washington. After a few weeks he persuaded his doctors he was well enough to get out. Then he was off, flying again, and a few months later he was institutionalized once more at the same rustic sanatorium. By now it was early summer, and after a few weeks the reports on his progress were encouraging. Phil was coming along okay. In July, I got word that he was beginning to see a few people beyond the circle of his immediate family. He wanted to see me. I flew to Washington, and was brought to Chestnut Lodge by limousine.

Graham met me outside the white clapboard house where he was billeted with some other patients, and ushered me to a wicker chair on the edge of a field of grass. It was a lovely day, and as we chatted the long grass waved in the breeze and puffy white clouds glided by overhead. Someone on the porch of the white house was yelling obscenities. I chose not to notice, and we continued our talk. A few minutes later, louder this time, came the same string of filthy epithets: "Shit, cocksucker, fucking asshole." Now there was no ignoring the angry voice.

"How do you like my friend?" asked Phil.

"Does he go on like this all day?"

"Most days, yes; and there's another guy who walks up and down the hall all day, saluting and saying to everyone, 'Yes sir, yes sir!' You know, when I first came in here a few weeks ago, the thing that scared me most was that I might sink to *their* level. But that hasn't happened." Phil went on to say that he was feeling better. In wondering admiration, he told how Kay was coming to visit him every day, bringing picnic lunches and playing tennis with him. "Sometimes," he said, "when you've shat on as many people as I have in the past year, you wonder if you shouldn't call it quits. But now, while I can't yet *see* the shore on the other side, I know it's there—and I think that's a sign of progress, don't you?"

I said that if I were ever as sick as he had been, it would

do me a lot of good knowing that there was such an army of people rooting for me as he had rooting for him.

"That's nice to hear, especially from you," Phil said. "I've always figured your bullshit quotient was pretty low."

Just a day or two before I came to Chestnut Lodge, *Newsweek* had completed the research on its first major exploration of Black America. I had brought with me an inch-thick stack of computer printouts, tabulating the findings of a poll that *Newsweek*'s house pollster, Louis Harris, had conducted for us to determine black attitudes across the land. I had found the results fascinating, and I thought Phil would, too—depending on his state of health. Clearly, at least clearly to me, he was rational and on the mend. I showed him the Harris findings, and after a few minutes he asked me to leave them with him. He was excited by the project, and wanted to study the results.

As Graham walked me to the car, he spotted a copy of *Time* on the backseat. "Why don't you leave that with me, too?" he said. "I've already read *Newsweek* this week but I haven't seen *Time*. And make sure you come back to see me in a few days. A guy can get awfully isolated in a joint like this." I said I was just leaving for a couple of weeks' vacation, but would see him as soon as I got back.

A few days later, at lunch with my family on Long Island, I was telling about my visit with Phil, and how I was sure he was getting better. I thought he'd be out in a few weeks, and back at work by fall. We went out to play golf. On the second fairway I saw someone running toward me from the caddie house. There was an emergency call. I ran back to the caddie house and breathlessly picked up the phone. It was Lansner. Phil had killed himself. He had apparently persuaded his doctors once again that he was well enough to be let out for the weekend. Alone with Kay, he had gone to their farm in Virginia. While she was in the bedroom, he found a .28-gauge shotgun, placed himself on the edge of a bathtub, and pulled the trigger.

The memorial service, in the National Cathedral, was attended by all the notables of Washington, including John Kennedy—who himself would be dead, a bullet through his head, within four months.

A meeting of the board of The Washington Post Company was called at Kay Graham's request. Sadly, Fritz Beebe—by then chairman of the company—called the meeting to order and gave the floor to Kay. She sat there looking ashen, dressed in black, her eyes downcast. The rest of us could sense the strain as she gathered strength to speak. She sat erect. Then she looked up and in a low but level voice began to speak. "I want you all to know," she said, "that I am aware of what you all have been through in the past year or more, and I want to thank you for conducting yourselves as professionals throughout. I also want you to know, despite whatever rumors you may hear, that this company is not for sale, and no part of it is for sale. This is a family company, and there is a new generation coming along."

It was an impressive display of bravery and grit.

When Kermit Lansner wrote the obit for *Newsweek,* he began with a quotation from Phil himself:

> "I came to journalism quite by chance, from another ancient and honorable calling—that of the law. It is said—in explanation of the inner torment of that minority of very good lawyers—that the law is a jealous mistress. No doubt that is a good statement of what stretches good men who engage in any precariously intellectual vocation. When I think of a few serious journalists I have known, I know that the jealous demands of excellence in our calling have borne down on them heavily and deeply while also elevating and enlarging them.
> "I am insatiably curious about the state of the

world. I revel in the recitation of the daily and weekly grist of journalism. Much of it, of course, is pure chaff. But no one yet has been able to produce wheat without chaff. . . . And not even such garrulous romantics as Fidel Castro or such transcendent spirits as Abraham Lincoln can produce a history which does not rest on a foundation of tedium and detail—and even sheer drudgery.

"So let us drudge on about our inescapably impossible task of providing every week a first rough draft of a history that will never be completed about a world we can never understand."

This, as Lansner noted, was pure Phil: "When he spoke, he had a wit which could dissolve pomposity and lighten tedium; a high seriousness which could endow the most trivial problem with dignity; a certitude that stemmed from an instinct for the highest standards; a sympathy which extended to the great and the weak alike."

In a stroke of editorial genius, the Washington *Daily News*, in its salute to Graham, quoted the familiar poem by Edwin Arlington Robinson:

> *Whenever Richard Cory went down town,*
> *We people on the pavement looked at him:*
> *For he was a gentleman from sole to crown,*
> *Clean favored and imperially slim.*
>
> *And he was always quietly arrayed,*
> *And he was always human when he talked;*
> *But still he fluttered pulses when he said,*
> *"Good morning," and glittered when he walked.*
>
> *And he was rich—yes, richer than a king—*
> *And admirably schooled in every grace:*
> *In fine, we thought he was everything*
> *To make us wish that we were in his place.*

· *Phil* ·

So, on we worked, and waited for the light,
And went without the meat, and cursed the bread;
And Richard Cory, one calm summer night,
Went home and put a bullet through his head.

•II•
END RUNS

Even in his craziness, this glowing Phil, this glittering Richard Cory of ours, remained our sun and moon and stars. And now he was dead, and we wept at his loss. We wept out of love: How much joy he had given us all. And out of resentment: How could he do this to us? And out of fear: What would become of us now?

After the funeral, I sat morosely in Ben Bradlee's Georgetown garden gazing into the uncertain future. What next? At the board meeting the day before the funeral, Kay had made it clear that there would be no change, no sale of the company or any of its parts. Yet we knew that she viewed *Newsweek* as some foreign body, some irritating mote, some bauble acquired at the bazaar in a moment of her husband's madness. Did she really mean what she had said?

She may not have known herself. She had worked as a reporter for the *San Francisco Chronicle* after graduating from college, and had spent some time reporting for her father's *Washington Post* as well. But mostly her life had been that of wife and mother of four children; she knew little about business, almost nothing about management—and here she was, suddenly in control of a huge and growing communications empire. No doubt she was tempted to unload *Newsweek* and settle back into the more familiar surroundings of the *Post*. She went off for a cruise on a yacht with her formidable mother, Agnes Meyer. Kay pondered. Should she assume command of the company? How could she fill the void left by her brilliant father, her dazzling husband? What did she know about business and big-time journalism? And how could she deal with all those men in the organization, those hard-eyed professionals who seemed to know so much? But what kind of a life lay before her anyway? She decided to take over the company. She decided to keep the magazine. At the age of forty-six, Katharine Graham began life anew.

Back in New York, the day after Graham's funeral, I gathered the *Newsweek* editorial staff and the top people on the business side to tell them what Kay had said at the board meeting: No change, no sale. Remembering the jangling uncertainties of three years before, when *Newsweek* was on the block, I did my best at that meeting and in a memo to the staff outside New York to reassure all hands—although of course I wasn't all that reassured myself. "Fritz Beebe," I said, "outlined the terms of Phil Graham's will . . . a minimum of fifty-five percent of the voting stock in the company goes to his widow. Fritz went on to explain . . . that there would be no necessity of liquidating any assets in order to pay death duties or inheritance taxes." I ended on this note: "What Phil brought to *Newsweek* was what he brought to everything he touched—a marvelously invigorating gust of fresh air. It has been fun standing in the wind these past two and one half years, and I have every intention and expectation that we shall continue to keep the breezes blowing freshly and in the right direction. I expect all of you—all of us—to continue to turn out a courageous magazine marked by honor, integrity, fairness, and eloquence."

And so we drudged back to "our inescapably impossible

task of providing a first rough draft of history." At least, I told myself, Phil Graham had been around long enough to see the first fruits of our efforts—"Thunder on the Right," our coverage of the Cuban missile crisis, the beginnings of our close scrutiny of Vietnam. And only a few days before he died, Phil had seen our precedent-setting exploration of Black America—the first in a series of racial reports that we were later to describe, quite proudly, self-servingly, and I think accurately, as "the deepest study of the American dilemma since Gunnar Myrdal."

· · ·

When Graham moved in to buy *Newsweek* in 1961, the magazine had been an anomaly: a reasonably successful publishing venture based on a rather weak editorial "product"—a Madison Avenue term that we all abhorred. ("We're not just in the business of canning sausages," was the way Gordon Manning put it.) The magazine had first appeared as *Newsweek* in 1937, the result of a merger between two struggling journals. One of these was *Today,* which had been launched by Vincent Astor and Averell Harriman, and which provided a graceful egress from the New Deal for Raymond Moley, who became *Today*'s editor. (Moley had been a member of Franklin Roosevelt's Brain Trust, but he split with FDR as the president began to launch increasingly vituperative attacks on big business.) The other publishing venture, called *News-Week,* had been started by a former *Time* man, Thomas C. J. Martyn. When neither fledgling magazine showed much promise of succeeding—losses at *Today* ran as high as $200,000 a month— they entered a *mariage de convenance*, with Moley remaining as editor of the merged magazine. Malcolm Muir, who had started *Business Week* at McGraw-Hill, was brought in as president and publisher, and the dehyphenated *Newsweek* was born. The new weekly aimed to please those who didn't like *Time*, by then already a bumptious, highly opinionated fourteen-year-old, and those who *did* like *Business Week*.

The early *Newsweek* had its successes. Its managers had the good sense, in those simpler times, to decide that its mission was to "separate fact from opinion"—a not-so-subtle dig at *Time*. The slogan later came to haunt us, but it was effective as an opening gambit. From the very beginning, instead of lacing its news stories with an editorial slant, *Newsweek* carried columns of political opinion by Moley, cultural criticism by the likes of George Jean Nathan, Sinclair Lewis, and John O'Hara, and, later, sports by John Lardner. It was "the magazine of news significance."

But for all its sparkling jewels in "the back of the book," *Newsweek*'s basic offering was a bland and unexciting rehash of the week's events. And while *Newsweek* was started as an alternative to *Time*, its managers never really considered it a competitor to Henry Luce's acid-tongued young Goliath. Indeed, when David Lawrence merged *his* two magazines into *U.S. News & World Report* after World War II, that was where the commercial battle lines were drawn by *Newsweek*'s management. I moved from *Time* to *Newsweek* in 1955, and I was dismayed to find my new magazine measuring itself not against *Time* but against the highly conservative and (to me) unimpressive *U.S. News & World Report*. At *Time*, we had never paid any attention to the other two newsmagazines; now I found *Newsweek* lowering its sights to do battle with No. 3. At a magazine publishers' dinner one night, the stand-up comic Mort Sahl put my feelings into words: "*U.S. News & World Report*," he said, holding the hybrid aloft for all to see, "now *that's* my idea of two magazines in none!"

It was Frank Gibney, who had left *Time* for *Newsweek* a

year before, who persuaded me to make the switch. I had
enjoyed working for *Time*; in my six and a half years there
as a business writer I had turned out a batch of cover stories
on subjects ranging from Texas oilmen Clint Murchison and
Sid Richardson to hotelman Conrad Hilton, General Motors'
Harlow Curtice, Procter & Gamble's Neil McElroy, fashion
designer Claire McCardell, Agriculture Secretary Ezra Taft
Benson, and Sears, Roebuck's General Robert E. Wood. I was
making $15,000 a year at *Time*, and doing fine. But I was in a
cul de sac, under a senior editor who showed no signs of moving either up or out. Gibney told me that he had run into my
boss, Joe Purtell, at the Rockefeller Center skating rink, and
that Joe had seemed hale and hearty as he glided around the
ice. "He said," Gibney insisted, "that his father hadn't retired
until he was ninety." With that—and a proffered $20,000
from *Newsweek*—I decided to make the move.

I joined *Newsweek* as business editor. The very first week in
my new job I had a cover story to edit—the Ford Motor Company had just signed a contract with the United Automobile
Workers granting what was loosely known at the time as a
guaranteed annual wage. It was big news, and I reacted in
the knee-jerk manner of any newsmagazine senior editor—I
ordered up research and reaction from the magazine's domestic
bureaus. As the reports came in a couple of days later, my
heart sank. *Newsweek*'s bureaus in those days were few and far
between. And instead of the rich background and "color"
that I had become accustomed to expect from *Time*'s news-
gathering network, there was only a thin gruel. Things improved a bit when the file from the Atlanta bureau came in.
Correspondent William Emerson quoted an anonymous Southern businessman as saying: "If the guaranteed annual wage
comes here, I'll get me a blonde, a goat, and a barrel of
whiskey, and take to the hills." That quote may have come

straight from Emerson's own fertile imagination, but I figured right then that he was headed for bigger things.

While *Newsweek*'s circulation and advertising people were
competing with David Lawrence's *U.S. News*, we editorial
types set out after Harry Luce's *Time;* we figured it was vul-
nerable because of its set ways, its predictable politics, its
snideness, and its cuteness of language (this last was beginning
to fade, by the mid-fifties, but the memory lingered on). But
how lightly armed we were for the battle! *Time*'s legion of
correspondents roamed the world making small talk and large
stories with the high and mighty everywhere, while *Newsweek*
made do with a scatteration of full-time staffers here and there
and a band of part-time "stringers" everywhere else. *Time*'s
top editors and public-relations and advertising people drank,
and lunched, and drank and lunched again at the "21" Club
while we drank our warm, sweet martinis and munched our
stringy spaghetti at Topps, a greasy spoon on Forty-second
Street near Broadway, across the street from our dingy offices
in the former Knickerbocker Hotel. On special occasions we
might patronize the Blue Ribbon, a stolid German restaurant
a couple of blocks away. And on Saturdays we would lunch,
cheek by jowl with *Herald Tribune* staffers, on the cheap but
excellent broiled chicken at Bleeck's—"The Artist and Writers
Restaurant" (nobody ever discovered who the artist was)
whose over-the-door sign also advertised to the world: "Formerly Club."*

---

* Taking off from the sign, a group of newspapermen formed their
own "Formerly Club" which met at Bleeck's at lunchtime every
Saturday—the club's chief function being to master a mathematical
and alcoholic exercise known as "the match game," played on the
table with wooden kitchen matches. Members included *Newsweek*'s
John Lardner, the *Trib*'s Homer Bigart, and free-lance writer Maury
Werner.

Every ten days or so *Newsweek*'s editor, John Denson, would take a few of us to the St. Regis Hotel for lunch in the spiffy King Cole Bar; because of Vincent Astor's joint ownership of both the St. Regis and *Newsweek*, we would get a 25 percent discount—which still left the St. Regis the most expensive place in town. Denson, favoring his dentures, would invariably order scrambled eggs, chocolate ice cream, and coffee; the rest of us would cup our hands and whisper into the captain's ear: "The small steak, please." After all, Denson—or rather *Newsweek*, or rather Vincent Astor—was paying. And we would sit in the glow of Maxfield Parrish's light-struck mural of Old King Cole and his fiddlers three, amused at the thought that King Cole's bemused expression, and the apprehensive look of his fiddlers, betrayed Parrish's little artistic joke: he had caught the king at the precise moment of committing a royal fart. So legend had it. We were all so knowledgeable then.

John Denson, our boss, was an amiable crank who combined deeply conservative political instincts with a circus barker's talent for getting the suckers under the tent. He was picky, and like almost every other editor he considered himself an expert on the press. So it was no surprise that he considered *Newsweek*'s Press section his particular turf and paid especially close attention to its contents. One Saturday night Denson called Gordon Manning, then the senior editor in charge of Press, into his office to dissect a piece he didn't like. For protection, Manning took along a new young researcher, fresh out of Radcliffe. For fifteen minutes, gnashing his false teeth, Denson picked the story apart, put it back together, and finally let Manning return to his other editorial chores. On the way back upstairs, Manning's researcher said: "That was very interesting. I'd never met Mr. Denson before. What were those nuts he was chewing?"

"Mine," said Manning.

Denson was a genius of sorts. A product of the Deep South, he had little formal schooling and became a journeyman reporter at an early age; he went on to hold more top editorial jobs than anyone else in U.S. journalism.*

Given the limited resources he had to work with at *Newsweek*, Denson did a remarkable job doing battle with *Time*. "We've gotta end-run 'em," he used to say. That meant big acts and special issues—such as the December 1955 economic special edition featuring "The Big Surge . . . the New America," which was written mostly by Clem Morgello and shepherded to press by me as *Newsweek*'s new business editor. Chronicling the big boom of the fifties, that issue was, we proudly announced, "the biggest story . . . of its type that we have ever attempted." Wide-eyed, we reported on how Americans were "buying new cars, TV, hi-fi, building new houses (some with swimming pools), and vacationing in Europe. . . ."

John Denson's "end runs" also meant exclusive stories; he knew that *Time*, so frozen in its highly professional, highly successful, highly impersonal mold, simply didn't know how to cope with an exclusive. As *Time*'s managing editor Roy Alexander once said: "*Time* with an exclusive is like a whore with a baby. We don't know what to do with it." But Denson

---

* By the time he came to *Newsweek* in 1953, he had been a reporter on *The Washington Herald*, *The Atlanta Constitution*, and *The Miami News*; Washington correspondent for the New York *Herald Tribune*, *The New York World*, and the *World-Telegram*; assistant managing editor of *The Washington Post* and of *The Chicago Times*; correspondent for the International News Service; assistant chief of the Washington bureau of *Time*; associate editor of *Fortune*; assistant executive editor of the *Chicago Herald-American*; managing editor of the *Kiplinger Magazine* and of *Collier's*. When he left *Newsweek*, Denson went on to become editor of the New York *Herald Tribune*, adviser to the publisher of the New York *Journal-American*, and editor of the *Los Angeles Herald Examiner*. His last job, which he took in 1978 at the age of seventy-three, was as editor of New York's short-lived tabloid, *The Trib*.

knew: You play it big, you slam it on the cover, you promote
it within the magazine, and you shout about it in advertising.
Denson laid the groundwork for what was to become a most
successful advertising slogan—describing *Newsweek* as the
"world's most quoted newsweekly."

John Denson sometimes made the magazine exciting at the
sacrifice of good judgment and good taste. One notable (and
horrible) cover that I later used in pep talks to show how
far we had come, was a picture of a bright red tomato—illus-
trating a story on the seed business. Another time Denson
had a cover drawn up purporting to map the New South,
complete with pickaninnies eating watermelons (we dis-
suaded him from running that one). But when all was said
and done, in the half dozen years John Denson was *Newsweek*'s editor, he took a dull, gray, pallid imitation of *Time*,
turned it upside down, and shook until all the nuts and bolts
came tumbling out. With *U.S. News* suddenly breathing down
Newsweek's neck, Denson may well have saved the magazine.
And when he left to become editor of the *Herald Tribune*, he
worked prodigiously in a similar vein. John Hay ("Jock")
Whitney, the *Tribune*'s owner, later said to me: "If this paper
survives, there should be a plaque to John Denson in the
lobby." Unhappily, there never was a plaque: For reasons
mostly unrelated to the editorial "product," the *Herald
Tribune* died in 1966.

By the time Phil Graham bought *Newsweek*, the magazine
had already moved to Madison Avenue from its (even then)
rather tawdry Times Square headquarters. Now Topps and
Bleeck's and the Blue Ribbon were replaced as eating places
by the wood-paneled bar of the New Weston, where any
trench-coated foreign correspondent would feel at home; by
Le Chanteclair, a hangout for racing-car drivers and enthusi-
asts; by Giambelli's, Clos Normand, the Berkshire, the ele-

gant Le Cygne, the Waldorf's hearty Bull and Bear, the pretentious Forum of the XII Caesars—even, on occasion, by the "21" Club. On Friday nights, if the Jewish vote carried, we editors would eat at Chandler's, a nearby steakhouse that seemed transplanted from Miami Beach; and on those rare occasions when the Gentiles prevailed, we'd go to Charley O's for soused shrimp and roast beef. If the week was easy (or particularly hard) we might treat ourselves to a Chinese dinner way over on Second Avenue, at the Shun Lee Dynasty, where senior editor Dwight Martin, an old Far East hand, would do the ordering and wash things down with vodka and beer. Occasionally I would take a staffer to lunch at the Racquet & Tennis Club, that Romanesque bastion of Ivy League Waspdom on Park Avenue—until I found its stuffy surroundings and unstated racism too much to take. My father had been a member for many years, and for his sake (I tell myself), I didn't make a fuss when I just quietly resigned.

If I dwell on our eating places, it is because they were so important a part of our professional lives. Journalistic hours are odd and long and often tense, and newsmen seek each other out as natural allies in a world that is so much part of them, but which they visit so randomly. There is another reason journalists like to drink and eat together: They simply cannot think of any better company. At *Newsweek*, the eating places were where we forged our team, kicked around ideas, and made our plots. It was at the Algonquin, lunching with Lou Harris one day in 1963, that I first hatched the idea— originally suggested by my friend Schuyler Chapin—of a survey of Black America; it was at the Gloucester House, eating expensive fish (on the company tab) that Lansner, Manning, and I spent hours that same year asking one another what we would say if called upon to testify in any family lawsuit aimed at dethroning Phil Graham from his seat of power. Was he merely an amiable and brilliant eccentric, as we had considered him for so long? Or was he certifiably insane?

. . .

By November 1963, sixteen weeks after Phil Graham's death, his widow, Katharine, was beginning to edge her way gingerly, unsurely, deferentially, into the affairs of The Washington Post Company. She spent one Friday night at my elbow, as I self-consciously edited copy, killed stories, ordered up new leads, picked and cropped pictures, and tried to show her how the magazine finally came together each week—all under the sure and skillful hand of its editor, of course. I always read every line of *Newsweek* before it went to press—how else could one edit a magazine? "You look pretty pro-y to me," Kay said—which was exactly the impression I had tried to convey.

In the weekly cycle of a newsmagazine, Friday is the key day. For most staffers, the week starts on Tuesday, with story conferences, picture conferences, cover conferences. Stories for the next week's issue are selected and assigned, and detailed queries are sent to the magazine's news bureaus around the world. (By 1963, thanks to the infusion of money by Phil Graham, *Newsweek* had sixteen bureaus and some forty correspondents.) Every Tuesday, in this weekly cycle, there are telephone discussions with Washington and other bureaus, and Telex conversations with such remote outposts as Moscow, Tokyo, and—back in the sixties—Saigon. At midweek, writers can be seen strolling the corridors of the New York editorial offices, wondering anxiously when the raw material from correspondents in the field will come chattering over the wire machines. By Friday, the reporters' "files" are flowing to New

York in avalanche proportions, and the writers are hunched over their typewriters. Those few who can still be found stalking the corridors now are gazing into the middle distance, searching out a new lead, or a better transition, or a more felicitous turn of phrase.

Because of the weekly rhythm of business, political, and other world affairs, in most weeks most of the news has been "made" by Friday afternoon, which enables newsmagazine editors to "fix" their magazine in semifinal form, with only minor changes reserved for Saturday. But wars are often made on weekends, and natural disasters have a way of picking their own time to happen. Likewise, assassinations.

November 22, 1963, was a Friday, and a few of us editors were scheduled to lunch in the editorial dining room that day with Katharine Graham, Arthur Schlesinger, Jr., and John Kenneth Galbraith. Kay had invited the New Frontiersmen in to talk about *Newsweek,* particularly about how its "back of the book" sections might be improved. I wasn't looking forward to the session; after all, who were these people to tell us how to run a magazine? Galbraith arrived late from Cambridge and Schlesinger from Washington, and so we were all still having drinks in Kay's office, after one-thirty, when the door suddenly opened. Al McCollough of the copy desk poked his head in. I noticed that his shirtsleeves, as always, were neatly and precisely rolled to just above the elbows. He had some AP copy in his hand. "I'm sorry to interrupt," McCollough said calmly, almost in a whisper, "but the president has been shot."

We dashed down the hall to my office, where there was a television set, and flicked on CBS. Wire-service flashes and bulletins were brought in. Ben Bradlee was on the phone from Washington. More bulletins. Additional bits and pieces by telephone from Charles Roberts, our White House correspondent, in Dallas. Galbraith and Schlesinger sat there crushed, unbelieving. And finally, the muffled-drum voice of Walter Cronkite: "The president is dead."

It was after 2:00 p.m., Friday—very late in the week for a newsmagazine to be ripped apart for such a colossal story. I had given up smoking three months before; now I sent out for a carton of Chesterfields.

The editing of a newsweekly is normally an exercise in planned improvisation. If the editors are at all sharp, they can plan major stories weeks in advance to coincide with such known events as space shots, political conventions, opening nights, elections, and the like. That week in 1963, the planned cover story was on Vice-President Lyndon Johnson's protégé Bobby Baker, just then the center of a growing political scandal. The Baker story, clearly, was the first thing that had to go—and before we were through another twenty pages of the almost-completed magazine would be swept out to make room for coverage of the assassination. But first we had to deploy our troops.

We decided that Chuck Roberts, already in Dallas, should stay with Lyndon Johnson—and as a result of his sure journalistic instincts, Roberts was one of only two reporters to witness LBJ's swearing-in on *Air Force One* and to accompany the new president, and the murdered president, back to Washington. To cover the Dallas scene, we dispatched Bill Brink, our Chicago bureau chief, and Bob Young, one of Brink's reporters, as well as Joe Cumming from Atlanta and Dick Mathison from Los Angeles. We sent Boston's Jayne Brumley to Hyannis Port. Brink assigned Young full time to the Parkland Hospital, where John Kennedy had been brought—and Young was finally able to get an interview with the first physician to attend the president. Brink himself staked out the second floor of the Dallas police station where Lee Harvey Oswald was being held. This stakeout paid off at about six o'clock Saturday morning, when Brink got the Dallas police chief and the chief of detectives to sit down and lay out what they knew about the events and what they were reasonably sure of. "Our story," Brink recalled laconically years later, "was pretty damn accurate."*

Meanwhile, in New York, we editors were shaping the flow and layout of the assassination "package." In this case the lead article, the "violin" (*Newsweek* jargon deriving from the tone-setting concert master's fiddle in a symphony orchestra,) would be the "running" story of the assassination. We allotted seven pages, or twenty-one columns, to this article and assigned it to the magazine's star writer, Peter Goldman. There would, of course, be a biographical sketch of Oswald; Jack Kroll, our cultural editor, volunteered to handle that, and turned out a gem under the headline, THE MARXIST MARINE. We apportioned ten columns to a review of Lyndon Johnson's career, six to worldwide reaction, four pages to a picture-and-text retrospective of Jack Kennedy's life. Emmet Hughes and Ken Crawford set about rewriting their columns, and young Ed Kosner—later to become my successor as *Newsweek*'s editor but at that point not yet even listed on the masthead—spent the night writing the piece on JFK's presidential years. "That was my vigil," Kosner said later.

There was one story I knew we must have, and I knew that only one person could write it. I called Ben Bradlee and asked him to write a personal appreciation of his friend Jack Kennedy. Through his tears, Bradlee agreed to undertake the toughest assignment of his career. But from then through Saturday, every hour or two (it seems in retrospect), Ben was on the phone saying he just couldn't do it. You've *got* to,

* Brink later became managing editor of the *New York Daily News,* where he concocted the famous headline, during New York City's fiscal crisis of 1975: FORD TO CITY: DROP DEAD.

I would say, in different words each time. At last, Bradlee
produced an intimate prose poem, "He Had That Special
Grace . . ." Kennedy, wrote Bradlee:

> . . . [was] a graceful man, physically graceful in his
> movements—walking, swimming or swinging a golf
> club—and had that special grace of the intellect that is
> taste. . . . John Kennedy had a Walter Mitty streak
> in him, as wide as his smile. On the golf course, when
> he was winning, he reminded himself most of Arnold
> Palmer in raw power, or Julius Boros in finesse. When
> he was losing, he was "the old warrior" at the end of a
> brilliant career, asking only that his faithful caddie
> point him in the right direction, and let instinct take
> over. . . .

As the full scope and horror of the events in Dallas sank in,
we threw out *Newsweek*'s regular sections, right and left—and
still, insisted my assistant, Rod Gander, we weren't giving
enough space to the assassination story. I killed another section; still not enough, said Gander. Finally, even Newsmakers
and Periscope, the magazine's two most popular features,
went by the board.

What to do for a cover picture? Ten months before, to
illustrate Walter Lippmann's first article for the magazine, we
had run that handsome color profile of Kennedy. Bert Chap-
man, our production manager, dug it out, and cover editor
Bob Engle routed out the Lippmann type and patched in the
words "John Fitzgerald Kennedy, 1917–1963." Off went the
new layout to our main printing plant in Dayton, Ohio, and
to our overseas printers in London and Tokyo.

By dinnertime Friday, the stories were assigned, the reporters at their posts, the photo coverage planned—including arrangements to pick up any late pictures that we might need

from the Dallas papers. On the makeup desks in New York, dummies of the semifinished magazine were laid open for major surgery. "There we were," recalled makeup chief Ralph Paladino, "blocking out a story on the murder of the president and at the same time saying to ourselves, 'This can't be, it just can't be!' "

Over that weekend, *Newsweek*'s correspondents filed more than seventy thousand words on the assassination—from Dallas and Washington and from news bureaus around the country and overseas. The writers in New York waded through this material, as well as the wire-service and newspaper accounts, and began to pull their stories together. Peter Goldman got a little sleep and came in at dawn Saturday to start writing the main piece. In the best of times, Goldman's mien is so dour as to have inspired a nickname: We used to call him "the one-man cortege." Now he had good reason to perform in character. But from the moment the main story was assigned, I knew it was safe in Goldman's hands; I knew it again when I saw his classic opening sentence late that Saturday afternoon: "In one sudden, swift, awful convulsion of history last week, the majesty and the burdens of the presidency of the United States shifted from one man to another. . . ."

Skillfully, movingly, Goldman told the intricate, painful, grotesque tale, resorting on occasion to the often tricky device of italics for emphasis and unity:

> *The President was dead . . .*
> *. . . The suspect was caught . . .*
> *. . . The order was changing . . .*
> *. . . The fabric was preserved . . .*

Of all the eloquent words that the fallen president had spoken in his short and unfulfilled career [wrote Goldman at the end of his story], his successor chose a single sentence for his proclamation of mourning:

"The energy, the faith, the devotion which we bring to this endeavor will light our country and all who serve it—and the glow from that fire can truly light the world."

It was left to Lyndon Baines Johnson to be the keeper of the flame. It was left to a sorrowing nation to answer his call for help—and to pray with him for God's.

Newsweek's normal deadline for final transmission of copy by Teletypesetter to the main printing plant in Dayton was 8:00 p.m., Saturday; this week, of course, much of the copy was yet to be written at that hour—and everyone was determined that it must be written well, if late, and that all the stories must be edited into a smooth-flowing and sense-making whole. Everything had to be special—from the cover picture to the final word. There was the problem, for example, of what to do with our table-of-contents page, the so-called "Top of the Week" feature, where normally the editors boast each week of their various feats of derring-do. At Kermit Lansner's suggestion, we turned the space over to an excerpt from Walt Whitman's "When Lilacs Last in the Door-yard Bloom'd," written after Abraham Lincoln's assassination a century before:

Coffin that passes through lanes and streets,
Through day and night, with the great cloud
* darkening the land,*
With the pomp of the inloop'd flags, with the cities
* draped in black . . .*
With processions long and winding, and the flambeaus
* of the night . . .*
With the waiting depot, the arriving coffin, and the
* sombre faces . . .*
With the tolling, tolling bells' perpetual clang;
Here! coffin that slowly passes,
I give you my sprig of lilac.

that was to be a
d decreed that no
t through to the
granted, and our

d ten, had been
ation in January
come with me to
grounds—but as
ly, we were able
l made our way
eing challenged.
aptains and the
son—Jacqueline
Gaulle, Ikeda,
only a few feet
ves—so lax was

evision in Kay
ts of the past
of her office,
nd *Newsweek*
nd Taps split
l known only
nd colleague
him, during
New York's
e magazine's
would have
y fixed him
n't you tell
thought of
es in 1960,
ge as Jack

e-setting room
rom New York
vels. I remem-
as in charge of
ce an early age,
ut this night, as
s to the printing
Finally, by three
by had been trans-
home.

e back in the office
ow the presses were
de to correct major
rough what we had
done it well, and
enty-five blocks away.
Cathedral, next door
what was going on. A
y. When I got home, I
s pouring myself a stiff
Jack Ruby shooting Os-
date the story with this
ote the story, procured a
The Dallas Morning News
aid off—and wired all the
percent of the press run,
ewsweek, with the new de-
. Special flights carrying the
ere already on their way to
and rerouted to "less impor-
Dayton were reloaded with
o Washington.

d. Subscriber copies for the
to arrive at the New York post

office at 5:00 a.m., Monday, but because
national day of mourning, the post office h
bulk mail would be delivered. A call wei
regional postal director; an exception was
magazines were delivered on schedule.

My two older daughters, then thirteen a
with me at John Kennedy's ice-cold inaugui
1961, and I thought it appropriate that they
his funeral. I had tickets to the White Hous
it turned out, we didn't need them. Incredib
to slip between two huge television vans and
almost to the White House portico without b
And there, on the driveway, we watched the
kings depart on foot behind the funeral cais
Kennedy and Jack's two surviving brothers; d
Baudouin, Erhard, Mikoyan. They all passed
away, such easy targets for assassination themse
White House security even on that day.

It was only later, watching the burial on tel
Graham's *Washington Post* office, that the ever
three days caught up with me. I sat in the bacl
now crowded with perhaps a dozen other *Post* a
people, and watched as the coffin was lowered a
the autumn air. And I thought of this man I hac
slightly, but who had seemed such a friend a
just the same. I thought of my first meeting with
the primaries of 1960, at a *Newsweek* dinner in
elegant Links Club. Malcolm Muir, then still the
boss, was huffing at the candidate about how he
to "do something" about organized labor. Kenned
with a cold eye, and said: "Mr. Mew-ah, why do
me what *you* would do about organized labor?" I
Muir, at the Democratic convention in Los Angel
tearing up his delegate-counting scorecard in a ra

Kennedy went over the top to win the nomination. And I thought of Kennedy so elegant (and Phil Graham so drunk) at the inaugural ball in 1961.

As I watched the television tube, watched the coffin sink into the ground, I was wracked by sobs. I hadn't had much sleep. I loved that president. I was glad I was in the back of Kay's office, where nobody could see me. I had wept that way only once before in my life—my parents were still alive then— and that was at Phil Graham's funeral less than four months before.

· · ·

Next day, when we *Newsweek* people had a chance to look at the "product" of our arch-competitor, *Time*, we found some professional consolation, at least. *Time* had devoted a mere thirteen pages to the assassination story versus *Newsweek*'s twenty-five; in unfeeling deference to an old tradition of never putting a dead man on its cover, *Time* featured a picture of Lyndon Johnson instead of Kennedy. And where *Newsweek* had used its editorial promotion space to run an excerpt from Walt Whitman, *Time* indulged itself in a tasteless bit of self-congratulation: "The President [said *Time*'s publisher's letter] had a special feeling about *Time*. . . . [He] got his copy early, and sometimes within an hour was on the phone to our White House correspondents with comments. . . . He said on several occasions that he regarded *Time* as the most important magazine in America. . . . *Time* and its staff greatly valued the relationships—both professional and personal—with its No. 1 subscriber."

And so, just as we believed *Newsweek* had led the way with our earlier exposé of the radical right, and then with our special issue on Black America, now, going head to head on a breaking story, we felt we had bested *Time* on the biggest news event since the war. "You did it right," said my friend Dick Clurman, then chief of correspondents for *Time,* "we did it wrong."

Newsweek, we believed, had arrived. Cockily, we began to refer to *Time* as "Brand X."

•III•
FORWARD
PASSES

L ittle did most of us realize it, but for all her wealth and new station in life, Katharine Meyer Graham was a pitiful figure in those early-sixties days. A poor little rich girl, she was born and raised in the shadow of powerful parents, who had little time for their children. She went to Vassar, transferred to Chicago for a taste of less traditional education—putting some distance between herself and home. She learned that she was half Jewish (on her father's side) only when someone told her so in a college bull session. She had married the sparkling Phil, and was outshone by him for years. In her own eyes, she had been an ugly duckling all her life.

And now, in the fall of 1963, she was the uncertain, neophyte boss of a huge communications empire, with her top executives pushing and pulling and pressing for decisions that had gone unmade in Phil Graham's final year. I hardly knew her, and had no idea how she might perform in her new job. Soon after she took over, I inflicted a long memo concerning *Newsweek*'s future on her and Fritz Beebe.

A key factor in any magazine's economy is the circulation guarantee that it makes to advertisers—a figure upon which its advertising rates are based. Unlike newspapers, magazines can, to a large degree, "control" their circulations by spending more or less money on direct mail and other promotion. If your promotion is good, the more you spend on it, the more new subscribers you get. But the big catch is the "renewal rate" three months or six months or a year later: How many of those new subscribers can be persuaded to renew their subscriptions, and at what cost in promotion? One of the great publishing mistakes of the 1960s was the decision by both *Life* and *Look* to go after huge numbers of subscribers, in order to compete with the populace that television was delivering to advertisers. The result was that both *Life* and *Look* took on many marginal subscribers and had to spend millions to keep them aboard as their trial subscriptions expired. As much as anything else, that was what skewed the economics of those magazines and brought about their ultimate demise. Not so incidentally, the new *Life* and *Look*, which appeared in 1978, both aimed at far smaller audiences.

At *Newsweek*, in the fall of 1963, the decision had been made to boost the magazine's circulation guarantee ever so slightly the next year. For a variety of reasons, I thought this decision was far too timid, and my purpose was to force The Washington Post Company's new managers into a much bolder course of action.

The opening line of my memo to Kay and Fritz set the tone —"Subject: 1964, 1965, 1966, 1967, 1968." I said that the "feel" of things was right—newsstand sales and subscriptions were up, advertising pages were on the rise, and people along Madison Avenue, in their special lingo, were talking about *Newsweek* as "the hot book." On top of that, 1964 would be a presidential year, and election years are always good for newsmagazines. Furthermore, there would be 2,300,000 students in college in 1964, a record high: "Here are the business, professional, scientific, and political leaders of tomorrow—the people who will *count* in the seventies. So why shouldn't we be slugging it out on the campus in the sixties on an equal footing with *Time?*"

I argued that we should spend heavily to boost our circulation: "The question . . . is not whether we can afford to spend the money . . . in order to lift this magazine to new plateaus. . . . The question really is, can we afford *not* to spend, and thus run the risk of letting opportunity—and the competition—pass us by for good?"

I have unearthed no written reply to this memo from either Kay or Fritz; that was not the way we operated. Probably Kay rolled her eyeballs skyward and said, "Oh Gahd, Oz." And probably Fritz cocked a lawyerly eye and said nothing. But seemingly the memo had an effect. *Newsweek's* circulation guarantee went up, as planned, by only 25,000 (to 1,550,000) in January 1964—but in March it was raised by another 50,000, and in January 1965 it leaped ahead by 150,000 to 1,750,000. Steady increases followed, year by year, until the magazine's domestic circulation reached 2,900,000 in 1974, and there the management decided to keep it for the next five years.

All this circulation growth cost money—and so did the editorial improvements that went with it. Kay and Fritz did not hesitate to pour the money in. The editorial budget, which was $3.4 million in 1960, increased to more than $10 million by the time the decade ended. And whereas there had once been no money at all for four-color illustration inside the magazine, hundreds of thousands of dollars were soon being lavished on this image-improving venture.

Phil Graham had brought Beebe into the company soon after he bought *Newsweek* in 1961; Eugene Meyer had advised his son-in-law always to have a partner in business, even though you may own the company. Now, with Graham dead,

Kay and Fritz were the partners—and they complemented each other nicely. Kay was bright, impulsive, tentative at first; Fritz was infinitely patient, almost dogged in his approach to his job. "He may look like a square," Graham once said, "but he isn't."

Beebe came from upstate New York, and went on from the Utica Free Academy to Dartmouth and the Yale Law School. He had become a partner in Cravath, Swaine & Moore—the Tiffany of Wall Street law firms—and served as the Meyer family lawyer. Fritz was married to a European beauty, Liane, whose family background was so complicated that she insisted the only way it could be explained was that her grandfathers were sisters.

Fritz Beebe combined Wall Street smarts with small-town decency. Early in the sixties, *Newsweek*'s Middle East correspondent Tom Streithorst was engulfed by a horrible tragedy. While driving on vacation in Turkey, he had a head-on collision with a truck; his wife, in the front seat beside him, was killed. Streithorst was clapped in a Turkish jail—and Beebe flew to Istanbul, hired the best attorney in the country, and managed to spring Streithorst from jail. When Fritz died of cancer at the age of fifty-nine in 1973, I wrote a eulogy for this brave and gentle and unpredictable man.

> . . . He was firm enough to hold a point long into the night; more often than not he would win the point. He was flexible and graceful enough to concede when he was wrong—just as opponents were beginning to think he might be right. . . . He had a wonderful feeling for people—and that was a reflection of his deep emotional nature. He had a great passion for the right—and that was an affirmation of his deep intellectual commitment to justice.

The additional money that Kay and Fritz poured into *Newsweek* made it possible to pay better salaries, and attract new talent. The changes in personnel, of course, had started the moment Phil Graham bought control—first with the appointment of Manning and Lansner and me as "Wallendas," and Ben Bradlee as Washington bureau chief. Other changes followed rapidly. The booming Bill Emerson was brought up from the Southland to run the "back of the book"; our elegant and energetic foreign editor, Arnaud de Borchgrave—who had given up his Belgian title to become an American citizen* —became chief European correspondent. Three old colleagues from my days at *Time* became important members of the team—Lester Bernstein, a brilliant and witty wielder of the pencil, as national-affairs editor; the scholarly Bob Christopher as foreign editor; and the cool and competent Jim Cannon as chief of correspondents.

The acquisition of Bernstein was fortuitous. At a dinner party in 1963, I met NBC's chairman, Bob Sarnoff, for whom Bernstein was then working as PR man and speechwriter. "How's Lester?" I asked, seizing upon one of the few subjects Sarnoff and I had in common.

"Oh, you know Lester," said Sarnoff, "always restive." Next day I called Bernstein and asked him, as a fairly recent alumnus of *Time*, for suggestions as to who at "Brand X" might be available to fill *Newsweek*'s key national-affairs spot. When Bernstein called back the following day, he said: "Were you sending me some sort of a message?" I told him I was but his reflexes seemed to have slowed down, and that worried me. Within weeks, Bernstein was on board—leaving Sarnoff, as Sarnoff himself noted, quite literally speechless. Lester was later to leave a lot of other people speechless. He rose to managing editor in 1969, returned to RCA as a vice-president

---

* His full name and title: Arnaud Paul Charles Marie-Philippe, Comte de Borchgrave d'Altena, Comte du Saint Empire, Baron d'Elderen, Seigneur de Bovelingen de Marlinne, et d'autres lieux.

in 1973—and six years later, in one of the more unusual shuffles in magazine history, Kay Graham abruptly brought Bernstein back to replace Ed Kosner as *Newsweek*'s editor. When Kermit Lansner, by then long gone from *Newsweek* himself, heard the news of Lester's 1979 rebirth, he called Bernstein with a three-and-a-half-word reaction: "Unbelievable. *Unbe-lievable! Un-fucking-believable!"*

In the early days of Graham's *Newsweek* ownership, scarcely a week had gone by without a potential editorial disaster. Not infrequently, cover stories and other hefty projects would land on the Wallendas' desks on Saturday, barely breathing and clearly wanting resuscitation or a total rewrite; more than once I was reminded of the note Tom Matthews, the managing editor of *Time*, had scribbled on some dismal piece of copy years before: "This story is badly written, badly edited, and badly typed."

But gradually, as the new senior editors attracted better writing talent, things became more orderly and professional, and we could concentrate not just on getting the magazine out every week but on making it better at the same time. More and more, we probed beneath the surface of events to find their meaning, and we moved increasingly to longer, more analytical stories ("blockbusters") —on Southeast Asia, the Atlantic community, the Mideast, the U.S. economy, poverty, unemployment, even the pros and cons of fallout shelters in those cold war days. In retrospect, we were making a risky bet—that we could elevate the intellectual level of the magazine and still keep readers buying it. We hardly gave it a second thought. And the bet paid off. Newsstand sales set record after record, subscription-renewal rates improved, and thousands of people were taking the trouble to write letters to the editor—4,500 in the first quarter of 1964 versus 3,200 in the same period a year before.

"*Time*," I said in a Knute Rockne-style pep talk at our 1964 sales meeting in Puerto Rico, "is the competition, and I propose to beat its increasingly pudgy posterior every time we have the chance—which is exactly once a week." And *U.S. News?* "If David Lawrence's wrinkled rump happens to be in the line of fire, so much the better."

We demanded excellence and thoroughness and long hours of our new writers and reporters. To one young reporter in the Washington bureau, Ben Bradlee wrote "some blunt thoughts . . . triggered by your question yesterday—'Is this a six-day week?'—which struck me dumb and [thus] deprived you of my profane answer: you bet your ass it is!"*

---

* Frank Trippett, then a reporter in our three-man Atlanta bureau, recalls a classic telephone conversation with Bill Emerson in New York. Trippett was in New Orleans in April 1962 when Emerson telephoned. The Religion section, he said, was doing a story on the confrontation between Archbishop Joseph Rummel and an excommunicated parishioner named Mrs. Una Gaillot over school desegregation. The confrontation had taken place on the archbishop's lawn, and Emerson needed just two questions answered.

"Number one," he said, "what does the archbishop's house look like? Is it wood, or stone, or brick? Is it Victorian with ivy on the walls? What kind of day was it? Was it balmy and overcast, or hot and muggy? What does the archbishop look like? Is he old and bespectacled or what? How did he walk when he came out of the house? Did he stride angrily? Or did he walk haltingly, leaning on a cane? How was he dressed? What is the walkway like? Is it concrete, brick or gravel? What do the grounds look like? Are there oak trees and rose bushes, magnolias and poppies? Were birds singing in the bushes? What was going on in the street outside the house? Was an angry crowd assembled? Or was there the normal business traffic, passing by oblivious to the drama inside? What were Mrs. Gaillot and her friends wearing? Did they have on Sunday best or just casual clothes? What happened when the archbishop confronted Mrs. Gaillot? Was he stern and silent? Or did he rebuke her? What was the exact language she used?

"Now," Emerson said, "question number two . . ."

We placed great stress on our cover treatment, for that, after all, was the magazine's face to the world. We simplified the format; we abolished the screaming-yellow headline slashes that used to clutter more than inform; we gradually reduced and finally removed the red "coat hanger" that had run around three sides of the *Newsweek* cover for many years. At length, Francis ("Hank") Brennan, another old colleague from *Time*, designed a new, more authoritative logotype which announced the magazine's title with simplicity and force. Under our indefatigable cover director, Bob Engle, more and more we used color photographs instead of gimmicked-up designs and drawings. We believed, I explained at another sales meeting, that "color photography is closer to the truth, and thus a closer reflection of what *Newsweek* is all about." *Newsweek*'s first overall "bleed" cover, with the picture extending to the borders of the magazine, was a dramatic photograph of Igor Stravinsky. The date was May 21, 1962.

We did not hesitate to change covers late in the week—once as late as Sunday, in the winter of 1965 when Winston Churchill died. Kay Graham and I happened to be in Japan and Kermit Lansner was in charge of the magazine (I always delegated full authority when I was away). I will never forget our pleased surprise at finding *Newsweek* on sale in Kyoto with a color photograph of Churchill on the cover, seemingly only hours after his death.

During one year in the early sixties, *Newsweek* made late cover switches no fewer than fifteen times. Robert Taft, Jr., of Ohio, running for the Senate, was scheduled for cover treatment one week in October 1964—poor fellow, that was the week that the Russians orbited three cosmonauts, the Chinese exploded their first A-bomb, Harold Wilson came to power, and Khrushchev was deposed. Leonid Brezhnev, the new man in the Kremlin, replaced Taft on *Newsweek*'s cover. Twice Ian Fleming's *Goldfinger* was scheduled and twice it was bounced—by riots in Harlem one week and by the Gulf of Tonkin incident another.

In the old Denson tradition of "end-running" the competition, we were sometimes like the fresh kid on the block, making faces at the local bully and scampering off before he could catch us. When *Time*'s own Henry Luce died in 1967, we had the temerity to picture him as a *Time* cover subject—superimposed on the cover of *Newsweek*. In the obituary that accompanied our cover, senior editor Dwight Martin, himself a former *Time* hand, dusted off a little of his old *Time*-style. He quoted Luce on the then current "God Is Dead" controversy:

"The real question about God is, of course, 'whose God?' or 'what God?' After all the argumentation is done, I believe that God revealed in the Scriptures is, quite simply, God; and therefore, not only living, but the creator and source of all life." Last week the questioning, probing, prodding soul of Henry Luce was off to get the final answer. God had better be prepared.

People frequently ask why *Newsweek* and *Time* so often "have the same covers." The answer is that mostly they don't. But when the world is in a period of fast-breaking and cataclysmic news events, as it was in the sixties and early seventies, the newsmagazines will understandably put those events on their covers simultaneously. But what about such subjects as pop music, films, the dance? There is a certain rhythm to the news in the cultural world, as well, and editors of newsmagazines like to take advantage of it. After laying a series of heavy cover stories on their readers—on taxes, say, or nuclear disarmament—editors like to "get off the reader's back" by featuring some new and topical cultural event, such as the American debut of an opera singer, or the opening of a photographic exhibit by an Avedon.

Occasionally photographers and reporters from the news-magazines run across each other's traces in the course of their work, and report back to the editors that the opposition is apparently planning the same cover story. In such cases, more often than not, efforts are made to speed up production—with the result, sometimes, that both magazines will appear with the same cover simultaneously. One case in point was the double-billing of Liza Minnelli in *Cabaret* on the covers of *Newsweek* and *Time* in the last week of February 1972; another, in May 1975, was the dual appearance of the dancer Mikhail Baryshnikov.

As we at *Newsweek* gained confidence—and financial resources—we moved from the old "end-run" techniques of John Denson to some long-distance forward passes of our own. What most differentiated *Newsweek* from its competition in the sixties and early seventies was its continuous exploration of social issues and cultural changes. Race and poverty were paramount concerns, and we covered those matters with compassion and in great depth. There were many other issues, ranging from the growing permissiveness of society to the newest fads in child-rearing. One cover story featured a not-so-angelic baby decked out in his Dr. Dentons, clutching a flower and bemedaled with a variety of buttons: "Don't Trust Anyone Over 7"; "Down With Mom"; "Up Against the Wall, Mother." IS DR. SPOCK TO BLAME? asked the headline.

Sometimes we clucked at the permissive society—and sold a lot of magazines in the process. A 1967 cover, for instance, showed a nude Jane Fonda (from the waist up, and from behind) in *Barbarella*. Fonda was looking over her shoulder seductively, holding a feather ready to tickle any male fancy—or something. The headline: ANYTHING GOES. The accompanying story talked about the increasing permissiveness in the arts as a reflection of "a society that has lost its consensus on such crucial issues as premarital sex and clerical celibacy, marriage, birth control, and sex education." Thousands of offended readers wrote in and hundreds canceled their subscriptions; but no one will ever know how many thousands of others bought the magazine and started new subscriptions as a result of the Fonda cover. Eighteen months later, we returned to the theme of sexual liberality in the arts —everything from *I Am Curious (Yellow)* to *Portnoy's Complaint* and *Oh! Calcutta!* We didn't moralize, except to say that in a mass society there are bound to be excesses, and repression is not the answer.

Another cover story on campus morals, written by Mel Elfin, then a writer in "the back of the book," cleverly sketched the evolution of American sexuality by citing passages from three vintage works of fiction:

1911
Stover at Yale

He put out his hand and gently took the end of a scarf which she wore about her shoulder, and raised it to his lips. It was a boyish, impulsive fantasy, and he inclined his head before her.

—Owen Johnson

1920
This Side of Paradise

"Isabelle!" he cried, half involuntarily, and held out his arms. As in the story-books, she ran into them, and on that half-minute as their lips first touched, rested the high point of vanity, the crest of his young egotism.

—F. Scott Fitzgerald

1962
Love With a Harvard Accent

They were sitting in Mark's bedroom . . . he saw her
blue eyes fastened on his . . . then Mark reached over
and brought her face to his . . . Within seconds they
were unbuttoning each other's shirts, and in less than
a minute, beneath the covers of his bed.
                                        —Leonie St. John

Newsweek's story noted that for growing numbers of college
students, the question of chastity "has become academic."

We visited the drug scene and the hippy world early and
often. We recorded the nonviolent and mystical activities of
the flower children from Haight-Ashbury to the East Village
to Woodstock, and reported on their bizarre *lingua franca* as
the freaks grooved on confrontations with up-tight pigs, and
the heads got their stuff together no matter what their hang-
ups. You know, like that, man. We did cover stories on pot
and LSD, and most of us at least experimented with the lesser
hallucinogens. One night, senior editor Ed Diamond called
home to tell his wife he'd be late, because he was going to a
pot party at a researcher's Greenwich Village apartment—just
a little necessary fieldwork for that week's cover story on
marijuana.

As the Space Age dawned, we launched a new *Newsweek*
section, Space and the Atom, and as the U.S. involvement
grew in Southeast Asia, we started a section called The War
in Vietnam. This forced us every week to pay editorial attention to those two continuing stories. Ed Diamond, our expert
on science and space (as well as pot), wrote or edited scores
of pieces, first on America's fizzling rocketry, then on the race
to the moon. In July 1969, when Neil Armstrong finally made
that "giant step for mankind," we pulled off a technical coup
that made us proud. In addition to its U.S. circulation, *News-*

week prints in Europe and Asia; I was determined to display an actual photograph of the first man on the moon on our cover, in all our editions around the world. We kept the magazine open an extra couple of days that historic week, and stationed photographers in front of television sets in Dayton, Tokyo, and London (our major printing locations) as well as in New York. They were all instructed to shoot continuously as the fantastic moon story unfolded on their television screens.

At about 1:00 a.m., New York time, I was shown a hundred or so pictures shot off the television screen by the photographer in New York; these were supposed to show us what—we hoped—the other three photographers, near our printing plants, were shooting. As I bent over the contact sheets with a magnifying hand viewer, I was seized with gloom; the quality of the pictures was very poor. I learned a lesson in optics that night: Watching a moving picture on the television screen, your mind tends to put the thing together, even though the reception may be bad; but when a still camera freezes the action on the screen, the whole image falls apart. At length I selected one picture that I thought might possibly be cropped and blown up for cover use. It showed an astronaut in the foreground, walking away from the camera, the left-hand side of his backpack in shadow, the right side in the light. In the background on the left, the landing module and a second astronaut could be hazily discerned. I told our photo editors to crop down to the single astronaut in the foreground, and blow him up until his helmet obliterated the final two "e's" in the *Newsweek* logotype.

Within half an hour the layout was on my desk, and I knew we had a serviceable black-and-white domestic cover—provided our photographer in Dayton had shot the same scene at just about the same moment. It turned out he had. But what about the overseas editions, to be printed within

hours in London and Tokyo? At about 2:00 a.m., Bud Korengold, our London bureau chief, called in. "How're you doing
on the cover takes?" I asked. "Well, the quality is pretty
lousy," said Korengold, "but I think we have one picture
that might *possibly* be usable." I asked him to describe it.
"There's an astronaut in the foreground, walking away from
the camera. The left-hand side of his backpack is in shadow,
the right side is lighted. In the background, on the left, I
think you can make out the other guy and the LEM." It was
extraordinary—out of the scores of pictures *his* photographer
had shot, Korengold had picked almost exactly the same
image that *we* had selected in New York—and these two
matched a photo that had been shot in Dayton as well. I told
Korengold how we wanted the picture cropped, and waited
anxiously to hear from Tokyo.

Half an hour later, Bernie Krisher, *Newsweek*'s Tokyo
bureau chief, called in with bad news: his pictures were very
poor. "Anything usable at all? *Anything?*" I asked. "Well,
there's one possibility. We have one picture that shows an
astronaut walking away from the camera in the foreground,
and in the left background . . ." "Bernie," I said, "you're a
goddamn genius. We've picked the same shot in New York,
London, and Dayton, and here's how I want you to crop
it. . . ."

So it was that *Newsweek* was able to appear that week, in
Asia and Europe and North America, with seemingly identical
photos of the man on the moon—but actually three different
pictures, taken at almost precisely the same split second from
three different locations and cropped on the basis of a fourth
picture snapped in New York. I was happy indeed when *Time*
appeared on the newsstands that week with an artist's render-
ing of what the moon walk *probably* looked like.

That also turned out to be a sadly lucky week for *Newsweek*
on another story. Because of the moon landing, we had kept

the magazine open long after its normal deadlines. And that enabled us to do a thorough job of reporting the tragic events that played out that Friday night on Chappaquiddick Island, off Martha's Vineyard. As luck would have it, three *Newsweek* staffers were on vacation in the area; Teddy Kennedy's accident had hardly hit the wire services when the *Newsweek* people arrived on the scene. Not only was our reporting from Chappaquiddick thorough; we editors also had in our possession two long, confidential memos from correspondents detailing a couple of recent Kennedy drinking bouts—one on a trip to Alaska, the other on a European visit. Editors in those pre-Watergate, pre-Wilbur Mills days were loath to print such information about public officials. But our story that week was tough:

> . . . when the man in question is a U.S. senator, a Kennedy whose star is ascendant; when at least eight hours elapse between the tragedy and his reporting of it—and when the senator's closest associates are known to have been powerfully concerned over his indulgent drinking habits, his daredevil driving, and his ever-ready eye for a pretty face, then the incident cries out for precisely the explanations which, as Teddy went into seclusion . . . were left bafflingly obscure.

Newsweek's story the following week was equally strong; it carried the headline: GRIEF, FEAR, DOUBT, PANIC—AND GUILT.

The reaction was predictable—a mountain of pro-Kennedy mail denouncing *Newsweek*. There were some exceptions, of course, including a letter from Kay Graham's mother, Agnes Meyer, whom I had met once or twice. "Dear Os," she wrote (Ray Moley used to spell my name and pronounce it that way, too), "I must write you a word of congratulation on last week's coverage of the Kennedy tragedy. *Newsweek*'s account was a brilliant job of reporting and its objectivity showed great courage because the Kennedy crowd is absolutely violent about [it]."

Indeed they were. Teddy's sister Jean Smith made a scene about *Newsweek*'s coverage at a New York dinner party we both attended. At length, I wrote the senator, saying that *Newsweek* wanted no vendetta with the Kennedys. He wrote back, still objecting to the Chappaquiddick stories, but peace was finally declared.

· · ·

One of *Newsweek*'s most ambitious undertakings in the sixties was a thirty-two-page special report in October 1969 on "the troubled American"—an account of the discontents of the nation's white, middle-class majority. What we found in this survey—the poll itself was conducted for us by the Gallup organization—was that "after years of feeling himself a besieged majority, the man in the middle . . . is giving vent to his frustration, his disillusionment—and his anger." That report served as an obituary for the sixties, and ushered in the sour mood of a new decade.

While chronicling the great upheavals of those years, we seized every opportunity to provide our readers with lighter fare. *Lolita*, Sid Caesar, Edward Albee, Liz Taylor, Zero Mostel, Truman Capote, Catherine Deneuve—they all appeared on *Newsweek*'s cover. Much of the comic relief, in those days, came from England. Ours was the first American magazine to feature the Beatles—the cover, a photomontage based on a horribly drawn sketch by me, showed only their eyes and moppy hair. The story was highly critical of this pop group that was to captivate an entire generation of young Americans and whose work remains popular today. "Sartorially," *Newsweek* said with great authority, the Beatles "are a nightmare: tight, dandified, Edwardian-beatnik suits and great pudding bowls of hair. Musically they are a near-disaster: guitars and drums slamming out a merciless beat that does away with secondary rhythms, harmony, and melody. Their lyrics (punctuated by nutty shouts of 'yeah, yeah, yeah!') are a catastrophe, a preposterous farrago of Valentine-card romantic sentiments. . . ." *Newsweek* was also the first American magazine to feature Twiggy, the wafer-thin waif from London: "She is a magic child of the media. Where there are no cameras, she ceases to exist. . . ." Mary Quant, Jean Shrimpton, Julie Christie all got their share of attention —and sold their share of magazines for us.

Gradually, we made our reportage more personal by identifying writers and reporters with their stories. We used internal by-lines ("The President, reports *Newsweek*'s Benjamin C. Bradlee. . . .") and increasingly we gave credit to staffers through the device of italicized introductions to articles. Top of the Week, the table-of-contents page, was moved to page 3 of the magazine and served to showcase the staff. And then, in October 1966, we undertook a dramatic new departure by allowing our cultural critics to sign all their art, theater, book, movie, and music reviews. We had debated this move for years, and had long shied away from so radical a departure from newsmagazine tradition. Would "by-lines" reduce the magazine's aura of authority? Would they make the writers unmanageable? What would happen to morale in those sections of the magazine where by-lines were *not* the normal routine?

We made this big move in the issue dated October 17, 1966; so cautious were we that we didn't call it to the attention of our readers until December 5, and even then in a rather back-handed way. We need not have been so cautious. The new policy made for better writing and better morale—but it was another three years before we extended the by-line policy to the entire magazine. I believe that this move, in February 1970, significantly increased *Newsweek*'s credibility among its readers at a time when the American press was frequently under attack. A couple of years after that, to give readers greater access to the magazine, we launched the My Turn column, where outsiders could express their views.*

While granting by-lines to the staff, we also changed the "balance" among our regular by-lined columnists. Early in 1961, Ernest K. Lindley's Washington column had been replaced by the old pro Kenneth Crawford, whose move into column-writing had also conveniently made room for Ben Bradlee to become Washington bureau chief. After adding Walter Lippmann and Emmet Hughes early on, and thus balancing the predictably conservative views of Raymond Moley, I thought it equally desirable to counter the antediluvian economics of Henry Hazlitt with something closer to current-day reality. Accordingly, early in 1965, Hazlitt was phased down to a biweekly cycle, and Yale's middle-roading Henry Wallich began to write about economics for us in alternate weeks.

So far, so good—but I thought even more variety was called for, and so I approached John Kenneth Galbraith at Harvard; would he care to join the *Newsweek* group? He would not, Galbraith said; he just couldn't write as short as that. From Harvard I went across the river to MIT and put the question to Paul Samuelson. "You have to realize," he said, "that as a result of my textbook [carrying the pre-emptive title *Economics*] I'm well-to-do and don't need the money." I said I was sure that a paltry few thousand dollars a year would be of no interest, but perhaps he *might* be interested in reaching

---

* The standard payment for a My Turn piece was $500. Art Buchwald, an early contributor, insisted on being paid more than anyone else, so I sent him a check for $501.

Newsweek's audience—an estimated 14 million people when "pass-along" readership was included. Samuelson's ears pricked up, and he said yes—so now I had a liberal economist, a centrist, and still a dull right-winger. I approached the lively conservative Milton Friedman of the University of Chicago, but he would have none of it—too busy to write for *Newsweek*, he said. But both Wallich and Samuelson agreed to lean on him, and soon Friedman was in—and Hazlitt was out. For years this new triumvirate performed effectively for *Newsweek*, giving the magazine great insight and balance in its coverage of economics. Two of the three—Samuelson and Friedman—later won Nobel Prizes, and Wallich became a member of the Federal Reserve Board.

Ever since the death of John Lardner in 1960, *Newsweek* had felt the need for a column of humor, but we had never been able to fill that gap. I hired young Peter Benchley, long before he became famous as the author of *Jaws*, and we experimented unsuccessfully with a light feature for a while. Now I thought I saw another opportunity. For months I took Tom Wolfe of the *Herald Tribune* to lunch on the Gloucester House's fancy fish, and finally persuaded him to write a column for us. At our sales meeting in 1964 I proudly announced the "acquisition, just this week, of the brightest young writing talent that has appeared on the scene in many a year." A contract was duly drawn, and duly signed, a sample column was written and put into type—and then Tom Wolfe disappeared. He never gave a reason; he just flew off to Paris, and within a few months I terminated the contract unilaterally. Not long ago, I ran into the talented Wolfe on the street one day, and asked him what the hell had happened. Well, said Wolfe, it wasn't just that he feared our two-column format would be too confining for his prolix style; he had been overwhelmed by a lunch with Kay Graham and me in our executive dining room—"complete with salad forks."

Our happiest acquisition in those years was the gentlemanly Stewart Alsop, who started writing a weekly back-page column for *Newsweek* in August 1968. Alsop was uniquely gifted as a columnist, combining the good reporter's eyes, ears and legs with the precision of a true stylist and the wisdom of a mature observer. One of Stew's earliest columns, in a single sentence, summed up how the promise and idealism and commitment of the early sixties had disintegrated into a tragicomic farce as the decade drew to a close. It was October 1968. The Democratic Party had almost gone under at its Chicago convention. That odd couple Nixon and Agnew were heading for their victory. Campus rebels were seizing buildings and professors. The Yippies were to the fore of the "revolution." Alsop asked Yippy Abbie Hoffman what were the goals of the revolution.

"Eternal life and free toilets," came the reply.

·IV·
BLACK AND
WHITE

O ne of the big, continuing stories of the sixties was Black
America's fight for civil rights, and *Newsweek* took the lead
in covering it. Why I became so caught up in this drama,
and pushed the magazine so deeply into it, I do not know.
Certainly there was not much in my background to suggest a
deep interest in racial equality.

I grew up in a whites-only cocoon of private schools—Browning in New York, St. Paul's in New Hampshire—and attended
a college where the only black I had even a nodding acquain-
tance with was a handyman who used to tend bar at Harvard
cocktail parties. He was enormous, black as coal; we called him
"Snowball." As a teenager, when I was starting to smoke, anyone who puffed on your cigarette and left it wet on the end
had "nigger-lipped" it. I served in a World War II Navy where
black people were relegated to the lowly ranks of steward's
mates, i.e., servants to white officers like myself. On a transport
crossing the Pacific, I lost a wristwatch and reported it to the
master-at-arms. "Well," he said, "looks as if we're going to

have to shake niggers again." I reported this in a letter home, factually, flatly, with no editorial comment. There used to be jokes in the wardroom of my ship, the heavy cruiser *Boston*, about how the steward's mates washed their socks in the officers' coffee. They probably should have, if they didn't.

My parents were of New York's four hundred, or perhaps four hundred and fifty. They never had any black servants in the house—only Irish and one beauteous French-Canadian who I think was fired before my older brother succumbed to temptation—and certainly no black guests. Were my parents bigots? By the simple force of isolation, everyone in their set was.* I remember their cool reception to the news, in 1947, that I planned to marry a Roman Catholic. Yet after that marriage ended a quarter century later and I was living happily with a Jewish woman, they could hardly wait for us to marry—for propriety's sake. "It's quite obvious what's going on," my mother said reproachfully. I was forty-nine years old at the time.

Joe Alsop, Stew's brother, once suggested with a sneer that my interest in civil rights came from a sense of guilt. Perhaps he was right. But I think something else may have been at work, as well.

I sense a presence, a hulking gentle bear of a man, a son of the South—from Thomas Wolfe's Asheville, North Carolina. Bill Miller was my officemate and mentor when I arrived at *Time* in 1949, at the age of twenty-five. A product of the Depression and a founder of the Newspaper Guild, Miller had left high school to become a copyboy on *The Cleveland Press*. He

---

* In 1931, a study by the Episcopal Church showed that sixty-five out of eighty-seven Episcopalian churches in New York and New Jersey said that blacks should be segregated in their houses of worship.

covered sit-down strikes, worked in factories to get his stories on labor unrest, became the *Press*'s star reporter and won a Nieman Fellowship for a year's study at Harvard. Having covered the black slums of Cleveland, Miller had an encompassing sympathy for others, particularly the downtrodden. He had come to know misery at first hand and could find dignity and value in the lowliest being. "Whenever I had occasion to deal with a black," Miller once told me, "I did not see just that indistinguishable blur that Ralph Ellison calls 'the invisible man.' I always tried to learn *who* the man was and to remember him as a person." I hope some of Bill Miller's great compassion may have rubbed off on me.

Then there was another Southerner, a great, rangy, bodacious man who flapped his arms when he walked and enchanted when he talked. This would be Bill Emerson, who had opened *Newsweek*'s Atlanta bureau in 1953, and forthwith launched a tradition of sharp and sensitive *Newsweek* reporting from the South.

This great, booming Emerson was responsible for sensitizing *Newsweek*'s editors in New York to what was happening on the civil-rights front in the fifties and early sixties, and he had the good sense to hire such able colleagues and successors as Karl Fleming and Joe Cumming and Frank Trippett, all Southerners like him. Interestingly, Emerson—who later became editor of the *Saturday Evening Post* and now teaches journalism at the University of South Carolina—gives John Denson credit for much of *Newsweek*'s early success in covering the civil-rights story. "*Newsweek* was in on the secret of the South," Emerson wrote me not long ago. "The magazine was enlightened, partly by design and partly by accident. *Newsweek* did better than *Time* because *Time* did not like the South—Luce wanted it to behave the way he wanted it to behave—and could not understand the South. Southerners hated *Time,* and had diminishing respect for its reporters who increasingly lost credibility as their reports were edited out of shape and away from reality."

Emerson, it should be noted, was an expert at fostering this disenchantment with *Time.* In the fall of 1960, he was covering Lyndon Johnson's vice-presidential campaign aboard the "Cornpone Special" (as Emerson dubbed it), whistle-stopping from Culpepper, Virginia, to New Orleans. "Lyndon spoke out of the caboose of the train at every crossroads on the line," said Emerson, "and every time the train stopped they played 'The Yellow Rose of Texas'—must have been a thousand times. There were about twenty Time Inc. reporters and me on that train, and at each stop I'd slip the *Time* badge off a drowsy one and wear it as I circulated among the crowd come down to hear Lyndon. I'd walk along the tracks until I came to the inevitable group of yellow-eyed old men sitting down on their hunkers whittling ax handles. I'd get their attention about the time Lyndon was winding up, and I'd lay a booming salutation on them: 'LOOK A HERE, YEAH YOU. HENRY LUCE WANTS TO KNOW WHAT YOU WHITE TRASH ARE THINKING ABOUT!' They'd be after me in a split second and I'd get over the rail of that observation car and land on Lyndon's feet just as we left the old codgers with cinders in their eyes. Always said it left little pools of bitterness along that whole route and *Time* never since has been able to sell a subscription between Culpepper and New Orleans."

We editors in New York could not all share our Southern correspondents' love for their region, but we could let them tell the truth as they saw it—and individuals, as Bill Emerson said, "always have a better view of truth than organizations." Also, *Newsweek* was never the giant rewrite machine that *Time* was; delicate and subtle subjects were handled with more precision and sensitivity.

Newsweek's Southern correspondents, according to Emerson, "weren't 'segs' but we also weren't 'nigger lovers.' We were a rueful, sadder, but wiser bunch who had gone through a lot of process ourselves and understood the primordial blocks, snags, blind spots, hang-ups, etc., in the Southern mind and conscience." These reporters were not all cut from the same mold. Emerson had gone to Harvard; Joe Cumming, from an old Augusta family, was a graduate of the University of the South at Sewanee; and Karl Fleming grew up in a Methodist orphanage. But they were all wise enough, as Emerson said,

> to know that some men will behave as badly as you allow them to, and that life was rigged, society was tilted, so there was too much opportunity to oppress the black man and the worst men did it in the worst way. Southerners always have had a great tolerance for disagreement among themselves, and this allows for the creation of champions for unpopular causes of the strangest sorts and in the strangest places. So, the black man has always had fearless champions, and in the darkest, most feverish and miasmic swamps of Southern intransigence there have been streaks, stabs of light, and understanding. There was always some poor bastard who was the self-elected conscience of the area, and it was the worst and lowest-paying job on earth.

Sometimes economic expediency fueled the Southern conscience, as illustrated by a story Lyndon Johnson liked to tell about how Johnson City, Texas, came to be integrated. One weekend in the autumn of 1963, my wife and I and two of our children were staying with Kay Graham at her farm in Virginia. Lyndon and Lady Bird Johnson came to lunch, and the vice-president told his story.

Some years before, LBJ recalled, a highway contract was up for bids in Johnson City, and one man was able to underbid the competition because his work force consisted almost en-

tirely of underpaid blacks. Soon thereafter, the winning contractor was in the local barbershop one day, wrapped in a
sheet and all lathered up for a shave. The town bully, sitting
in the back, began to mumble: "Is that the sonofabitch who's
bringin' the niggers to Johnson City?" Then louder, and
louder, until finally the highway contractor jumped from his
chair, trailing the barber sheet behind him, and grabbed the
bully by the lapels. He pulled him out to the sidewalk,
knocked him flat, and began to pound his head rhythmically
on the pavement. "Can mah niggahs stay in Johnson City?"
cried the contractor. "Can mah niggahs stay in Johnson City?"
"Yeah," gasped the bully at last, "yo' niggahs can stay in
Johnson City." And that, said LBJ, is how Johnson City came
to be integrated.

Like good salesmen, *Newsweek*'s Southern reporters knew
their territory—and they knew their "customers" in the editorial offices up north in New York. They knew that there was
no ideological tilt among the top editors—though Emerson
put it a bit more harshly. He suggested that New York headquarters "was sufficiently disorganized and, in a sense, ama-
teurish, and thus lacked any pervasive values, goals, clarified
positions." I, in my innocence, would have said that we just
wanted good stories, and we wanted them straight.

And we got them—on the lunch-counter sit-ins, the freedom
riders, the "sound and fury" at Oxford, Mississippi, in the fall
of 1962, when James Meredith became the first black student
to enter the University of Mississippi after three thousand
troops put down the riots. By the spring of 1963, "Black
pride" had become a part of the language, and in May, as
Birmingham's forces of law and order let loose their dogs and
water hoses against the black protesters, Sheriff Bull Connor
was rejoicing: "Look at those niggers run!"

All these events, spilling nightly via television into the living rooms across the land, had a profound effect on millions

of Americans. I was no exception; for the first time in my life I found myself thinking deeply about racism in America. For the first time, I became conscious of the tight little island that had been my life. Suddenly, for example, I found myself writing a sermon to the headmistress of my daughters' private school in Manhattan: "I have a question that bothers me increasingly, as I am sure it does you. It has to do with your policy on the admission of Negro, Jewish, and other students. . . . It seems inconceivable to me that in a city of this size there are no Negro girls qualified to attend your school, no Negro adults to teach them. . . . As a parent, I don't think it's a good idea for my children to be segregated in a little world that no longer exists; as a teacher, I suspect you agree."*

At *Newsweek* I launched a program to recruit and train black journalists. Our first move, in 1967, was to convert our summer training program into an all-black activity, and in the next few years a stream of talented black students spent the summer months in our news bureaus. But hiring and keeping black staffers on a permanent basis proved to be no easy job. In 1970, John Dotson became our first black bureau chief (in Los Angeles) ; more recently another black, Vern Smith, has taken over the Atlanta bureau. But at this writing *Newsweek*, like almost every other news organization in America, is still woefully short of minority representation among its reporters, writers, and editors.

---

* The headmistress was apparently taken aback by this summer assault. "If the temperatures were not soaring already," she wrote, "your letter would have sent the temperatures at School sky-high. . . ." But a year later, I was writing a note of congratulations, expressing pleasure that the first black girl to be admitted to the school was in my eleven-year-old daughter's class. "So far," replied the headmistress, "everything seems to be going along well for Cindy's classmate . . . perhaps the particular pleasure that the children seem to have in returning this year was in part the result of having accepted [this] child."

We fared better in our civil-rights coverage—highlighted by our first big survey of Black America in 1963. In the spring of that year, as I was lunching one day with our pollster Lou Harris, the idea was developed. Why not combine Harris's polling resources with *Newsweek*'s journalistic expertise, and produce an authoritative study of Black conditions, attitudes, and ambitions throughout the land? For this survey Harris and I worked out the first successful marriage of the old art of journalism and the new pseudoscience of public-opinion polling.

It was a big undertaking, to which *Newsweek* assigned a task force of forty people under the direction of Ben Bradlee. Harris deployed 158 interviewers, almost all of them black and most of them teachers, principals, or graduate students. More than 1250 interviews were conducted, averaging better than two hours apiece; at the end an IBM 7094 computer counted up the results of three thousand man-hours of work in just eighteen minutes. No one was more excited by the results of the poll than Harris himself. "It's as though we were able," he said, "to photograph at split-second intervals an earthquake as it was taking place."

At the end of July 1963, *Newsweek* readers around the world found on the cover of their magazine a dramatically lighted photo of a striking black face, against a jet-black background. In extra-large white type were the words, THE NEGRO IN AMERICA, and in smaller type: "The first definitive national survey—who he is, what he wants, what he fears, what he hates, how he votes, why he is fighting . . . and why now?"

By way of an editor's explanation, I wrote:

> One of the most remarkable aspects of the biggest news story of 1963 is that so few facts about it are known. The surface evidence of the Negro's drive for equal rights can be seen on every front page, and heard on every television set as the song of revolution rings out

across the land: "We shall overcome." But what goes
on beneath the surface? Until now, not even Negro
leaders could say for sure what the Negro's goals are,
how deeply rooted is the drive—or even who the leaders really are. The factless void between whites and
Negroes is deep and dangerous. . . . *Newsweek* is
proud to present the kind of facts that are needed by
a democratic society as it seeks solutions for the major
issue of the day.

Essentially, what our eighteen-page report found was that
the Black revolution was rooted deeply and extended to every
corner of the land. It was aimed at ending discrimination and
establishing complete equality in every field. Much of its
strength came from the Black churches, which still preached
faith that justice could be won within the American system,
working cooperatively with white society and not against it.
The heroes of Black America ranged from Martin Luther King,
Jr. (with an 88 percent favorable rating), to Jackie Robinson
(80 percent), James Meredith (79), Medgar Evers (78), Roy
Wilkins (68), Thurgood Marshall (64), and Ralph Bunche
(62). Politically, 85 percent of the nation's blacks had voted
for John Kennedy in 1960, and 89 percent or more said they
would vote for him again—against Nelson Rockefeller, Barry
Goldwater, or George Romney.

In addition to all the statistics churned out by Harris, there
were moving personality sketches by *Newsweek* reporters of
some representative blacks—a sharecropper in South Carolina,
a trashman in Los Angeles, a postal worker in Atlanta, a slum
dweller in Chicago. And there was something approaching
poetry both in *Newsweek*'s prose and in the way many of the
blacks expressed themselves. The report ended on this note
by Peter Goldman:

As certain as the rhythm of the seasons, the Negro
revolution will outlive the summer of its birth. It will

not end when the leaves redden, when the cotton is baled, when night comes charitably early to hide the slums of Harlem and the South Side and Buttermilk Bottom from themselves. It will go on. . . .

The final question will be not so much what the Negro will settle for—he is united and insistent—as how much the white man will give him. Negroes think [the white man] will change, that he will start treating them better because of his conscience, because he fears their militancy, or simply because he is an American. But whether or not the white man is willing to open the final door, the Negro will not stop knocking.

"I want to be a whole man this very instant," says Dr. Daniel A. Collins, a Mill Valley, California, dentist. And Susie Huzzard, a Cleveland domestic, has her own definition of freedom: "I want some of these flowers before I die."

The special issue had an enormous impact. It was praised in Congress—someone inserted it, in toto, into the *Congressional Record*. The Kennedy White House approved, and so did blacks and whites around the country. There was a flood of complimentary letters and editorials. From Russ Wiggins, editor of *The Washington Post*: a "marvelous issue." From Abe Rosenthal, then in Tokyo, and later to become executive editor of *The New York Times*: "Probably the best, most meaningful survey on the subject I have ever seen."

Suddenly, *Newsweek* was the talk of the country; for many, it had become the magazine to turn to for full and accurate (and sympathetic) coverage of the civil-rights movement. When *Newsweek*, a few weeks later, covered Martin Luther King, Jr.'s huge March on Washington, it had this to say: "The March . . . for Jobs and Freedom was most eloquent in its wordless moments, in the living presence alone of 210,000 petitioners bearing silent testimony to the patience and to the urgency of the Negro revolt." Quite a contrast to the view of

David Lawrence, the editor of *U.S. News & World Report,* who wrote: "The march will go down in history as marking a day of public disgrace."

In October, just three months after our survey of Black America, we followed up with another report—"What the White Man Thinks of the Negro Revolt." We found that "the white American is divided within himself. He is biased against black skin—yet a sense of justice tells him he is incontestably wrong. He is pulled one way by his intellect, the other way by his emotions. Conscience whispers, 'Equal rights, freedom for all'; convention says, 'But a Negro is "different." ' The white man is eternally torn between the right that he knows and the wrong that he does. . . ."*

Newsmen are supposed to be thick-skinned and not easily moved by what they encounter. But as our work on the Black America survey progressed, we were all seized with a sense of excitement. For most of us, certainly for me, this was the discovery of another world, as strange as the other side of the moon—the dark side. We would not soon forget the things we saw, the people we met, and we were mightily proud of the results. For myself, no journalistic experience before or since has been as stimulating.

During the next decade, *Newsweek* was to return time and again to the theme of America's racial dilemma, charting the rise and fall of such black leaders as Stokely Carmichael and Malcolm X, reporting the changing rhetoric of the revolution as "we shall overcome" escalated into "burn, baby, burn":

1964

Lyndon Johnson signed the Civil Rights Act (using seventy-two pens) that year, and *Newsweek* sent Lou Harris's pollsters

---

* A few months later, the two surveys became the core of a book, *The Negro Revolution in America,* by Lou Harris and *Newsweek*'s William Brink.

out to determine the extent of the white "backlash" (we found it menacing but not yet a major force). For a feature to accompany a cover story on tense and retrograde Mississippi that summer, we sent Frank Trippett, himself Mississippi born, bred, and educated, to do an on-scene report. When Trippett arrived back home, a farmer friend said to him: "Frank, boy, I guess you'll go on back North and write another bunch of lies about us." Trippett replied: "Goner do something much worse than that. I'm goner tell the truth." Trippett's impassioned report on Mississippi revisited did indeed have the ring of truth. "Almost before he learns to spell the words," Trippett's story said, "a white Mississippi boy masters the braggadocio of racial conflict ('A nigger get smart with me I'll be on him like white on rice and turn that nigger every way but loose'), and he utters these words as clarion proof of his masculinity." Trippett's Mississippi friends and relatives were incensed. There were threats on his life, and the local Baptist minister in Aberdeen, Frank's hometown, read him out of the church. An uncle wrote: "Your aunt and I think you're lower than whale shit." Frank wrote back, congratulating his uncle on this new interest in oceanography.

1965

In February, *Newsweek* reported the results of a new Harris poll of Black America: "Negroes are experiencing a fresh surge of hope. They feel heartened that their fighting faith has been doubly rewarded—by the passage of the Civil Rights Act of 1964 and by the landslide burial of its most prominent opponent, Barry Goldwater. Black America has no illusion that the millennium has arrived—and no intention of relaxing its fight for full equality."

And then, the very next month—Selma. Marching across Edmund Pettus Bridge at Selma, Alabama, and heading for the state capital of Montgomery to petition for the right to vote, a column of 525 protesting blacks came face to face with a wall of state troopers dispatched by Alabama's Governor George Wallace. The bloody melee that followed, *Newsweek* said, linked "Selma's name forever with those of Little Rock, Oxford, Birmingham—the great battlegrounds of the American Negro revolt."

1966

The civil-rights revolution moved north, and *Newsweek* told its readers: "The victories in the South seem suddenly easy against the intractable urban tangle of poverty, joblessness, slum housing, inadequate schools, crumbling family life. . . ." From Harlem to Watts to Chicago's West Side, a score of urban ghettos exploded—and three years after its initial black survey, *Newsweek* once again sent Harris pollers out across the country to make a new portrait of the racial crisis. This time, we reported, "the old American dilemma of race . . . is more poignant and critical than ever, as the black man's insistent hopes confront the white man's stiffening resistance."

In covering this story, one of *Newsweek*'s star civil-rights reporters was missing. Karl Fleming, by then Los Angeles bureau chief, had been set upon by a gang of black youths in Watts, and pounded to the pavement by a four-by-four timber. For many weeks after that he was out of action, his broken jaw wired closed.*

The nonviolent tactics of Martin Luther King, Jr., were in-

---

* Fleming had had many close shaves before this. At the height of the Ole Miss riot in 1962, he borrowed a U.S. marshal's helmet, stepped out of the embattled administration building for a look, and heard a sniper rifle fire three times. The .22-caliber bullets crunched into the doorjamb inches from his head. "You know," said Fleming, "if I were James Meredith I wouldn't go to school with these people."

creasingly being challenged by younger blacks, and in the summer *Newsweek* produced yet another cover story—on the now fragmented leadership of the black revolt.

. . .

Ironically, just after this I was taken away by my friend Arthur Houghton for a cruise down the Dalmatian coast of Yugoslavia. There were ten of us on board his 190-foot chartered yacht, and 22 in crew, which meant that at any given moment 2.2 crewmen were at the ready to fetch you, personally, a vodka and tonic. Sailing from Pula to Hvar to Split to Dubrovnik, inspecting Roman ruins along the way, we were about as far as you could get from a black urban slum in America.

Then we put into a little port called Korčula, and my idyll was shattered. I was able to buy a European edition of *Newsweek*—and there in Korčula, Yugoslavia, for the first time I became aware of the full horror of the fire and riots that had just enveloped Detroit. "The trouble burst like a firestorm," reported *Newsweek*, "and turned the nation's fifth biggest city into a theater of war." I was deeply depressed. I feared that all the civil-rights progress of the past five years was literally going up in smoke, and from what I could tell the government's reaction was pathetically inadequate.

That night, I had a long talk on the afterdeck with Houghton, a man of huge intellect and tender, if sometimes camouflaged, concern. I poured out my apprehension and my disgust at the Johnson administration's reaction: "How does LBJ respond to this national emergency? He calls for a day of national prayer and asks a commission to report next July—by then we'll probably be in the middle of the riots of 1968!"

"Why don't you do something about it?" said Houghton.

"Why don't you use *Newsweek* to produce the definitive editorial on this whole subject of race relations?"

And so the decision was made, on a luxury yacht off the coast of Yugoslavia, that *Newsweek* would depart from all tradition. It had always been an article of faith that *Newsweek* would never editorialize in its news columns. Now I decided that, for the first time since the magazine's founding thirty-four years before, the moment for advocacy was at hand. When I got back to New York a few days later, I assigned Ed Kosner to head up a team to produce our most ambitious project ever. In the course of the 1960s, *Newsweek*'s writers, reporters, and editors had turned out a score of cover stories recording the progress of the black revolution: now their assignment was to go beyond analysis and seek out solutions to America's greatest domestic crisis since the Civil War.*

For many weeks the task force labored, interviewing more than 250 experts, sifting through a substantial library of books, reports, and papers, and piling up more than two hundred thousand words of research. Time and again, through the months of work on the project, one editor or another would come to me, saying that we had undertaken an impossible task that none of the experts, black or white, could

---

* In a speech to an Atlanta business group later, that summer, I quoted from Walter Lippmann: "The race problem as we know it is really the by-product of our planless, disordered, beddraggled, drifting democracy. Until we have learned to house everybody, employ everybody at decent wages in a self-respecting status, guarantee his civil liberties, and bring education and play to him, the bulk of our talk about 'the race problem' will remain a sinister mythology. In a dirty civilization the relation between black men and white will be a dirty one. In a clean civilization the two races can conduct their business together cleanly, and not until then." That, I noted, was Walter Lippmann writing—not in the summer of 1967, but almost fifty years before, in 1919.

agree on what should be done. That's precisely why we must keep trying, I would say. In the end, we turned out a twenty-two-page section that blended reportage with analysis, was highly critical of what we perceived to be Lyndon Johnson's abdication of leadership because of his preoccupation with Vietnam, and ended with a twelve-point program for action.

We called our landmark special issue—in November 1967— "The Negro in America: What Must Be Done." On the cover was a symbolic photo of two black hands, one extended beseechingly, the other in clench-fisted determination. Explaining our decision to move beyond analysis into advocacy, I described some of our premises:

> The entire project is founded on a number of premises.
> The first is that America so far has failed to deliver to many citizens, and particularly to many Negroes, that measure of equality that lies at the heart of the American idea.
> A second premise is that America has to make that delivery. . . .
> A third premise is more arguable: that America has, or can generate, the will to solve its racial problems. . . .
> We hope that this Program for Action will stimulate the thoughts and deeds that will not only point the way to a more peaceful racial prospect, but will finally bring those eighteenth-century truths, which all Americans supposedly hold self-evident, into twentieth-century reality.

Well, we could hope, couldn't we?

Newsweek was by then a journalistic voice respected throughout the world, and its first "editorial" made news everywhere. For that special issue we won many prizes, including Columbia University's National Magazine Award.

But events abroad and at home in 1967 and 1968 were soon to show that America's priorities, alas, lay elsewhere. The very next week *Newsweek*'s featured story reported the move to dump LBJ; within three months came the demoralizing Tet offensive of early 1968—and *Newsweek* was editorializing for the second time, urging a de-escalation of the Vietnam war. By March, Eugene McCarthy was winning the New Hampshire primary, and Bobby Kennedy was throwing his hat in the ring. By April, Lyndon Johnson had bowed out of presidential politics and Martin Luther King, Jr., was dead. And by June, Robert Kennedy lay dying on the kitchen floor of a Los Angeles hotel. Someone called me from the coast at 4:00 a.m., June 5, to tell me the awful news of Bobby's shooting. As it happened, I was scheduled to make the commencement speech at my daughter's (now somewhat integrated) school that very morning, so I spent the next few hours rewriting the talk.

Gazing out on the pleasant graduation scene, the girls in their white dresses and the proud parents beaming up from the audience, I found it hard to keep my mind on the happy academic proceedings we were there to celebrate. My mind kept going back to that hotel kitchen in Los Angeles, to that motel balcony in Memphis where Martin Luther King had been gunned down, to the wasteland of urban slums and the violence that pervaded them. "We yearn for calm," I said in my commencement talk, "yet we are beset by tumult; we are blessed with material bounty, but afflicted with a poverty of the spirit."

Something was terribly wrong.

· · ·

As *Newsweek* was covering the civil-rights movement during the sixties, I came to know a number of black leaders as acquaintances, and a few of them as friends. Some of them, strangely, I first met in Africa, at conferences sponsored by the African-American Institute. It was at such a meeting in Nairobi that I met Bayard Rustin, the tough and gentle and brilliant disciple of Gandhi, organizer of the 1963 March on Washington, and head of the A. Philip Randolph Institute. At a reception in Nairobi, we were watching Kenya's president Jomo Kenyatta leave the university campus. There were perhaps a dozen motorcycle cops as escorts; a black band in kilts was playing martial airs, and flags fluttered from the Cadillac that carried Kenyatta, fly whisk and all, off in a cloud of dust. Rustin leaped to my side on the balcony overlooking the scene. "You know what I was thinking when he drove off?" Rustin asked. "I was thinking, Go, black boy, go!" (Later, at a similar conference in Lagos in 1971, the Urban League's Whitney Young died while swimming in the ocean, and it fell my lot to break the tragic news to Rustin. Bayard just sat there in his hotel room, overcome with grief.)

But while I had come to know some of these black leaders over the years, the first real taste I ever had of ghetto life didn't come until the spring of 1969. That was when Whitney Young had the bright idea of assembling a group of fifteen leading journalists and sending them on a tour of black ghettos around the country—in Cleveland, Detroit, Chicago, San Francisco, Oakland, Los Angeles, and Atlanta. For me, this trip—during which we ate and slept in the black slums and never saw the downtown areas—was a life-changing experience. It gave me a feeling for Black America that I had never had before, and that I'm sure will never fade away.

In each city we journalists would be paired off and assigned a black guide who would stay with us throughout our visit.* We would go to his local bar with him, have breakfast with him, perhaps sleep in his home. The first night, in Detroit,

---

* One of my fellow travelers was William F. Buckley, Jr., who seemed to attract crowds of admiring blacks everywhere we went. I asked him why. "Perhaps," Buckley said self-mockingly, "they're finally seeing the value in my philosophy."

Joseph C. Harsch of *The Christian Science Monitor* and I were brought to the clapboard home of a sixty-six-year-old United Automobile Workers official. By remarkable coincidence, our black host's last name was the same as my first. "Now I imagine," said Andrew Osborn, "that after all that traveling, you'd like something to put body and soul together with." Eyeing a nearby bottle of Johnnie Walker, Joe Harsch answered in the clipped accents picked up during his many years in London: "Mr. Osborn, if you have in mind what I *think* you have in mind, it sounds like an absolutely *splendid* idea." We sat up for hours as our host told us about his partly Choctaw heritage ("but I consider myself a plain ordinary Negro"), his middle-class way of life, and his views on the racial situation, which no doubt would mark him as an Uncle Tom among the more militant. "I don't think the blacks should take it out on white grandsons for what their grandfathers did," he said.

In that week in ghetto America, we listened to the anger of black students, the rhythmic preaching of Chicago's Jesse Jackson—"I am *somebody*"—the weird incantations of Ron Karenga, speaking from his zebra-striped throne in Los Angeles, through a wisp of incense smoke, of "a nation becoming." And we heard the street-smart wisdom of community organizers from Watts to Atlanta. A particular friend that I made in Atlanta was Tom Evans, a union organizer, community worker, and amateur artist who had been active in many civil-rights organizations and whose wife worked for the Urban League. "You don't see me wearing a dashiki and beads and sandals," Evans said with a smile. "Hell, it costs more to *dress* for the revolution than to run it these days."

From a lightning-like tour of this sort [I wrote in *Newsweek*], it is difficult to draw many broad conclusions. But some are possible. First, that the spirit and the quality of the black people are tremendous. Second, that white America has a long, long way to go before it makes the American dream a reality for millions of its citizens. At the end of the trip, an Urban League official asked if what we had seen was a revolution or even a rebellion—and then answered his own question. "What we're seeing," he said, "is no more than a regurgitation of what the ghetto has been fed. . . ."

I return from this trip impressed, depressed, enriched—even exhilarated by seeing the world for a few days through the eyes of my black friends. But there was a difference between my view and theirs.

For I knew, all along, that I was going to get out.

· · ·

Soon the nation became so obsessed by the Vietnam war and then by Richard Nixon and the horrors of Watergate that it was difficult to keep attention focused on the racial problem. By February 1973, in fact, in order to justify putting the handsome face of Vernon Jordan, successor to Whitney Young as head of the Urban League, on the cover of the magazine, we devised this headline: WHAT EVER HAPPENED TO BLACK AMERICA? That week, Jordan was traveling all over the country, and everywhere he went—in airports, hotels, on street corners—there was his picture staring back at him from the cover of *Newsweek*. He got to like it. The following week he called up with a complaint.

"I'll never forgive you, Oz Elliott," he said.

"What have I done now?" I asked.

"Why, you took my face off the cover of *Newsweek*."

I hope Vernon makes it to the cover again.

For that might be a sign that America once more is directing its attention to the racism and discrimination that are the nation's enduring shame.

·V·
THE
VIETNAMIZATION
OF AMERICA

Before long, the civil-rights revolution was being pushed off the front pages by the war in Vietnam—which was not, of course, confined to the rice paddies and jungles of Southeast Asia. As the disaster gathered momentum in the Far East, its poison seeped through the entire American nation, turning families against themselves, setting young against old, students against teachers, the poor against the largely draft-proof rich, and finally bringing about what Bill Buckley aptly described as a "massive seizure of national self-hatred." It also caused major rifts within the journalistic fraternity. *Newsweek* was no exception.

My own involvement with the Vietnam war developed on several levels—as a journalist and occasional visitor to Saigon, trying not very successfully to figure out where the truth lay; as the leader of an editorial organization whose staff was increasingly at war—over the war—with itself; as an Overseer at Harvard, where monthly visits confirmed the growing anger and alienation and confusion of the young; and as a father whose own eldest daughter, Diana, was a Harvard undergraduate at the time.

Beginning with its very first cover story on the Vietnam war in 1961, *Newsweek* had taken a skeptical view of prospects for U.S. success. As early as then, because of his critical reports from the field, *Newsweek*'s François Sully, a Frenchman who had lived in Vietnam for most of his adult life, was expelled from the country.*

Hell hath no fury like a journalist censored. Upon receiving word of Sully's expulsion, we had Ben Bradlee, then *Newsweek*'s Washington bureau chief, push as many buttons as possible. He talked with McGeorge Bundy, Averell Harriman, Pierre Salinger, Roger Hilsman. Hilsman, then director of the State Department's Bureau of Intelligence and Research, said that any reporter who had been in Vietnam more than two years had been there too long—Sully included. But Harriman, then assistant secretary of state for Far Eastern Affairs, agreed to instruct the U.S. ambassador to Saigon, Frederick Nolting, to protest Sully's expulsion. Phil Graham sent a cable to President Ngo Dinh Diem, noting archly that

NEWSWEEK'S MOSCOW BUREAU CHIEF [Whitman Bassow] WAS EXPELLED BY RUSSIA ONLY THREE WEEKS AGO. BUT SUCH CONDUCT IS NOT TO BE EXPECTED FROM FREEDOM-LOVING COUNTRIES LIKE YOUR OWN.

All to no avail. It was more than a year before Sully was readmitted by the regime that succeeded Ngo Dinh Diem's, and thereafter sporadic efforts were made by both Vietnamese

* The particular story at issue was a Sully interview with the French-born military analyst Bernard B. Fall, who even then was suggesting that the United States might "win the military battle but lose the political war."

and American officials to discredit him as being not just a journalist but a French-government agent.

(Sully ultimately was killed in 1971, in the crash of a South Vietnamese helicopter near the Cambodian border. Before his funeral, two jeeploads of Vietnamese police drove up to the memorial room where Sully's body lay. His *Newsweek* colleagues had removed thirty-eight framed cover pictures from Sully's office and placed them on the wall of the memorial room. A police officer ordered Kevin Buckley, then *Newsweek*'s bureau chief, to remove each and every cover that showed the face of Ho Chi Minh. Buckley reluctantly obliged.)

But while *Newsweek* had been critical and skeptical of American strategy and tactics in Vietnam almost from the beginning, we—I—rarely questioned the basic wisdom of America's commitment to "holding Southeast Asia." For that matter, few Americans did. Most people in the sixties, including a succession of American presidents, were still thinking in terms of European-style "containment" of a monolithic Communism; indeed, even when the Soviet-Chinese split took place, many viewed it as some devilishly clever Communist dissemblance. And those relatively few Americans, like me, who were able on occasion to observe Vietnam at first hand were subjected to an impressive display of American professionalism in the field.

I first visited the war zone with Kay Graham in 1965. In the few days we were in Vietnam, we had sessions with General William Westmoreland, Ambassador Maxwell Taylor, and a number of other top American and Vietnamese officials, including McGeorge Bundy, who was in Saigon on an official visit. Our stay there happened to coincide with the surprise Communist attack on the American barracks at Pleiku. And so we were on the scene when a major escalation of the war took place, with the United States sending its planes off for the first time to bomb North Vietnam in retaliation for the Pleiku raid. We visited "strategic hamlets"; we toured recently "secured" areas and Delta villages surrounded by Viet Cong. We helicoptered to one Green Beret outpost, at a place called Black Virgin Mountain, not far from Saigon. The Green Berets held the top of the mountain, the Viet Cong the foothills. Years later, I visited Black Virgin again. Damned if the VC weren't holding the *top* of the mountain, by then, and the Americans the *bottom*.

In early 1965, America had only 25,000 "advisers" in the field, and I was thoroughly impressed by those advisers. Returning home, I made a series of speeches to this effect. In my talks, presented to groups of *Newsweek* advertisers or advertising prospects or leading businessmen in various cities around the country, I gave a cautious prognosis on the course of the war. I didn't think our intelligence was good enough. I didn't think our press coverage was adequate. I thought morale among the South Vietnamese needed improving. I noted that political instability in Saigon no doubt was having a damaging, but hard to measure, effect in the field. I said the pacification program, as it was known, was enjoying a spotty success at best. But to the most crucial question of all—"Is the United States following the right course, and will it be successful?"—my answer was loud and clearly affirmative.

George Romney had also been to Vietnam in 1965; two years later, running for the presidency, he confessed to having had "the greatest brainwashing that anybody can get . . . not only by the generals but also by the diplomatic corps over there. . . . I no longer believe that it was necessary for us to get involved in South Vietnam to stop Communism in Southeast Asia."

Romney made these remarks on a Detroit television talk show, and *The New York Times* buried a brief wire-service account of the interview far inside its pages. That probably

would have been the end of the matter, had not Gordon
Manning, by then with CBS News, ripped out the little story
and ordered up a tape from Detroit for showing on the
Walter Cronkite show that night. Within hours, the wolves
were at Romney's heels. Democratic National Chairman John
Bailey was one of the first: "Romney aspires to be president,
but can't you just see him coming back from a conference
with Kosygin, yelling that he had been brainwashed by a
Russian?"

Gamely, Romney stuck to his guns. "Yes," he said, "I was
brainwashed. We're all brainwashed. The administration
simply does not tell the truth about Vietnam. . . ." But the
polls that autumn of 1967 soon spelled the end of Romney's
presidential bid. After having led all the other Republican
contenders against President Johnson for almost a year,
Romney plummeted overnight to fourth place in the Harris
survey—from a mere four points behind LBJ to a sixteen-
point deficit. Nelson Rockefeller became the leading Republican (trailing Johnson by only two points), and Richard
Nixon and Ronald Reagan were second and third. As a candidate, Romney was dead.

The American commitment to the South Vietnamese regime
grew rapidly, and by the time I paid a second visit to Saigon,
in 1966, the number of U.S. troops (now no longer "advisers") had swollen from 25,000 to 225,000. What had impressed me the year before was the professionalism and dedication of the Green Berets; now it was the sheer massiveness
of the American presence, including a proportionately ex-
panded press corps. The *Newsweek* bureau in Saigon, which
had been established as a one-man operation in 1963, now
had four correspondents. They had laid out a heavy schedule
for me—including a day in the field on an infantry operation;
a day and a night on the aircraft carrier *Kitty Hawk*, and a

ten-hour day at the side of General Westmoreland as he flew the length and breadth of the country for a series of top-secret briefings on military operations.

My day with the infantry was on a sweep from a place called Cu Chi, headquarters of the first brigade of the U.S. 25th Infantry Division, about twenty-five miles northwest of Saigon. For years Cu Chi had been one of the Viet Cong's strongest bastions, and from the moment the 25th had landed two months before, it had had to fight for its bivouac area. Night after night, there had been a rain of incoming mortar fire now, in "Operation Waikiki," the goal was to sweep out through a wider radius and secure more of the surrounding territory. I went in by helicopter with *Newsweek*'s Mert Perry.

As the chopper was just spiraling down to land, a sharp crackle of sniper fire came from the thicket somewhere below. When we landed, the Viet Cong were nowhere to be found.

Along with a company of the 25th, Perry and I walked and waited, walked and waited, through an endless expanse of dry paddy fields for about three hours; the only "action" was another brief volley of sniper fire, which sent us all flopping to the ground. After we had walked until we thought we'd drop in the tropical heat, we climbed into an armored personnel carrier and jounced around for another three hours in temperatures above 110 degrees. In that heat and dust and insect-ridden discomfort I could think of just two things. One was the fact that for the dozen other men in that vehicle this was just another miserable day in their lives; the other was the cold beer that we had been promised at journey's end.

My day with Westmoreland began with a flight over Camranh Bay. (Only months before, the area around Camranh had contained nothing but sand, rocks, wild boars, and a couple of tigers. Now, we looked down upon a six-thousand-man military complex including a jet airstrip, a hospital, communications installation, oil storage tanks, and inflatable "bubble" warehouses like so many indoor tennis courts.) The jut-jawed "Westy" was, I thought, the very model of a modern four-star general. At one outpost, as he entered the briefing tent, a dozen senior officers snapped to attention. Then, one by one, they filled him in on an operation that was about to be launched in an area long controlled by the Viet Cong. At the end the tent fell silent, and the general began his questioning.

Would there be enough air support? Yes, sir, detailed arrangements had been made with the Air Force. Had the B-52 bombers been ordered in to soften up the area? They had. Shouldn't there be some diversionary B-52 strikes to keep the enemy off-balance? Perhaps. How about some strikes *during* the operation? How good was security? Landing zones in this area were few and poor, said the general: "We'll have to create our own." Were there enough power saws? How handy were the engineers with those saws? "I don't want to see any six-foot tree stumps left around." How about hospital facilities? Shouldn't patients be evacuated from the nearby hospital to make room for the new casualties that were sure to come in? Any complaints about the new M-16 rifle? Any shortages?

At last Westmoreland was satisfied. "Well, gentlemen," he said, "I think you have a good sound plan and I expect a successful operation." With that, he was on his feet, out of the tent, and into his helicopter.

·   ·   ·

Aboard a heavy cruiser in World War II, I had seen hundreds of air strikes launched against the Philippines, Formosa, Iwo Jima, Japan—even, come to think of it, Indochina. But I had never been aboard a carrier in action, so I particularly looked forward to my visit to the *Kitty Hawk*, operating at "Yankee Station" off the coast of North Vietnam. The operation was dramatic in its routine precision. For sixteen hours a day, seven days a week, the *Kitty Hawk* was sending its planes on strikes into North Vietnam. Every hour and a half—on the dot—the ship would turn into the wind and launch a strike. And just as the last plane of each new strike was taking off, the first plane of a returning strike would come in to land. The roar of jets on the flight deck was so thunderous that you couldn't hear a man if he screamed right into your ear. The flight directors used a code of graceful, almost balletic signals to direct the pilots with their hands and bodies.

After the last plane of the final strike had slammed down on the flight deck at midnight, I sat in a ready room talking with some of the pilots. One twenty-four-year-old ensign, on the *Kitty Hawk* for only four months, was already a veteran. He told me of the terror he had felt the first time he ran into antiaircraft fire. Had he become used to it? "Well," he said, "it's a kind of calculated fear now." His fingernails were bitten to the disappearing point.

What conclusions did I draw from this second visit to Vietnam?

I thought, and said in speeches back home, that we had "moved from an unwinnable war to an unlosable war," whatever the hell *that* meant. I was a bit more accurate when I predicted we might have as many as 400,000 men in Vietnam within another year—"about the same number as we had in the field when the guns fell silent in Korea."* The idea of the United States pulling out, I insisted, was simply inconceivable.

Years later, I heard a brutally absurd story that may, in its way, say more about American capabilities, sensitivities, and

* By June 1967 the actual figure was about 460,000.

insights in Vietnam than I ever gleaned from visiting the place. In 1974, William Westmoreland was running for the governorship of South Carolina. At a big political rally, so the story went, an admirer approached the candidate and thrust a notepad into his hand. "Good luck, Westy," the scribbled note said. "Sorry I can't talk. Have laryngitis." Westmoreland took the man's pencil and pad, flipped a page, and wrote: "Many thanks. Appreciate the good wishes." The fan recaptured his notepad, and wrote his reply: "I can *hear*, General, it's just that I can't *talk*." Once again, Westmoreland took the pad. "Well," he wrote, "I sure hope you recover soon. So long."

As the years dragged by in Vietnam, America could see and hear what was going on, well enough. But it didn't seem to understand.

· · ·

My last visit to Vietnam was in the spring of 1970, and just as I had witnessed a major escalation of the war after Pleiku on my first trip, now came another dramatic turn. Richard Nixon was sending U.S. troops and planes across the border into Cambodia, in an "incursion" that would, in the end, be blamed for the destruction of that country. The very day before, I had had a lengthy interview with President Nguyen Van Thieu, whose South Vietnamese troops had already crossed the Cambodian border in a sector known as Parrot's Beak.

o.e.: Are you satisfied with the degree of American assistance in this Cambodian operation?

THIEU: Yes.

o.e.: You don't want U.S. troops?

THIEU: We don't need them in such a ground operation because mainly these ground operations now are
taken care of by the Vietnamese.

Next day, twelve thousand American troops went plunging
into the "Fishhook" sector of Cambodia to wipe out enemy
"sanctuaries" that were never really found.* By some con-
torted logic, the action was also supposed to be a signal to
the Soviet Union, whose pilots were by then flying operational
missions in the Middle East. Late that night, in *Newsweek*'s
Saigon bureau, I listened in growing disgust as Richard
Nixon sounded his tinny horn. "If, when the chips are down,"
he said, "the U.S. acts like a pitiful, helpless giant, the forces
of totalitarianism and anarchy will threaten free nations and
free institutions throughout the world."

For the better part of a decade, frustrations over the Vietnam war had been steadily rising, and the antiwar movement
had been gaining strength and passion. I felt absolutely sure,
as I listened to that presidential speech twelve thousand miles
away, that it would trigger an explosion of furious protest.
In the aftermath, it also unleashed a volley of deadly rifle fire
at Kent State University in Ohio. *Newsweek* was not exagger-
ating when it reported the next week:

> A mass of Americans rose up against their President.
> Rarely had the nation's citizens seemed so divided,
> their confidence in its leaders so shaken, their temper
> so rankled, their young people so driven to despera-
> tion and despair. Mr. Nixon had plunged American
> troops into Cambodia in hopes of shocking the Com-
> munist enemy and stabilizing a turbulent world. In-
> stead, he had shocked his fellow countrymen and

* A day or two later, I visited the Fishhook area, and as someone
who had served as a lowly ensign in World War II, I was delighted
to discover that the Army had assigned me the rank of lieutenant
general.

brought on the most serious domestic crisis of his career. . . . The Cambodian invasion bespoke a President perilously insensitive to the expectations of millions of his countrymen that the war would be steadfastly wound down rather than suddenly cranked up. And the abrupt manner of his decision suggested that Mr. Nixon had allowed himself to become isolated from the American people, not only from their representatives in Congress but also from many of his own chief advisers.*

Nixon himself seemed surprised at the outrage that surrounded him, and one sleepless night he wandered out of the White House on one of the weirdest missions in presidential history. A week before, he had referred to student protesters as "bums." Now, he set out for the Lincoln Memorial at around 4:35 a.m. to mingle with some of the young protesters. "I told them," he said later, "that I know you think we are a bunch of so-and-sos—and I used a stronger word." One of the youths, sophomore Joan Pelletier of Syracuse University, gave this version of that remarkable predawn conversation: "I hope it was because he was tired, but most of what he was saying was absurd. Here we had come from a university that's completely uptight—on strike—and when we told him where we were from, he talked about the football team."

Long before the 1970 Cambodian "invasion," the Vietnam war had been eroding America's confidence in itself and its institutions, and taking its toll in every aspect of American life. For *Newsweek*'s Fourth of July number in 1967, we had put out a special issue entitled "The Vietnam War and Ameri-

---

* *Newsweek*'s cover that week featured the famous photo of an anguished young woman kneeling by one of the dead students at Kent State. She turned out to be a fourteen-year-old runaway named Mary Ann Vecchio, and her parents were able to track her down when they saw the cover picture on a newsstand.

can Life," which explored the effect of the war and the depths of the divisions that it had brought about. In science, in medicine, in religion, in business, in small-town life, in politics and diplomacy, in education, even in the arts, the war had left its searing imprint. There were few Americans, I wrote in an introduction to that issue, "who do not find this year's Fourth of July somehow clouded by the frustrations and agonies of the battle, somehow dulled by a new understanding of a nation's power—and its limitations."

Those limitations grew ever more evident as 1968 dawned, bringing with it the Tet offensive—and subsequent demands for 206,000 more American troops for Vietnam. For some time *Newsweek*'s editors had been considering a second effort at advocacy, following our special issue on Black America in the fall of 1967. Some of us wanted to produce a similar "editorial" on Vietnam. But until the Tet offensive in early winter which showed the enemy far better organized and more resilient than the U.S. military or government had imagined— it was impossible for *Newsweek*'s senior editors to reach a consensus. Tet changed all that. In March 1968, we produced a special section, edited by Bob Christopher and entitled "More of the Same Won't Do," which argued in favor of de-escalation and ultimate withdrawal.

That we were finally able to reach consensus on Vietnam was notable, for *Newsweek* itself had not escaped the anger and frustration that divided the nation as the war dragged on. Week in, week out the Saigon bureau would report its generally downbeat view of events in the field; week in, week out the Washington bureau—understandably reflecting the views of the administration more closely—would weigh in with more optimistic reports. It was up to the editors in New York to try to strike a balance—and since we tended to be less in sympathy with the war, there were frequent fights with

Washington. On one occasion Mel Elfin, by then our Washington bureau chief, was so furious with a *Newsweek* interpretation of the mood in Washington that he flew to New York, his resignation in hand; we talked him into staying.*

During one antiwar march on Madison Avenue, a large part of the New York editorial staff stood silent vigil outside the *Newsweek* building. And after the Cambodian invasion, a group of antiwar activists on the staff distributed a questionnaire polling editorial workers on their views of the war. The activists asked if they could use the company meeting rooms at the top of the building for an antiwar rally, and I said no —but I permitted them to hold an open forum on the war there, provided all sides could be heard.

Things were tense as the staff convened for the meeting. Most of *Newsweek*'s writers, researchers, and editors were by then strongly opposed to the war, but a few editorial people, and many more on the business side of the magazine, felt quite differently. In the end, everyone who wanted to be heard was allowed to speak. But when news of the meeting (and the questionnaire itself) reached Asia, some of our correspondents let their unhappiness be known.

From Maynard Parker in Vietnam: "All of us in the Saigon bureau . . . were extremely disheartened (actually the reaction ranged from anger to ridicule) by the news of the Vietnam war protest meeting. . . . No doubt the war has become a tremendously emotional issue in the United States; probably in many ways it is, in fact, a more emotional, polarized issue

---

* *Time* magazine, not known in those days for letting the facts from the field interfere with its editorial views, lost Charles Mohr, one of its best Vietnam correspondents, when the editors in New York ordered up a story that attacked the American reporters in Vietnam for being totally biased and negative in their coverage of the war. Mohr quit, and later joined *The New York Times.*

to people in the States than it is to those of us who live in the midst of it. But if the *Newsweek* staff cannot keep some objectivity and coolness on the subject, then who can?"

And from Bernie Krisher, our Tokyo bureau chief: "I was quite upset at receiving a poll on Vietnam by a group of *Newsweek* employees. . . . If this movement at *Newsweek* succeeds, I fear correspondents, like myself, will begin to be labeled by our sources—and once identified with a cause, those who oppose that cause will hesitate to confide in us. . . ."

I couldn't have agreed more, but I also feared the effects of totally throttling the staff. I wrote Parker and Krisher accordingly. "One never knows, in a highly politicized situation such as this, just what is the right thing to do. In retrospect, however, I believe that we acted properly and that the divisions and passions among *Newsweek* employees would have been exacerbated had we denied the turf for this purpose."

Dick Boeth, one of *Newsweek*'s senior writers and the moderator of the mass meeting, wrote to me privately about the Parker and Krisher complaints:

> What no one seems to have begun to grasp is that a substantial majority of edit people here in New York either wanted to set up a strike for peace or take out an ad in the *Times*, or hit you with a well-publicized petition for (free) advertising space. . . . The wheels were in motion. Now the poll . . . shows that (1) a majority of Newsweekers oppose the war and (2) a majority of them hold exactly the same opinions about company activism as Parker and Krisher do. So what the hell is wrong with finding this out, or even telling the world about it, for that matter? And not incidentally the likelihood of another rump movement among edit activists—with all its dilemma-horns for everyone—is now extremely remote . . . much more remote [than] if last month's movement had been answered only by . . . upright posturing.

For our correspondents in Vietnam, covering the war was a difficult, exhausting, and often dangerous business. In addition to François Sully, three others died while on assignment for the magazine. After taking some spectacular color photographs of the bombardment of Khe Sanh in March 1968, twenty-three-year-old freelance photographer Robert Ellison died in a C-123 transport plane shot down by enemy gunners; he was on his way back to Khe Sanh, carrying a case of Coke for the beleaguered Seabees there. In 1971, photographer Keisaburo Shimamoto was killed while on assignment in Laos. And in 1972, Alexander Shimkin, after carrying a wounded South Vietnamese to safety, was felled by grenades.

Somehow, the men in the field were supposed to keep track of an infinitely complicated guerrilla war and at the same time keep on top of the political, social, and religious upheavals that were continuously disrupting Vietnamese society. If they wrote too critically—as François Sully discovered early on—they were targets for expulsion; and if they wrote too uncritically they were suspect among the editors in New York. Ending his tour of Vietnam duty in July 1972, bureau chief Nick Proffitt offered some advice to Rod Gander, who was by then chief of correspondents: "I really don't care if a blue-assed baboon replaces me as long as I get out. . . . Whoever he or she may be, look for someone who is stable (to begin with anyway), doesn't mind working in the face of official hostility and obstacles, and who has a healthy skepticism which stops short of being cynicism. If you find such a person, to hell with Saigon, make him foreign editor or run him for President."

Not infrequently, the magazine was banned in Vietnam because the authorities objected to some story or other. My files are full of cables like this one to President Thieu in 1971: "I MUST STRENUOUSLY PROTEST YOUR GOVERNMENT'S MOST REGRETTABLE ACTION BANNING 5TH APRIL ISSUE NEWSWEEK. I

SINCERELY HOPE THAT IN THE SPIRIT OF TRUE DEMOCRACY NO
SIMILAR ACTION WILL BE TAKEN IN FUTURE." There was, of
course, no answer. And this one, in the early sixties, to Am-
bassador Henry Cabot Lodge: "NEWSWEEK STRONGLY PROTESTS
THE ACTION OF THE SOUTH VIETNAM GOVERNMENT IN BANNING
THE CURRENT ISSUE OF THE MAGAZINE. NEWSWEEK HOPES AND
EXPECTS THAT YOU WILL MAKE URGENT REPRESENTATIONS TO THE
SOUTH VIETNAMESE AUTHORITIES DEMANDING THAT THIS ACT OF
CENSORSHIP BE RESCINDED IMMEDIATELY."

A lot of good these cables did. The fact was that many
American officials often would have liked the power to censor
us themselves.

A big flap was caused by an October 1967 story by Mert
Perry, assessing the capabilities of the South Vietnamese
Army. His article ran under the headline, THEIR LIONS—
OUR RABBITS:

> At Dak To in the central highlands of Vietnam, an
> entire South Vietnamese regiment has taken itself out
> of action in order to concentrate on supplying the
> 173d U.S. Airborne base with beer, prostitutes, and
> laundry service. A Vietnamese Ranger unit performs
> a similar function for the Fourth U.S. Division near
> Pleiku. And in Bien Hoa, next to a sprawling airfield
> crowded with GI's, another enterprising Ranger unit
> has built a red-light district known as "Tijuana East."
> All across the shell-pocked face of South Vietnam
> these days, a distressing fact is evident: an uncomfort-
> ably large number of South Vietnamese fighting men
> have virtually opted out of the war. . . .
> The South Vietnamese Army . . . is sick. Like the
> society which created it, it is riddled with factionalism,
> nepotism, corruption, inefficiency, incompetence, and
> cowardice. . . . As a Vietnamese colonel recently re-
> marked to me over breakfast: "The North Vietnamese
> and the Viet Cong fight like lions while our soldiers
> fight like rabbits. . . ."

Shortly after this article appeared, *Newsweek*'s White House correspondent, Charles Roberts, was invited in for a private one-hour chat with President Johnson. It was a typical LBJ performance. Chuck listened as the president read aloud from Ambassador Ellsworth Bunker's weekly situation report. It fairly bubbled with optimism—and was quite at variance, Johnson noted, with Perry's story. LBJ went on to say that Bunker had complained to Perry about the story, and that Perry had said his copy had been drastically changed in New York, with "the caveats mostly eliminated." When we received similar word from the Pentagon, we cabled Perry and got this Telex back:

WHITE HOUSE AND DEFENSE DEPARTMENT ALLEGATIONS ARE ABSOLUTELY NOT RPT NOT TRUE. IN FACT WHAT EYE POINTED OUT TO THE TWO OFFICIALS EYE TALKED TO ABOUT IT . . . WAS THAT HAD IT NOT BEEN NECESSARY BECAUSE OF SPACE TO SHORTEN THE ARTICLE IT WOULD HAVE BEEN MUCH TOUGHER THAN IT WAS, IT WOULD HAVE BEEN CRITICAL OF WESTMORELAND PERSONALLY AND IT WOULD HAVE INCLUDED MANY, MANY MORE EXAMPLES OF CORRUPTION AND INCOMPETENCE. . . .

NO NO NO: THE ARTICLE WAS RIGHT ON THE MONEY. AS EYE POINTED OUT IN AYE MESSAGE TO OZ, IN WHICH EYE FURTHER DOCUMENTED THE POINTS MADE IN THE LEAD, GEN. SIDLE, IN FACT, ADMITTED THAT WHAT WAS PRINTED WAS TRUE BUT THAT EYE SHOULD HAVE "WRITTEN IT AYE LITTLE HAZIER." HELL, MY FEELING IS THAT THERE IS ALREADY ENOUGH "HAZE" IN CONNECTION WITH THIS WAR, MOST OF IT CREATED BY THE WESTMORELANDS WHO WILL NOT FACE FACTS. THE FACT THAT NEWSWEEK IS WILLING TO STRIP AWAY SOME OF THE HAZE IS GRATIFYING, NOT ONLY TO ME BUT TO MANY PEOPLE OUT HERE. THE RESPONSE TO THAT ARTICLE AMONG MILITARY

MEN AS WELL AS CIVILIANS—AMERICANS AND VIETNAMESE
—IS OVERWHELMINGLY IN NEWSWEEK'S CORNER. EYE AM
PROUD MY NAME IS ASSOCIATED WITH STORY. REGARDS
PERRY

Not only was that issue of *Newsweek* banned in Vietnam but the bureau in Saigon received anonymous telephone threats that it was about to be sacked. The semiofficial Vietnam Press Bulletin denounced the magazine in a story headlined: NEWSWEEK GIVES HELPING HAND TO THE VIET CONG. I cabled Westmoreland asking protection for our personnel, and he responded that we should not be "unduly alarmed."

Knowing that all cable traffic was read by the Vietnamese authorities, I also sent an open message to Mert Perry's boss, Saigon bureau chief Everett Martin: "DISMAYED TO HEAR OF CONTINUING HARASSMENT OF BUREAU. UNLESS IT CEASES VERY SOON WE INTEND TO SEE TO IT THAT THE WHOLE SITUATION GETS A THOROUGH AIRING BOTH IN U.S. PRESS AND IN CONGRESS OF UNITED STATES. WE HAVE NO DOUBT THAT THROUGH SENATORS [Robert] KENNEDY AND JAVITS AND THROUGH THE NEW YORK TIMES AND WASHINGTON POST WE CAN GET CONSIDERABLE PUBLIC ATTENTION. . . ."

And I cabled President Thieu for good measure.

Within a few days I received a letter (in Vietnamese) from Mai Van Dai, under secretary of the Ministry of Information, responding to my message to Thieu. We got somebody at the U.N. to translate for us:

> First of all, we are very surprised and wonder where did you get the news which would substantiate your allegation that "certain number of people which includes military servicemen are planning to sabotage your News bureau in Vietnam" because here on the spot we have not seen any signs which could give some

ground to your allegation. However, in view of your exaggerated concern we have informed military authorities and the security forces to see to your safety. The fact that you are so concerned about this threat is proof that you fully realized that the groundless slander printed in *Newsweek* is an insult to the people of Vietnam. . . .

I hope that the explanations given to you will tranquilize you and we hope that your newsmagazine will show more understanding and friendliness to our struggle in the defense of the free world.

Duly tranquilized, we set about trying to understand better the South Vietnamese struggle for the defense of the free world. These efforts, however, were rudely interrupted a few weeks later, in November 1967, by a Telex message from Saigon bureau chief Ev Martin: "NEWSWEEK HAS JUST BEEN PAID SUPREME COMPLIMENT FOR VIETNAM COVERAGE. AS BUREAU'S HEAD EYEVE JUST BEEN EXPELLED FROM COUNTRY AND MUST LEAVE BY NEXT MONDAY. . . .

There was another flurry of cables—to President Thieu, Prime Minister Loc, Vice-President Ky, Ambassador Bunker, Assistant Secretary of State William Bundy. My friend Dick Clurman, Time-Life's chief of correspondents, also weighed in with a supporting wire to Secretary of State Dean Rusk. I put out a statement to the press: "In the past two years, Mr. Martin's coverage . . . has been marked by objectivity, clarity, and sympathy—not to mention a notable degree of courage. To have his assignment abruptly ended in this shocking manner is to cast into doubt the true motivations of the South Vietnamese government, and its understanding of what democracy is all about." All this noble rhetoric was for naught. Within days, Martin was out of the country.

Not only was the American press often at odds with officialdom in Saigon and Washington; it was also locked in a fiercely competitive journalistic battle. Late in 1969, word began to leak out about the massacre that had taken place nine months earlier, at My Lai, in the area of Song My, and *Life* announced that it would be publishing eighteen color photographs of that bloody event. An American Army combat photographer, Ronald Haeberle, had photographed the massacre and was selling his pictures to publications around the world. *Life* had bought exclusive rights to his color photos. Determined not to be scooped by *Life*, I wired Defense Secretary Melvin Laird:

> I RESPECTFULLY URGE YOU TO ORDER THE RELEASE OF PHOTOGRAPHS BEING WITHHELD BY THE DEPARTMENT OF DEFENSE IN CONNECTION WITH THE EVENTS AT SONG MY. . . . THESE PHOTOGRAPHS, TAKEN BY AN ARMY PHOTOGRAPHER WHILE ON DUTY, ARE PROPERLY PUBLIC PROPERTY: COPIES ARE UNDERSTOOD TO EXIST IN YOUR DEPARTMENT'S FILES. THE POSITION THAT ISSUANCE OF THESE PHOTOGRAPHS BY THE DEPARTMENT WOULD PREJUDICE ANY FORTHCOMING LEGAL PROCEEDINGS SEEMS TO ME ACADEMIC AT THIS TIME IN VIEW OF THE FACT THAT THEY ARE ABOUT TO BE PUBLISHED BY ONE OF THE LARGEST-CIRCULATION AMERICAN MAGAZINES, AND BY A NUMBER OF PUBLICATIONS ABROAD. . . . RELEASE OF THE PHOTOGRAPHS WOULD BE IN KEEPING WITH THE CLEAR SIGNALS THAT OUR GOVERNMENT, FAR FROM SUPPRESSING THESE EVENTS, IS PURSUING EVERY MEANS OF BRINGING THIS DARK MATTER TO LIGHT AND BRINGING JUSTICE TO THOSE RESPONSIBLE.

Back came a letter from the deputy general counsel of the Army. In the interests of a fair trial, he said, "even though a number of the photographs in question have already been published, it would be inappropriate for us to encourage their dissemination." *Life* got its scoop.

Sometimes our arguments with the administration bordered on the ridiculous—in part because of Lyndon Johnson's perception of the press. LBJ always viewed the press with suspicion. "Unhappily," wrote his friend and assistant Jack Valenti in *A Very Human President,* "it was LBJ's unvarying view that all reporters had a tilt that showed all too clearly."

But LBJ thought they *could* be manipulated, and figured he knew how to deal with most of Washington's leading journalists. As he told Doris Kearns toward the end of his life:

> You learn that Stewart Alsop cares a lot about appearing to be an intellectual and a historian—he strives to match his brother's intellectual attainments—so whenever you talk to him, play down the gold cuff links which you play up with *Time* magazine, and to him, emphasize your relationship with FDR and your roots in Texas, so much so that even when it doesn't fit the conversation you make sure to bring in maxims from your father and stories from the Old West. You learn that [Rowland] Evans and [Robert] Novak love to traffic in backroom politics and political intrigue, so that when you're with them you make sure to bring in lots of details and colorful description of personality. You learn that Mary McGrory likes dominant personalities and Doris Fleeson cares only about issues, so that when you're with McGrory you come on strong and with Fleeson you make yourself sound like some impractical red-hot liberal.

At Christmastime in 1967, Lyndon Johnson decided to fly from Prime Minister Harold Holt's funeral in Australia to visit Pope Paul VI in Rome, thus offering the world the reassuring spectacle of a Yuletide meeting of two men of peace. When it was over, *Newsweek* reported that the meeting had been "less than completely harmonious," that it had been "correct but impersonal," and that the pope had pressed the president to extend the twenty-four-hour Christmas truce and suspend the bombing indefinitely. The very day the story appeared LBJ was on the phone to right-hand man Valenti, who had arranged the logistics of the papal visit and had himself sat through the audience. LBJ, Valenti later reported in his book, was "mad as hell." He ordered Valenti to call Kay Graham "and find out how she tolerates such stupidity on her magazine. Any idiot that writes a story like that ought to be confined."

So Valenti called Kay, and Kay told him to call me. We were on the phone for forty-five minutes or so. Valenti said the *Newsweek* story was totally wrong, that he had been there, that the meeting between pope and president had gone swimmingly—and if I wanted any proof, he would show me his handwritten notes. I said that I had confidence in *Newsweek*'s reporters and their sources. "Are you saying," he asked, "that you refuse to believe the president of the United States?" That was about what I was saying. Valenti called back, a while later, having talked in the meantime with his chief Vatican contact, the American-born Monsignor Paul Marcinkus, who had told him that the *Newsweek* story had come from Ellen Sullivan, a part-time Vatican "stringer" for the magazine. I told Valenti that I myself had also checked back, and was satisfied that the story had been nicely "triangulated" by other correspondents. "I don't care if you've resurrected Euclid to do your triangulating," Jack Valenti said, "the story's just not true."

We at *Newsweek* did not, of course, take this matter lightly. But what Valenti didn't know was that our sources for the story were not in the Vatican but on the U.S. side of the talks.

Here the most basic lesson in journalism was driven home once again: The truth is an elusive quarry, and different persons will find different realities in the same set of seemingly objective facts.

As the war ground on, most of *Newsweek*'s correspondents came to agree that things were not going well; more and more they became convinced that the United States should pull out of Vietnam. The most notable exception was Arnaud de Borchgrave, by 1966 our senior foreign correspondent, whose Vietnam experiences went all the way back to covering the French defeat at Dien Bien Phu in 1954. While columnists Walter Lippmann and Emmet Hughes, and our correspondents in the field, were writing downbeat pieces, in June 1966; Borchgrave weighed in with "A Dissent From the Dissenters." He argued that the United States must stay the course in order to "contain the expansion of Chinese Communist imperialism." A familiar refrain at the time.

Borchgrave is one of the most extraordinary journalists of our time. Trim, dapper, suave, and perpetually tan (he carries a sun reflector and a warehouse of lotions wherever he goes), this transplanted Belgian nobleman has long been known affectionately to his *Newsweek* colleagues as "the short count." He is endlessly energetic. He is well connected. He is sometimes imperious—but is caring, too. He is godfather to my youngest daughter, Dorinda, and wherever he has found himself over two decades—in the Congo, in Vietnam, in the Middle East—he has never forgotten her birthday. He can be devious—so much so that former *Newsweek* editor John Denson used to say that Arnaud was the only person he knew who would plant a story against himself just to see how it would come back to him. And Borchgrave has incredibly good luck, much of which he creates for himself by figuring out exactly where to be, and when.

Mostly he is known in news circles for his journalistic coups in the Middle East, his exclusive interviews with a whole series of Arab and Israeli leaders, his scoops on Soviet missiles in Egypt. But he has scored numerous beats in Africa and Europe as well, and whenever he came to Asia, *Newsweek*'s bureau chiefs there knew that he was likely to pull off something dramatic. They did not always welcome his visits. Thus it was with pleasure that, in 1966, I received a letter from Ev Martin in Saigon agreeing that Borchgrave should visit Vietnam at regular intervals. Likewise, it was no surprise when, eighteen months later, I received a letter from Martin saying he would like to "unequivocally withdraw the multiple-entry visa I personally gave [Borchgrave] in my letter to you after his first trip."*

Two of Borchgrave's Vietnam coups are worth recording here—one military, the other diplomatic.

Because of the sensitive feelings of the local correspondents, I had been most reluctant to permit him to visit Vietnam, and wrote to him in August 1966 that the idea of any married man with children going off there and taking a lot of risks still bothered me very much. "I am also, quite frankly, concerned about the morale of the Saigon bureau—with all its special and continuing tensions—as Mr. Hot Shot White Silk Scarf moves into the area, shooting at parakeets—as a friend of mine used to say—waving at his friends, and plucking fruit from the overhanging branches."†

As soon as he got to Vietnam, Borchgrave made his way with a Marine Corps outfit to an area just south of the De-

---

* I wrote back to Martin: "Your reference to multiple-entry visas made me feel as though we were dealing with the South Vietnamese Foreign Office all over again. Leave us not attempt to abridge freedom of the press intramurally, eh?"

† This line was stolen from a memo written years before by *Time* writer Paul O'Neil, describing how newsmagazine editors get all the glory while the writers do all the work.

militarized Zone. There, for a night and two days, he found himself in the middle of one of the war's fiercest actions—The Battle for Hill 400. The first we knew about it in New York was a Telex message from the Saigon bureau: "ARNAUD BACK WITH FANTASTIC STUFF. HE HAS BEEN WITH UNIT THAT WAS FIGHTING FOR 100 YARDS FOR TWO DAYS. HE WAS NICKED BY SHRAPNEL, HIS HELMET QUITE BADLY HIT. HE OKAY."

Before seeing Borchgrave's file on the battle, I fired off a rather stern admonition: "THOUGHT EYED MADE IT CLEAR THAT WE LOVE YOU TOO MUCH AND VALUE YOUR BODY IF NOT YOUR MIND TOO MUCH FOR YOU TO TAKE SUCH RISKS. WHILE WE ANTIC-IPATE FINE STORY FROM YOU THIS WEEK EYE EXPECT THIS TO BE LAST SUCH ENDEAVOR. STANDING ORDERS TO ALL NEWSWEEK COR-RESPONDENTS IN VIETNAM ARE NOT TO RISK LIFE OR LIMB UN-NECESSARILY. YOU MUST NOT GO INTO FIELD AGAIN RISKING NECK IN THIS FASHION. CONCENTRATE HENCEFORTH ON POLITICAL AND STRATEGIC COVERAGE NOT GUNGHO STUFF. ALL BEST ELLIOTT."

From Borchgrave came a crisp reply: "AYE AYE SIR. AP-PRECIATE YOUR CONCERN BUT WISH POINT OUT THIS WAS NOT GUNGHO VENTURE NOR DID EYE TAKE UNNECESSARY RISKS. EYE WAS DOING INDISPENSABLE REPORTING FOR TAKEOUT ON WHOLE DDDMMMZZZ CAMPAIGN. . . . EYE HAVE NEVER TAKEN UNNECES-SARY RISKS DASH ONLY CALCULATED ONES. . . . DONT FEEL EYE HAVE ACTED AGAINST YOUR STANDING ORDERS. . . ."

His story, in diary form, was gripping and dramatic and full of the pathos and gore of combat. With Borchgrave's own photos for illustration, we gave it three full pages in the maga-zine. I cabled my congratulations, told Borchgrave I had spoken with his family, and urged him to "ARRANGE ARM IN SLING AND MAYBE EYEPATCH FOR SPEAKING TOUR. WELL DONE AND DONT DO IT AGAIN. AS EVER." When Arnaud arrived back in New York, we gave him a hero's welcome in the lobby of the *Newsweek* building—complete with a towering Irish bag-piper, all decked out in kilts and busby and playing the "Marine

Corps Hymn." Borchgrave was limping from a sprained ankle suffered a few days before, while leaping out of a helicopter. As he made his way into the building and down the ranks of his applauding colleagues, a bunch of flowers in his arms, his limp grew noticeably worse. Or so it seemed to me.

Borchgrave's biggest diplomatic coup in Vietnam came almost exactly six years later, in October 1972. To his great surprise, he was invited to Hanoi to interview North Vietnam's Premier Pham Van Dong, and came away with an exclusive account of Dong's terms for peace. "ANCIENT JACKPOTS," cabled Borchgrave in his own special code for his exclusive, would arrive in time for our deadline—but he might have to spend $2000 for a chartered flight from Hong Kong to Hanoi. I cabled back: "WHILE WE ARE NOT ANXIOUS TO SPEND TWO THOUSAND CLAMS YOU ARE AUTHORIZED TO USE YOUR BEST JUDGMENT IN MAKING CONNECTIONS SO THAT JACKPOTS WILL BE IN OUR HANDS IN GOOD TIME." The next week, *Newsweek* carried Borchgrave's two-page interview, which he had conducted in French.

Over the years, eight Newsweekers served as bureau chief in Saigon, and they and their colleagues filed millions of words of copy.* By August 1974, with the U.S. armed forces withdrawn, staffer Ron Moreau reported: "Saigon has fallen on hard times economically. The trees in front of the *Newsweek* villa have been stripped of bark by those in search of fuel. Even trees in our garden and the fence itself have been attacked. And this week the cars of the *Time* and AFP bureau chiefs, parked at the villa, had their gas tanks punctured and drained. Now I have a police guard at the gate.

"I am closing the bureau with regret, but perhaps it's a good

---

* William Tuohy, who went on to win a Pulitzer Prize for *The Los Angeles Times*, was the first bureau chief. He was followed by Everett Martin, Joel Blocker, Maynard Parker, Kevin Buckley, Nicholas Proffitt, Lloyd Norman, and Loren Jenkins.

time for the *Newsweek* exodus, before our furniture ends up as fuel for someone's cooking pot—and before the next offensive kicks off."

·   ·   ·

The post-mortems on Vietnam are still continuing as this is written—with the Shawcrosses and the Kissingers doing battle, and many others yet to be heard from. I concluded, rather belatedly, that it was a tragic misadventure. Others have yet to be convinced. In December 1978, I happened upon General Westmoreland at a resort hotel in Florida, where he was attending an economic conference. I asked him if he thought the Vietnam war had ever been winnable. Yes, he said firmly. And when might that have been? "After the Tet offensive in 1968." In Westmoreland's view Tet had actually been a great military defeat for the Communists, and the American media had totally misrepresented the affair. If only he had been sent those troops he wanted.

Old soldiers never die, they say.

Neither, it seems, do their dreams of glory.

•VI•
FAIR HARVARD,
THY SONS—AND MY
DAUGHTER

Civil rights and Vietnam so dominated the 1960s that at a distance of fifteen years or so, it is hard to remember that the first stirrings of campus unrest had little if anything to do with those events, or with any other great political issues of the day. Rather, many of the early student protests were a simple cry against the ballooning size and growing impersonality of American institutions, particularly the universities themselves. They also represented a revolt against an encompassing materialism and what my own daughters scornfully perceived as "the middle-class trap." In some universities, many hundreds of students were herded into giant lecture halls for their instruction, sometimes delivered by closed-circuit television; later the cold computers would spew out a reading on how well they had paid attention. "Do not fold, spindle, or muti-

late," said an early poster of protest in Berkeley, "I am a human being." As late as 1967, a rallying cry of the hippies in
San Francisco's Haight-Ashbury district echoed a weird varia-
tion on this theme: "The psychedelic baby eats the cybernetic
monster."

It was only later that campus demonstrations focused on
civil rights, the draft, the universities' ties to military research,
and the war. "In the eyes of the politicized students," *Newsweek* reported in 1968, "the university has become the surro-
gate for the ills of society, and they want to turn it around
and use its powers and resources to cure those ills."

One of the greatest ills, as the students saw it, was a political
system that had plunged America into a brutal war; a notable
phenomenon of early 1968 was the army of young people,
suddenly shorn and "clean for Gene," who swarmed into New
Hampshire to help Senator Eugene McCarthy topple a president from power. For a while, it looked as if they might indeed
bring about the changes they sought by working "within the
system." But within weeks came the assassination of Martin
Luther King, Jr., and within months the murder of Robert
Kennedy, and "the system" seemed to many to have some
self-sealing mechanism to protect itself against peaceful
change.

As spring 1968 rolled by, Americans were treated to the
spectacle of gun-toting black students marching out of a building at Cornell, and striking students swarming over the statue
of Alma Mater at Columbia, where they seized the president's
office and peed into his wastebasket.

Late that summer, when the Democrats gathered for their
national convention in Chicago, mayhem seemed inevitable—
and was made so when Mayor Richard Daley's blue-coats allowed themselves to· be taunted into a police riot. Gazing
down from his hotel room at the violent street scene far be-

low, Hubert Humphrey wept as he watched his chance for the presidency drift away in a cloud of tear gas.*

Some thought that the events in Chicago had marked the high tide of youthful protest, but the tide kept rising. In the spring of 1969, the nation's oldest university went on strike. I was afforded a close-up view of the events at Harvard, equally as the father of a student there, as the editor of a publication closely following the action on campuses all over the country, and as a member of Harvard's venerable Board of Overseers.

· · ·

"The Reverend and Honorable the Board of Overseers" is Harvard's senior governing body. It was established by the General Court of the Massachusetts Bay Colony in 1636, and the following year the court appointed the board's first members: Governor Winthrop, Deputy-Governor Dudley, four magistrates, and six clergymen. Over the years, the board has grown to thirty members, each elected to a six-year term by the 140,000 persons now living who are qualified to vote by virtue of holding Harvard degrees.

The process of nominating Overseers is shrouded in mystery, and the election is usually unpredictable. Although blacks and women later proved to be eminently electable, in the mid-sixties the board was predominantly ultra-Establishment: Waspish, bankerly, lawyerly, and male. If my own election in 1965 was any standard, academic credentials were no criteria. I

---

* *Newsweek*'s news editor Hal Bruno, in charge of the magazine's convention task force, ordered his reporters to travel in pairs around Chicago, carrying prominent press identification, and wearing riot helmets on the streets. Six of Bruno's reporters fell victim to police billy clubs nonetheless.

had been propelled through Harvard by the Navy in a little more than two years during World War II, getting mostly C's and concentrating mostly in hockey.

After the war, when I was working as a writer for *Time*, I thought I might make up for what I had missed in college by applying for a Nieman Fellowship, which would provide a full and unhurried academic year at Harvard. My application got only as far as the managing editor's desk. "What the hell does Elliott want a Nieman for?" asked *Time*'s managing editor, Roy Alexander. "He's already got the two things a Nieman has to offer." "And what," asked my sponsor, "might they be?" Said Alexander: "A membership in the Harvard Club and a job on *Time*."

Harvard's Board of Overseers does not have a great deal of direct power; the university is run, on a day-to-day basis, by the seven-man "Corporation," a self-perpetuating body made up of the president and the treasurer of the university, and five outside "fellows." But the Overseers do have a veto power over acts of the Corporation, and they possess unquantifiable but very real powers of suasion. It is a distinct honor to serve as an Overseer—aside from anything else, it entitles you to wear a silk hat and a cutaway at Commencement—and more than once the office has lent unexpected and welcome prestige to one member or another.

Donald Hornig, science adviser to President Johnson and later president of Brown University, was a case in point. One day in the White House, Hornig was locked in a policy dispute with LBJ. Suddenly the president exploded: "Why, what do you know about public policy, Hornig? You've never been elected to office."

"Yes I have, Mr. President," protested Hornig.

"Which office?" the president wanted to know.

"I was elected an Overseer of Harvard," Hornig replied.

"And what in hell kind of election is that?"

"That, Mr. President," said Hornig triumphantly, "is the kind of election that Bobby Kennedy once lost." From that moment on, Hornig told me later, he rose rapidly in the president's estimation.*

So pervasive was the war in Vietnam that as early as 1966 it intruded into the classic, eighteenth-century faculty room of University Hall, where the Overseers hold their monthly meetings. Up for consideration at a winter meeting that year were the Corporation's nominations for honorary degrees. A subcommittee of the board, headed by Neil McElroy—chairman of Procter & Gamble, former secretary of defense, and that year's president of the Overseers—had studied the list and recommended that fourteen of the fifteen proposed honorary degrees be approved. Among the candidates were a Cabot and a Coolidge and a Gardner; a scatteration of scholars; the dancer Martha Graham; and Averell Harriman. But the committee balked at one New England nominee: the poet Robert Lowell. The reason was that the previous autumn, when Lyndon Johnson held a White House reception for American artists, Lowell had refused to attend, in protest against administration policy in Vietnam. McElroy and others feared that if Harvard awarded Lowell a degree, the act would be interpreted as endorsing the poet's position. What followed was a two-hour battle royal among the Overseers in University Hall.

There were those who strongly agreed that Lowell's degree should be rejected. One lawyer, just then trying to raise millions for the Harvard Law School, said: "Look, I'm having

* In 1967, Robert Kennedy ran tenth in a field of ten candidates for Overseer. John F. Kennedy had been elected a Harvard Overseer ten years before, and soon after he became president, he invited the board to hold a meeting in the White House.

enough trouble fund-raising, without being burdened with *this!*" Another Overseer noted that it was now midwinter, and by Commencement the casualties in Vietnam might be running high. How would Harvard look in *that* case? Some wondered what would happen to the university's research contracts with the government should the poet be honored.

But Lowell had his defenders, too. Craggy-faced John Crocker, retired headmaster of the Groton School, said: "Year after year I have been going to Harvard commencements, and year after year I have seen the same predictable people up there on the podium, getting the same predictable honorary degrees. It seems to me it's time we honored the *yeast* of this society, someone who appeals to our young people as Robert Lowell does." Jesse Greenstein, a scientist from Cal Tech, turned out to be the poet of the day. "Gentlemen," he said, "as I flew in from California at dusk last night, I gazed down on the snowy New England countryside and my mind went back to our forebears and the people who founded this institution. I thought of what they believed in, and their central commitment to freedom. And I think, quite frankly, that this very discussion is an insult to the men who held those ideals."

What seemed to be the *coup de grâce* to Lowell was delivered by a lean and leathery New York lawyer, who rose toward the end of the discussion, grabbed his lapels, and peered over his half-glasses—assuming the prescribed Overseerly stance when a major statement is about to be uttered. "Gentlemen," he said, "when I saw Mr. Lowell's name among those to be honored, a little bell went off in my head. I seemed to remember something that had appeared in what I believe *The New Yorker* calls its—uh—Funny Coincidence Department. So I asked one of my associates to do a little research—and sure enough . . ." Reaching dramatically into his inside pocket, the attorney pulled out a nineteen-year-old clipping from

The New Yorker and began to read aloud. The item compared Lowell's famous "The Quaker Graveyard in Nantucket" with "Cape Cod," by Henry David Thoreau.

Lowell:

> *The corpse was bloodless, a botch*
> *of reds and whites,*
> *Its open, staring eyes*
> *Were lustreless dead-lights*
> *Or cabin-windows on a stranded hulk*
> *Heavy with sand. . . .*

Thoreau:

> . . . the coiled-up wreck of a human hulk, gashed by the rocks or fishes, so that the bone and muscle were exposed, but quite bloodless,—merely red and white,—with wide-open and staring eyes, yet lustreless, dead-lights; or like the cabin windows of a stranded vessel, filled with sand.

The similarity was striking. "So I submit, Mr. President," said the accusing Overseer, "that if we were to honor Mr. Lowell, we would be honoring a plagiarist." He sank back into his leather chair, full of pride at having discharged his Overseerly duty.

Then Nathan Pusey, Harvard's president, rose to explain why he and the Harvard Corporation believed a degree should nonetheless be granted to Lowell. "I would like to dispose of the last charge, that of plagiarism, first," Pusey said. Calmly and with authority, Pusey pointedly explained that anyone who knew anything about Lowell's poetry must know that his "Graveyard in Nantucket" was deliberately structured to reflect the work of Lowell's literary forebears in New England. The particular excerpt cited by *The New Yorker*, said Pusey, showed how well Lowell had succeeded in that aim.

Left, Straight arrow: A battalion commander in World War I, my father was wounded in France and remained loyal to the army and to Harvard for all his eighty-eight years.

Bundle of energy: My mother (left) marched for women's suffrage, rose to the top of the New York real-estate world, and was still working at the age of eighty.

A hockey major at Harvard.

First job: O.E. (center) in the Dickensian city room of *The Journal of Commerce*. "That's the way it's done, Oss."

Friday-night fever: Which twin is the editor? *Newsweek* colleagues marched into my office one evening, wearing fright masks. (*Newsweek*, Robert R. McElroy)

Above left, With Phil Graham: witty, brilliant, electric—and manic depressive. (*Newsweek,* Vytas Valaitis)

Above right, Phil and partner Beebe: Were Fritz's grand-fathers-in-law really sisters? (*Newsweek,* Vytas Valaitis)

A Flight of Wallendas: Kermit Lansner, Bob Christopher (bottom), Lester Bernstein climbing aboard. (*Newsweek,* Robert R. McElroy)

A flattering *New Yorker* cartoon: "Now, confidentially, just between my government and your government and 'Newsweek . . .'" (Drawing by Alan Dunn; © 1967 The New Yorker Magazine, Inc.)

Story conference: We tried to keep things airy and informal; there would be tensions enough later in the week. (*Newsweek,* Robert R. McElroy)

"Going Through the Book": On Saturday, the editors would review the dummy for last-minute makeup changes. (*Newsweek*)

With Kay Graham and Deirdre (head turned) in Japan: The emperor received her, and she moved into the world.

At Harvard: Overseers get to wear silk hats and cutaways at commencement. (Geoffrey Biddle)

While it may not have seemed so to me in 1966 *(above)*, Nixon turned out to be "the one" at the G.O.P. convention in Miami two years later. (*Newsweek,* Robert R. Mc-Elroy)

Above left, Ben Bradlee at my fiftieth-birthday party: "Ozzie baby, I know where the smart money is." (Geoffrey Biddle)

Above right, Hubert Humphrey at *Newsweek* (1964): Four years later, he was a different man. (*Newsweek,* Phil MacMullan)

Oval Office, 1974: Gerald Ford gave *Newsweek* his first interview as president. (*Newsweek,* Wally McNamee)

With Bobby Kennedy at *Newsweek*: The editors were in their cups. (Vytas Valaitis)

At the Elysée Palace: being charmed by Giscard. (T. Boccon-Gibod)

Beach Bums: Dorinda, Diana, Alec, Inger, O.E., Kari, Cynthia (Molly absent). (Geoffrey Biddle)

Some Women in My Life: with Kay Graham and Eleanor Holmes Norton as *Newsweek* signed a deal with its editorial women in 1970. (*Newsweek*)

A Gag in Drag: For Gib McCabe's farewell film, I stuffed my cheeks with cotton and made like a salacious old newsstand lady. (*Newsweek,* Bernard Gotfryd)

Ave Atque Vale: Kay Graham's farewell speech did me no injustice; I helped her write it. (*Newsweek,* Robert R. McElroy)

As Abe Beame's Deputy Mayor: A bird flew in the window. (Tony Rollo)

Commencing at Columbia, 1979.

The accuser was abashed. Rising halfway to his feet, he mumbled: "Well, Mr. President, I—er—if that's the case, of course I withdraw the charge of plagiarism." Pusey went on to review Lowell's work, and how strongly the faculty felt in his behalf, and at length a vote was taken. Lowell won, 13 to 12. (At lunch that day, Neil McElroy said he was reminded of the time a company's board of directors met with one of its members absent. The missing man was in the hospital, and the board deputized one of the directors to visit the patient and report that they had passed a resolution expressing their hopes for a speedy recovery. He did so, duly informing the patient that the motion had passed by a margin of a single vote.)

·   ·   ·

Outside the walls of University Hall, passions about Vietnam were rising among young and old alike. Sometimes they exploded in the most unlikely places. After the Harvard-Yale football game one year, I was with my family at President Pusey's cocktail party. Making my way across the crowded room with a bunch of drinks in my hands, I bumped into my old friend Blair Clark, who introduced me to David Halberstam, the fiery young bull-in-a-china-shop who won a Pulitzer Prize for his Vietnam reporting. "What *Newsweek* did to Mert Perry was inexcusable," exploded Halberstam from out of the blue. I was taken aback. After serving *Newsweek* with distinction for years in Vietnam—including, incidentally, that day and night with me in Cu Chi—Perry had been transferred to Chicago. He wanted London, but for a variety of reasons we had decided against it. At that, Perry quit the magazine and moved to Mexico to write a book. There the poor man, who had long been heavily overweight, died of a heart attack, and now Halberstam was more than implying that *Newsweek* was responsible for his death. "I don't have to take this kind of shit from you," I said elegantly, and made my way across Pusey's living room. Since then, passions have cooled and Halberstam and I have become friends—so much so that I told him far too many anecdotes for his book *The Powers That Be*; that was, of course, before I knew I would be writing this book myself.

As the first rumblings of student protest were felt in Cambridge in the mid-sixties, various of the Overseers, a pretty stuffy lot in those days, often complained to Pusey—and Pusey would frequently come to the students' defense. At one meeting, someone rose, assumed the accepted major-statement-about-to-be-delivered stance—hands clasping lapels, eyes peering over glasses—and proclaimed: "Nate, it seems to me that when a fella is up here just to tear the place down, he ought to be expulsed." That was a new verb to me, but Pusey was unfazed. "Charlie," he said, "there's hardly a day that I don't wake up mad at somebody. But we've got to keep reminding ourselves that we're here to *educate* people, not to *expel* them." This, of course, was not the Nathan Pusey the students knew. To them, he was a gray and cold and distant figure. Someone once described him as looking like a retouched photograph of himself.

Harvard's explosion came late—nine months after the Chicago convention of 1968, a full year after Columbia erupted, five years after the first troubles at Berkeley. As *Newsweek*'s Boston bureau chief Frank Morgan reported: "Always flexible, open-minded, sophisticated, Harvard had in the past not only smothered crises with just enough measured response to undercut the radical demands but also anticipated them by as much as a year."

But on April 9, 1969, Harvard's wile and guile and style ran out. At a noontime rally of the local chapter of the Students for a Democratic Society, outside University Hall, a proposal was made to take over the building. The object was to advance the cause of the SDS, which had assembled a rather disparate array of demands, ranging from the abolition of the Reserve Officers Training Corps (ROTC) from the Harvard campus to the rolling back of rents in Harvard-owned housing, and a halt to the university's expansion into Cambridge's black neighborhoods nearby. A crowd of some five hundred students voted down the proposal, but sixty to eighty Maoists and other hard-liners charged into University Hall anyway, physically ejected nine deans and their secretaries, and settled into the faculty room for a siege. As afternoon faded into evening, the crowd grew to three hundred. Students came and went, bringing in blankets and food—and carrying out copies of university files.

I had spent most of that day in cap and gown in New York, helping celebrate the centennial of the American Museum of Natural History, of which I was a trustee, and didn't hear of the events at Harvard until my freshman daughter, Diana, called that evening. She told me what had happened, and was clearly worried about what might happen next. She had reason to be. At 4:55 the next morning, responding to a request from the Harvard administration, local police and a contingent of state troopers arrived on the scene at University Hall. The cops charged, clubs swinging. In twenty minutes, it was all over: 197 students arrested, 45 injured badly enough to require treatment.

Diana was on the phone again at 8:00 a.m. She had been up all night, and had witnessed the police "bust." "Daddy," she said, "it was like Chicago all over again."

This would naturally be a major story for *Newsweek*'s upcoming issue, and I faced a serious conflict of interest. As an Overseer, it was my duty to protect and support Harvard—even though I strongly disapproved of Nathan Pusey's decision to call in the police; but as an editor I was duty-bound that *Newsweek* should pull no punches. I put out a memo to the top editors, and sent copies to Pusey and to Douglas Dillon, then president of the Overseers: "Because of my role as a Harvard Overseer, I have decided that it would be improper for me to become involved in *Newsweek*'s handling of this week's story on the events in Cambridge. Accordingly, I shall not engage in any phase of the reporting, writing, or editing of the story—secure in the knowledge that *Newsweek*'s guiding light, like Harvard's, is Veritas."

As I have said, Overseers could be a pretty stuffy lot in those days.

The following Monday, five days after the bust, the Overseers were scheduled to gather for their regular monthly meeting. It was decided, a bit pusillanimously I thought, that to meet in University Hall might invite more disorders, and so we trooped to a secret location across the Charles River, in the library of the Medical School. It was, said Douglas Dillon, a "momentous" occasion. But you would hardly know it, reading the minutes of that meeting today: "On behalf of the Executive Committee, Mr. Amory reported with regret the deaths of two former members of the Board, John Mason Brown . . . and Edward W. Forbes. . . . Mr. Amory stated the Executive Committee, upon recommendation received from the Committee on Committee Assignments . . ."

I had flown up from New York on a Sunday-night shuttle with my friend and fellow Overseer Teddy White, and it turned out that each of us had drafted a statement for consideration by the board. His was a bit perfervid, I thought, took too hard a line. He believed, for instance, that the police action had been absolutely necessary. I thought, after many talks with Diana, that it had been precipitous, and that Pusey should have allowed time for student and faculty sentiment to rally behind him and against SDS.

When we arrived at the Medical School, we discovered a third draft statement had been drawn up by Judge Ammi

Cutter, a crusty New Englander who went so far as to suggest in his draft: "The Board expresses regret, shared by every Harvard man, that the conduct of some Harvard students made necessary the use of police to end the violent invasion of a university building and that, as a consequence, members of the police and others were injured." If anything was calculated to inflame the situation even more, I thought, Judge Cutter's statement would surely do the job.

Pusey spent an hour reviewing for the Overseers the events of the past few days; he said he thought it likely that another building would be seized, perhaps that very day. Midway through the morning session, we got word that three moderate student leaders wished to be heard, and they were admitted to our august presence. They were an impressive trio—one black, two whites—who obviously were concerned that their own political power was slipping through their fingers as more radical students stole the limelight.

These students asked that we pass a resolution endorsing a university-wide referendum on ROTC. At that point, Elliot Richardson, just named as under secretary of state, became incensed. Chin outthrust, voice trembling, and color rising in his face, Richardson fairly spat out his response. Didn't they remember the plebiscites in the days of Hitler? Richardson's outburst seemed curiously off-target. It was embarrassing.

Dillon appointed a drafting committee, including Teddy White and Judge Cutter. Just before they left the room to go to work, there was some discussion as to what the statement should say. I said the Overseers would be making a big mistake if they specifically endorsed the police action: "This Board has a number of constituencies, including students, faculty, the alumni, and the whole field of higher education in this country. If we make such a specific endorsement we will automatically lose one of our constituencies—the students—and vitiate what we have to say in the rest of the statement."

No one else seemed to agree. Washington lawyer Jim Rowe in particular argued against me, and others said that Pusey must have all-out support.

The drafting committee was out of the room for the better part of two hours—Teddy White at a typewriter, tie askew and looking for all the world as if he were churning out a chapter in *The Making of the President*. At length they filed back in with Xeroxes of a new draft resolution, and the full Board proceeded to vote on it, line by line.

I objected: the statement said the occupation had "necessitated" the calling of the police. Finally, Dillon put the key paragraph up for a vote. "All those in favor?" Every hand but one went up. "Opposed?" Feeling rather lonely, I stuck up my right hand. Jim Rowe, sitting next to me, said: "Well, you satisfied your conscience and made your point."*

I went off to find Diana, feeling dejected.

. . .

As I had promised, I read *Newsweek*'s story on the Harvard strike only after it was in print. I was satisfied with what I read. "Both inside and outside the university," it said, "there is astonishment that, given other schools' errors to learn from, Harvard could do no better. In meeting the crisis, the administration had failed to consult its own faculty and student lead-

---

* The statement, as finally issued by the Board of Overseers, included an egregious grammatical error, which I can only believe was the fault of a harried typist and not of the distinguished drafting committee. "President Pusey," it said, "had to make a prompt and painful decision in an emergency. We support his action *unequivocably*." [Italics added.] A few months later, in a special section on the Harvard strike, *The Boston Globe* wrongly reported that I had proposed a vote of no confidence in President Pusey. They subsequently printed a retraction.

ers. Whether Pusey acted correctly or too quickly or too slowly was perhaps less important than the fact that he acted without seeking the support of the university community."

Later that week, I was back in Cambridge for a lunch with *Harvard Crimson* editors at Barney's: Nina Bernstein, daughter of my longtime colleague Lester (and now a star reporter for *The Milwaukee Journal*) ; James Fallows, now Washington editor of *The Atlantic;* three or four others. The *Crimson* people had been painted as all-out SDS types to me, but these particular students didn't strike me that way. Certainly they were opposed to Harvard's administration; but just as surely they were not aiming to tear the institution apart.

After lunch Diana came along and we went off to the football stadium where a mass meeting was getting under way. The crowd was handled beautifully by a husky, bearded, red-headed teaching fellow named Lance Buhl. Everything was strictly parliamentary—and most important, the sound system worked. At one point, the proceedings were interrupted by an amatory encounter between a couple of dogs who were nuzzling each other in the stands and finally consummated their passion in the fifty-yard line seats occupied by the Overseers at Harvard-Yale football games. The crowd went wild.

Later on in the afternoon, the students voted to suspend their strike.

But that was not the end of protest at Harvard or anywhere else. Almost a year later, as chairman of a committee appointed to inspect Harvard's East Asian studies program, I found myself embroiled again. One March evening in 1970, eleven members of my committee were dining with eight students in the library of the Faculty Club to hear out the students' complaints and criticisms with no faculty members present. Suddenly the library door burst open, and in marched half a dozen angry and rather scruffy young men who handed out Xeroxed copies of a flier:

Good evening,
Welcome to Harvard-East Asia, where the natives are
both quiet and informative. To make your dinner
even *more* pleasant, we would like to inform you that
the only information you need learn during your stay
here, is that more than 40,000 Americans have died in
the false cause of Imperialism. We would appreciate
your passing that along to the Board of Overseers.

Bon Appetit.

P.S. We did not elect you, nor were you chosen by the
Mandate of Heaven, rather, you were "elected" by the
monied elite of the Board of Overseers, & you therefore represent only yourselves here.

The sudden invasion was unsettling. I asked the invaders if
they were bona fide students, and one of them grunted yes.
"Well," I said, "in that case you've come to exactly the right
place, because this dinner is supposed to provide an exchange
of ideas with students. Why don't you sit down and join the
group?" Now it was *their* turn to be unsettled. As they pulled
up chairs, I glanced around at my committee and told our uninvited guests: "You seem to think this group is not legitimate.
Let me ask some of our members to stand and identify themselves." I selected carefully—skipping a general and a few
businessmen who were incontestably Establishmentarian.
Teddy White rose and told about his poverty-stricken boy-
hood in the Boston ghetto, and how he had been the first to
major in Chinese at Harvard, and how he had been fired from
Time Inc. for his presumed sympathy with the cause of Chinese Communism. Professor W. A. C. H. Dobson of the University of Toronto told about the abject poverty he had
suffered as a boy in the slums of London. The student invaders
sat silently for the next hour as the meeting proceeded, and at
the end I had to urge them to participate.

· · ·

What did all the protest and rebellion finally accomplish? In the months that followed the Harvard strike, any number of committees, made up of students, faculty, alumni, Overseers, administrators, churned out reams of reports analyzing the causes of the strike and recommending changes in the university's curriculum, disciplinary procedures, and "governance." For many hundreds of students, my daughter included, it was a traumatizing experience; a number of her friends have never fully recovered. "I wish I'd gotten an education when I was in Cambridge," one young woman said almost a decade later, "but as it is, all I learned was how to stencil armbands."

Nathan Pusey was of course a casualty. This eminently decent person, who had stood up nobly against Joe McCarthy's assaults upon academe in the early fifties, simply did not possess the political agility demanded of college presidents in the turmoil of the sixties. When Pusey, in 1970, announced his intention to retire two years early, Harvard's governing bodies geared up for the elaborate process of searching out and electing a successor—a procedure laid out by the university's three-hundred-year-old charter. As Senior Fellow, Boston lawyer Francis H. ("Hooks") Burr was in charge of the search, which turned out to be, as Blair Clark wrote, "the biggest thing of its kind since Hollywood's quest for a Scarlett O'Hara."

To begin with, the Corporation sent out two hundred thousand letters to students, alumni, faculty, and the rest of the "Harvard community," seeking nominees. About a thousand nominations came pouring in, from some three thousand respondents. Thirty persons nominated themselves, and were quickly purged from the list; one alumnus nominated his wife because "what Harvard needs is a Jewish mother." As Clark wrote, "it was the most public, complete, constituency-appeasing manhunt in academe's history."

By the fall of 1970, the list was pared to 169 names, and by Thanksgiving the number was down to 23, all of them with "a primary academic commitment." At that point, the Overseers' executive committee (of which I was a member) met with the Corporation for a progress report. Among the leading candidates: Overseer and Stanford scientist Donald Kennedy; Harvard's dean of the faculty John Dunlop, and Harvard Law dean Derek Bok. Ever jealous of their prerogatives, some of the Overseers were concerned that they might be considered nothing more than rubber stamps, and urged that the executive committee insist on seeing the Corporation's final candidate before a vote was taken. Jay Iselin, then a top editor at Harper & Row, wrote me a letter: "I am concerned that the cuckoo clock is going to go off one of these days—and a strange bird will pop out. . . ."

And so it was arranged, when the Corporation had finally zeroed in on Derek Bok, for the executive committee to lunch with him in New York in January 1971, two days before the formal vote was to take place in Cambridge. The creamed chicken, purée of peas, and Château Haut Brion were provided by Douglas Dillon in his handsome Fifth Avenue apartment. At the beginning of lunch, Dillon asked Bok to say a few words.

Bok started by saying that his life at Harvard had centered in the Law School and so he could not be expected to have opinions on all aspects of the university. But he wanted to make some general points. To begin with, he felt that all universities had lost the confidence of many people, including even their own students and faculty, and he thought that the top priority for the new president of Harvard would be to restore confidence in the institution.

He dwelt in particular on the needs of the students who ar-

rive on campus "expecting Nirvana," but soon find that the
reality nowhere nearly meets their expectations. Bok said it
was vital to bring the reality closer to the students' expectations by beefing up the faculty, reforming the curriculum, and
interesting the students in an academic commitment. He
thought that universities had been asked to do too much over
recent years; they should concentrate more on education, their
primary function, not on reforming society. Given the choice
between a poor teacher/excellent researcher and an excellent
teacher/poor researcher, Bok said he would go for the latter almost every time.

Then Bok invited questions from the group. I asked him:
"What lessons in crisis management were learned from the
events of April 1969?" The first lesson, he said, was that much
more information is needed to cope with any such situation:
"Not to criticize Mr. Pusey, but I don't think anybody at the
top level of the Harvard administration even knew what Harvard's housing policies were at that time—and housing was one
of the chief issues of the day." We were all favorably impressed
by Bok's presentation, and we looked forward to the ceremonial laying-on of hands the following Monday. But when we
arrived in Cambridge Sunday night, we discovered some dis-
sension in the Overseerly ranks. On Saturday, *The New York
Times* had printed a story that Bok was the final choice; a
number of Overseers felt they were being steamrollered by the
Corporation.* There were rumblings that some of them might

* Once again I faced a conflict of interest, and once again I removed
myself from the story—with some reluctance. At a New York Public
Library executive committee meeting earlier in the week, Time
Inc.'s President Roy Larsen, a loyal son of Harvard, leaned over
and suggested to me that *Time* and *Newsweek* should go with the
Bok election that week, and not wait for the formal vote the next
Monday. I agreed to call Hooks Burr to seek permission of the Corporation, but Burr feared a backlash from the Overseers if they
saw the story in print before they even had a chance to vote. When

try to block the vote, and the atmosphere was tense as we gathered at University Hall next morning. But matters proceeded smoothly. According to ancient custom, President Pusey was asked to escort the Senior Fellow, Hooks Burr, into the Overseers' meeting.

Reading from a yellow legal pad, and "speaking of the solemnity of the occasion"—as the minutes later recorded—Burr described Derek Bok's qualifications, reviewed his career, and cited his modest nature. "This is not a man," Burr concluded with a flourish, "who will mistake the rumblings in his bowels for the urgings of the Almighty."

The Reverend and Honorable the Board of Overseers then proceeded to vote. Harvard had its twenty-fifth president.

---

reporter Jack Rosenthal of *The New York Times* called me Friday to say he had the Bok story locked up, I did not try to dissuade him. It was one time I was perfectly happy to have *Newsweek* beaten by the *Times*, for the *Times* story freed me to tell *Newsweek*'s editors to go ahead with a major story that week. As it happened, our Boston bureau chief, Frank Morgan, already had pinned down the story by an interview with Derek Bok himself.

•VII•
SOME WOMEN
IN MY LIFE

W hile civil rights and Vietnam and the student revolt had dominated the news during the sixties, another mighty force began to make itself felt as a new decade dawned. This was the women's movement, whose new language of "raised consciousness," "sex objects," and "male chauvinism" began to echo through the corridors of *Newsweek* in the spring of 1970. The magazine's forty-six editorial women were in rebellion, charging management with a long and strong history of discriminating against them on the basis of their sex. I had come to view *Newsweek* as an exemplar of journalistic liberality, but here we were being accused by our own employees of sexist oppression. What was worse, though it took me a while to realize it, the women were right.

• • •

Like most American males of my generation, from an early age I had the earmarks of a male-chauvinist piglet. In the summertime, when we were kids, my brother Jock and I used to scramble around beneath the deck of the "ladies' court" at our beach club on Fire Island, peering up between the boards to see what we could see. Our research came to an abrupt halt one day when my brother found a comb in the cool, shadowed sand beneath the deck. Poking it up through a crack in the boards, he innocently inquired of the startled naked lady above: "Did you drop your comb, Mrs. Walther?"

My appreciation of the opposite sex tended to be rather basic. Joan I admired, at thirteen, for her deliciously full and tightly haltered bosom; Harriet, at fifteen—all names here are fictitious—for her willingness to take me in hand and relieve my teenage tensions; Hiroko, a girl in Nagoya, for finally making a man of me—in a manner of speaking—when I was twenty.

We used to do a lot of sailing when I was a boy, and the summer I was fifteen, my first mate brought along some cherry bombs for the July Fourth races. As we maneuvered around before the start, he lighted the fuse and lobbed a bomb across the water to another boat manned (or personned) by three girls. The mighty firecracker hit their mainsail, slid down, and bounced off the boom, coming to rest beneath the derrière of Mary, who was just then leaning over to coil a rope. There was an enormous explosion, and the girls sailed in to the dock for repairs.

A quarter of an hour later, when their boat appeared back at the starting line, I was vastly relieved to see that all three girls were still on board. "What happened, Mary," I yelled, "did you blow your ass off?"

The scene now shifts to the country-club dance that evening: the Pavilion Royal Commanders are playing "Deep Purple," "Honeysuckle Rose," and "String of Pearls," and I am suavely sipping a Cuba libre between puffs on my Chesterfield. A waiter tells me I have a phone call. "I think you'd better start home," my father says stiffly over the telephone. "But Jock has the keys to the car," I say, "and I don't know where he is." "You can walk," my father intones.

And so I walk the mile home, and he sits me down in the living room, and then this man, this beautiful, straight-arrow of a man—who has never in his life uttered so much as a hell or a damn—says to me: "Is it true that you said to Mary, 'Did you blow your ass off?' " I allow that that may have been the gist of my remarks, and the next morning I am riding my bicycle to Mary's house on Howell's Point Road, a bunch of roses in one hand. Her mother comes to the screen door; Mary, she says, is in bed. Thrusting the roses toward her, I blurt: "I'm-sorry-I-said-'Did-you-blow-your-ass-off.' "

"How's that?" (Mary's mother is hard of hearing.)

I shout: "I SAID I'M SORRY I SAID 'DID YOU BLOW YOUR ASS OFF!' " and wheel my bicycle down the drive.

In my family, sex was never discussed, any more than money. Long after I had absorbed the essential facts of life from my grubby schoolmates, I was given a birds-bees-and-flowers book called *Growing Up*. I remember once, when I was about twelve, trying to get my mother to tell me how babies are made, just to see what she would say. "Well," she said, looking the other way, "a man and a woman have to be very much in love."

"Do they have to be married?" I asked disingenuously.

"They have to be very much in love."

The night I left for college, standing on a steamy platform at Grand Central, my father cleared his throat and told me awkwardly that sex before marriage was not at all necessary; in fact, it was fraught with dangers of every sort. And the day before I was married—at twenty-three—he asked me, in excruciating embarrassment, if I knew about condoms and that sort of thing.

I never went to dancing school of the white-gloves-and-blue-suit variety. Instead, as the old song went, "Arthur Murray taught me dancing in a hurry." But I was forced to attend some horrible Christmas and Easter dances at New York's Plaza and Pierre hotels, and at the Colony and Cosmopolitan clubs. These were formal affairs to which the ladies and gentlemen of East Side Manhattan sent their children as if to reassure themselves that nothing had really changed since they were young, when the boys attended the Browning School and the girls went to Miss Spence's or Miss Chapin's and they all learned the waltz and the two-step at Mr. Dodsworth's dancing academy. Now, as they sent their own children off to tromp on each other's feet, it was as if there had been no crash, no Depression —and no Hitler already running amok in Europe.

To me, all the other boys at these dreadful dances seemed to be older and richer and better looking and more sophisticated; I would spend most of my time on the stag line, fiddling with my black tie and wing collar, running my fingers over my bumpy teenage complexion, and gathering courage to cut in on some poor creature who hadn't the faintest idea what Fate was about to inflict on her.

· · ·

I have always been surrounded by strong women. My longtime boss and friend, Kay Graham, whom I watched grow from shrinking violet to publishing power, was only one of them. There was, to begin with, my mother, a beautiful, auburn-haired, European-educated, compact bundle of inexhaustible energy. The energy must have been inherited; it could hardly have come from diet. In all her life my mother never tasted any fruit or fruit juices or jams, never tasted fish or shellfish, never ate any salads or cheese, never sipped a glass of wine or alcohol of any kind. She liked lamb chops and roast beef and steak and asparagus and peas and dark chocolate and milk. When she went out to dinner, she would take tiny portions and push her food around the plate and hide it under her knife and fork.

She spoke with something close to an English accent, and drove a Bugatti to Canada in 1912, when she was eighteen. Before World War I, she marched in parades on Fifth Avenue, demonstrating for women's suffrage. Later, she used to hustle her way to the head of the line at the movies and other events—which embarrassed the rest of the family but always paid off with the best seats in the house. When my father, a true gentleman of the old school, lost his partnership in Kidder, Peabody after the crash, my mother went to work in real estate. She became the leading woman broker of brownstones and cooperative apartments on Manhattan's East Side, was made a vice-president of her firm, Douglas Gibbons-Hollyday & Ives, at seventy-five, and was still working the telephones and pounding the pavements of Manhattan two years before she died, at eighty-two.*

My first wife was and still is a workingwoman. My sister-in-law has made a career out of volunteerism—serving for many years as chairman of the board of Barnard College, and more recently as the first woman board member of Celanese Corporation and CIT. My three daughers—Diana, Cynthia, and Dorinda—are independent spirits who let me know, early on, that they didn't want, ever, to be caught in "the middle-class trap," which I suppose reflected *their* view of *my* life. My step-daughters, Kari and Molly, are already showing similar signs of independence—and stepson Alec, the only boy in this crowd, seems to be surviving the ministrations of all these women—the most important of whom being his mother, Inger, the earthy, loving genius who is now my wife.

---

* During the Depression, my father arranged for scholarships to get my brother and me through college; later, when he re-established himself as an investment counselor with Scudder, Stevens & Clark, he paid back every cent of the scholarship money.

A scholar-turned-teacher-turned-photographer-turned-design-er-and-businesswoman, Norwegian-born Inger is the founder and chief executive of China Seas, Inc., which in a few years has become better than a million-dollar company. She will try anything. She photographed one of her own children, Molly, as she was being born. She climbs mountains. She water-skis. She wants to buy a motorcycle. She wants to act—even though she still commits such Norwenglish locutions as "Close the lights" and "Turn on the fire." And she still has nightmares about the Nazi occupation of Norway.

· · ·

One of the most interesting women in my life died long before I was born. This was my mother's mother. Her name was Josefa Neilson Osborn, and judging from the scrapbooks full of newspaper clippings about her, she must have been a tigress. When her wine-merchant husband lost his money in 1898, Josefa, then about thirty years old, went into business for herself. She set up a dress-designing and importing company, and soon was supplying costumes to Ethel Barrymore and other notables of the New York stage, as well as outfitting the fashionable matrons of Madison, Park, and Fifth.

She started a monthly column for the *Delineator,* the *Vogue* of its day. "Mrs. Osborn," the editors boasted, "does not contribute to any other magazine." In her columns, Josefa deplored the American woman's taste in clothes: The trouble was, there was no "knowledge of the importance of the *ensemble.*"

Josefa had such firm notions of *"ensemble"* that she dressed her little golden-haired daughter Audrey in nothing but black and white—"for effect," as my mother later told me. Together they would often lunch at Louis Sherry's chic restaurant on Fifth Avenue, and invariably after lunch a playlet would unfold. Mrs. Osborn would produce a cigarette, and Mr. Sherry would bustle to her table, imploring her not to smoke in his restaurant. Josefa would thereupon proceed to light up, and Mr. Sherry would arrange a screen around her table to protect his other guests from the awful spectacle of a lady smoking.

Josefa Osborn was both a smart businesswoman and a great self-promoter, as attested by the headlines.* One day she had the bright idea of bringing together the world of New York society and the world of the stage, in a revolutionary attempt to improve them both—not to mention her own business.

As the battleground for her great social revolution, Josefa selected the public rooms of the old Waldorf-Astoria, and chose as her weapons a pair of musical teas on two successive Sundays in Lent. NO SACKCLOTH AND ASHES FOR SOCIETY, headlined the *New York Journal*. But the God-fearing citizenry of New York was outraged. Angry "Sabbatarians" ripped her picture from the papers and sent it off to her with Biblical injunctions scrawled across her décolletage.

Josefa herself no doubt reveled in the controversy, and was only too happy to continue the fray. She released her anonymous hate mail to the press, and reminded one interviewer that she was just a poor woman trying to make a living by running these events.

Through it all, and through a divorce—a rarity in those days —Josefa's business prospered. Soon after the turn of the century, she vowed to earn as much, in a single year, as the president of the United States, who in those preincome-tax, preinflationary days was paid $50,000. She succeeded. The family scrap-

---

* From the *St. Louis Post Dispatch* (MRS. ROBERT OSBORN, CREATOR OF THE SHIRTWAIST) ; the *New York Journal* (BELLES IN BUSINESS) ; the *Boston Record* (MRS. OSBORN'S NEW TRADE) ; *The Nashville Tennesseean* (ARBITER OF FASHION) ; the *New York Evening Telegram* (PIONEER IN MANAGERIAL FIELDS)—and scores of others.

books end abruptly. Josefa Osborn died in 1908. She couldn't have been much over forty at the time.

. . .

With women like that in my background, I shouldn't have been as surprised as I was when, in 1970, *Newsweek*'s editorial women filed a complaint against the magazine with the Equal Employment Opportunities Commission. *Newsweek*, they charged, had been systematically discriminating against them for years.

The history of women at the newsmagazines is laced with irony. Back in the twenties, when Henry Luce founded *Time*, he created a new job category which proved to be a liberating force for women in magazines. The new job was that of "researcher," and for the first time young graduates of Radcliffe, Bryn Mawr, Wellesley, and other women's colleges could enter magazine work at a level somewhat more exalted than stenographer. When *Newsweek* came along a decade later, it structured itself along the same lines. But at both newsmagazines the catch was this: once a researcher, always a researcher. Male journalists would swagger in, their trench coats flapping, and work their way up through the editorial ranks from reporter to writer to editor. Not so with the women—with the exception of a very few who managed to become writers in the manpower-short years of World War II.

After the war, the only woman senior editor at *Time* was its head of research, Content Peckham;* and much later, the only woman senior editor at *Newsweek* was Olga Barbi, likewise the magazine's head researcher. Within a few years after World War II, the few women writers on both magazines had all but

---

* When asked how she pronounced her first name, Content would answer in no uncertain terms: "Like the adjective!"

disappeared. And when, in 1959, fresh out of Connecticut College, an aspiring young journalist named Elizabeth Peer came looking for a job at *Newsweek*, she was told flatly: "If you want to write, go somewhere else. The rules here are very firm." Liz Peer took a job anyway, on the mail desk, and on Friday nights ran copy for me as "an Elliott girl"—that's actually what they were called. As Liz was to recall later, with some bitterness, "Few bureaucracies are perfect, and by a series of oversights on management's part, one woman was given a writing tryout between 1961 and 1969. I was the recipient of this largesse, becoming a writer in 1962 and a correspondent in the Paris bureau in 1964. . . . Management was dazzled by its own boldness in sending a woman abroad. They'd never done it before, as Osborn Elliott repeated when I hesitantly asked if the job would mean a raise. It was, after all, a promotion. 'What do you mean?' he asked indignantly. 'Think of the honor we are paying you!' "

My own recollection of this conversation differs in detail, but I suspect Liz accurately caught the central drift.

A few years later, talking with another *Newsweek* boss about a possible transfer to Washington, Peer was told: "It's really too bad you're not a man, because the sky would be the limit. But of course as a woman you can never be a bureau chief— and you can never be Number Two in a bureau because we need two men to, you know, lock horns with each other. But because we think your work is so good, you can be Number Three in any bureau *Newsweek* has." Looking back on this interview, Peer said: "Even more shameful than *his* rationale was *my* reply: I nodded in agreement. Later I went home and threw plates around the kitchen, but those were, after all, the rules."

The "rules" were so well entrenched that we men never gave them a second thought. Speaking on a *Newsweek* editorial panel before a Cleveland business audience one day, I was asked why it was that so few women were to be found in the upper editorial echelons of either *Time* or *Newsweek*. "Oh," I said airily, "it's just an old newsmagazine tradition that goes back fifty years or so." After the panel discussion, our Washington bureau chief, Mel Elfin, asked me: "What would you say if you got that reaction from Senator Jim Eastland in response to a question about the plight of blacks in the South?" I had never thought of it that way.

Given the temper of the sixties, it was surprising that the women's movement was so late arriving—and burst upon the newsmagazines (*Newsweek* first) only after half a century of systematic, if mostly inadvertent, discrimination. In March 1970, *Newsweek* ran its first cover story on women's lib—and even at that late date we found it necessary to explain to our readers what it was all about, and who the new feminists were. They were, we reported, "thousands of women with lovers, husbands, and children—or expectations of having a few of each—talking about changes in social attitudes and customs that will allow every female to function as a separate and equal person."

Planning the story, we realized that it should be written by a woman—but as we looked around the New York staff we concluded (correctly) that we had no woman then qualified to do the job. And so, for the first time in *Newsweek*'s history, we commissioned an outsider to write the cover story—reporter Helen Dudar of the *New York Post*, who happened to be married to our own star writer, Peter Goldman.

Dudar found the assignment an eye-opener. "I came to this story," she wrote, "with a smug certainty of my ability to keep a respectable distance between me and any subject I reported on. The complacency shriveled and died the afternoon I found myself offering a string of fearful obscenities to a stunned male colleague who had 'only' made a casual remark along the lines of 'just-like-a-woman.' "

Dudar's story traced the origins of the new women's move-ment—one track deriving from Betty Friedan's *The Feminine Mystique,* another from both the civil-rights movement and the new left. In those two movements, Dudar wrote, "scores of young women . . . were learning what it was to have a college education and to be offered a porter's job. Their contributions seldom were allowed to go beyond sweeping floors, making cof-fee, typing stencils, and bedding down. 'The new left has been a hellhole for women,' says a Berkeley veteran. 'It's the most destructive environment sexually I've ever encountered, going as far as Norman Mailer's anti-birth-control posture. You know: "I don't want my chicks using pills—that demolishes my immortal sperm." ' "

Dudar concluded her piece on what was—to her as well as to us editors—an unexpected note:

> Halfway through an initial talk with Lindsay Van Gelder, a friend and colleague, she said almost as a footnote that a lot of women who felt established in male-dominated fields resented the liberation move-ment because their solitude gave them a sense of superi-ority.
>
> I came home that night with the first of many anxiety-produced pains in the stomach and the head. Superiority is precisely what I had felt and enjoyed, and it was going to be hard to give it up. That was an important discovery. One of the rare and real rewards of reporting is learning about yourself. Grateful though I am for the education, it hasn't done much for the mental stress. Women's lib questions everything; and while intellectually I approve of that, emotionally I am unstrung by a lot of it.
>
> Never mind. The ambivalence is gone; the distance is gone. What is left is a sense of pride and kinship with all those women who have been asking all the hard questions. I thank them and so, I think, will a lot of other women.

Among *Newsweek*'s editorial women, the fact that we had hired an *outside* woman to write our piece crystallized precisely their complaints about the magazine's personnel policies —and fitted neatly into their plan of attack. On the very Monday that *Newsweek*'s women's lib issue landed on Katharine Graham's desk, so did a letter from the women of *Newsweek*:

> Women have rarely been hired as, or promoted to, the positions of reporter, writer, or editor; they are systematically by-passed in the selection of bureau correspondents and are routinely given lower titles and pay. . . . Incredibly, *Newsweek* was unwilling to work with any woman on staff to write this week's cover story on the women's liberation movement. . . .
>
> In addition to the day-to-day atmosphere that discourages women as professional journalists, women are pointedly excluded from public functions which represent *Newsweek*. . . .

I had first heard about the women's revolt only a couple of days before, and learned that one of the leaders was Fay Willey —no wet-behind-the-ears radical, but a longtime, respected senior member of our research staff. I called her at home, and urged that we all get together to discuss the women's grievances before they went public with their complaint. Fay was civil. But Fay was firm. "Sorry, Oz," she said, "this thing is too far down the road to stop it now."

And so the women sent their letter to Kay Graham, and filed their complaint, and held their press conference, and made headlines around the world. *Newsweek* had the distinction of being the first media organization to be so confronted by the women's movement.

A couple of days after their press conference, I met with all forty-six of the angry women in *Newsweek*'s reception area, Top of the Week, a large room on the fortieth floor of the building. Informality, I figured, would help. And so, instead of sitting behind a green-baize-covered table and looking down at the assembled employees, I placed myself and Kermit Lansner, my No. 2, on a couch surrounded by concentric semicircles of chairs for the women. That was a tactical mistake; the couch was a foot or more below the level of the chairs. Lansner and I hunched there, gazing up at the women, our knees under our chins. "Before we start," I said, "I'd like to say just a few words. . . ."

"Sorry, Oz," came a cold and even voice. "We don't plan to talk until our lawyer gets here."

This was evidently to be a heavy session.

We sat in awkward silence for five minutes or so, and finally in came the women's lawyer—highly articulate, tough, militant, black—and pregnant. It was Eleanor Holmes Norton, who since then has become a top government official in equal-opportunity areas.

"Delighted you could join us, Mrs. Norton," I said, looking up at her in the front row. "First, I'd like to say a few words to the women of *Newsweek*."

"I'm sorry, Mr. Elliott," replied Mrs. Norton, "but this is *our* meeting, and on this occasion we must insist on the women's prerogative. *We* will do the talking."

Heavy stuff, indeed. And so Mrs. Norton laid out the women's complaints, and I expressed my concern, and we agreed to meet in a smaller group for the start of formal negotiations a few days later. Before that second session, I was relieved to receive a letter from Eleanor Norton saying that she considered our first meeting "enormously promising . . . because of your obvious sincerity and goodwill. . . ."

But as it turned out, no amount of sincerity or goodwill could undo overnight what had been almost a half century of institutional discrimination. Our negotiations—interrupted by sudden, dramatic, and quite effective outbursts of anger from the skillful Mrs. Norton—dragged on for months. And they were not helped by a residual resentment on the part of many men on the staff. At one point a "manifesto" was circulated anonymously by the *"Newsweek* Two," who thought they were being pretty funny at the time. These jokesters petitioned for . . .

> . . . a redress of grievance engendered by *Newsweek's* recent systematic discriminatory policy against us for:
>
> 1. Our tendency to become bemused and somewhat glassy-eyed when confronted with posters, slogans, interoffice memos and earnest solicitations from sundry persons, some of whom we're not sure even work here.
> 2. Our failure to employ with fervor such phrases as "Right On," "Up Against the Wall," and "Mea Culpa for 50 Years of Male Supremacy" either in our copy or during casual conversation around the coffee wagon. . . .

In the end, *Newsweek* reached an agreement with its women, and on August 26, 1970—a full five months after the original complaint was filed—I circulated the terms among the staff. Calling for "substantial rather than token changes," the agreement stipulated that management would "undertake an affirmative accelerated policy of recruitment of qualified women . . . for reporter and writer positions." Management further agreed to "substantially increase the number of reporting and writing tryouts granted to women," and to discover "if there is an untapped reservoir of talent among women already employed at *Newsweek*." The summer trainee program would be enlarged to include "at least three positions for *Newsweek* women [in] the U.S. bureaus."

In addition, *Newsweek* promised to "make affirmative efforts to employ men as researchers"—a job category that was still almost purely female. Management also agreed to "identify women . . . qualified for editing positions"—and to invite women to editorial lunches and other functions "when their assignments, interests, and background would contribute to the subject matter being discussed."

To most of us, men and women alike, the agreement seemed a truly historic breakthrough, promising new opportunities for women and a generally happier atmosphere around the magazine. But it was not to work that way. The old inertia was still there, and the agreement was phrased in such general terms that it was easy for management to ignore. At just about that time, I was moving out of editorial affairs and for the following two years served as president of Newsweek, Inc., mostly occupied with the business management of the company. I paid little heed to what was happening on the women's front. My mistake. When I moved back into the editorship in the spring of 1972, I found the women just as angry and unhappy as they had been two years before—and now their ranks had grown from forty-six to fifty-five.

Once again, they filed a complaint with the Equal Employment Opportunities Commission, charging that "*Newsweek* magazine discriminates against women in its recruitment, hiring, placement, promotions, and conditions of employment." This complaint cited some pretty dreary specifics:

> —Management refuses even to discuss when—if ever—a woman will become a senior editor of the magazine or part of top management.
> —In the past two years [management] hired only four women and more than twice that number of men as writers. Today there are five women and thirty-six men writing for *Newsweek*. . . .
> —Osborn Elliott . . . issued a statement to the press two years ago . . . in which he said that the "absence of discrimination against women at *Newsweek* is shown by the fact that *Newsweek* already numbers more than a dozen women among its foreign and do-

mestic correspondents, five in Washington alone."
Today there are exactly twelve women correspondents on the magazine (out of a total of seventy-
one), only three in Washington, D.C., and only one
in a foreign bureau.
—In research . . . there are seven men—and thirty-
three women—in this lowliest editorial position.

By this time the federal government had moved toward re-
quiring employers to establish more specific goals, timetables,
and even quotas—and the women of *Newsweek* were determined to capitalize on this. Again we sat down to a long round
of negotiations, with *Newsweek* represented this time by Joseph
Califano, and the women by a young Columbia University
lawyer named Harriet Rabb. It was almost a full year before
a new, twenty-two page agreement was hammered out, and this
one was loaded with specific commitments on the part of management.

We agreed that within seven months, *Newsweek*'s staff of
writers would include at least eleven women, and within eighteen months one third or more of the writers would be women.
We agreed that a third of all domestic reporters, and new
foreign correspondents, would be women—likewise two out of
the next six persons appointed chief of domestic bureaus. We
stipulated that "The percentage of all researchers who are men
shall be approximately equal to the percentage of all writers
who are women." And by December 31, 1975, we promised, "at
least one woman shall have been appointed a Senior Editor."*

In addition to all this, elaborate rules were set up governing
tryouts, settlement of differences, even specifying forms to be
used by management in reporting its progress to the women's
representatives, three times a year.

During the months that the new agreement was being

---

* She turned out to be Lynn Povich Young.

thrashed out, something else was happening that dramatically boosted the morale of the female staff. Two of our senior writers—Peter Goldman and Dick Boeth—launched an informal training program which they called "The Famous Writers School" and encouraged women to enroll. They admitted ten researchers at a time, and put them through eight-week training sessions. So great was the women's fear of failure that they wrote their assignments under such pseudonyms as "Jane Eyre" and "Emily Brontë," and were critiqued anonymously. But over a period of months, some fifty women went through the course. A number learned that they did indeed have a talent for writing and reporting, and later were given official tryouts by the magazine; equally important, others concluded that research was really their forte, and became more willing to accept that job as a worthwhile and respectable occupation.

This time around, *Newsweek* lived up to its new agreement, and in 1974 I received a memo from Liz Peer—who always had her doubts about women's lib—stating: "We have both toiled, from different starting points, through the women's movement. I concluded quite a while ago that your consciousness has been raised further than my own. . . . No one else in the business has done what you have and it [is] apparent to everyone . . . that women on *Newsweek*, by the mores of the day, are lightyears ahead of their sisters. . . ."

There is no question in my mind that as a result of all this, *Newsweek* became a much better place for people to work and that, in real but unquantifiable ways, it became a better magazine as well.

· · ·

It had been a long road from those cool sands under the ladies' court on Fire Island, from that cherry-bomb explosion and those early gropings so many years before. A much longer time since those turn-of-the-century lunches at Louis Sherry's. You might say that, symbolically, all those women in my life—the tightly haltered Joan, the helpful Harriet, the willing Hiroko, my independent wife and daughters and mother and grand-mother—had won a notable victory at long, long last. And so they had.

But then, hadn't we all?

·VIII·
THE MEAN
YEARS

O n the night of September 23, 1952, I sat with my wife, my
parents, and my brother and sister-in-law before a flick-
ering black-and-white television set to watch the Republican
candidate for vice-president defend himself and the "slush
fund" that supporters had made available to him for expenses.
As Richard Nixon's "Checkers" speech ended, members of our
little group, like thousands of other Americans across the
country, made for the telephone to wire their congratulations
to Nixon and their strong advice to Dwight Eisenhower to
keep this man on the GOP ticket. But to me the whole performance had been crass, mawkish, and dissembling. I was
disgusted.

With the exception of my mother, who usually voted on the
Democratic line for president, my family was Republican; my
father, in fact, only turned against Joe McCarthy when the
Wisconsin senator began to attack the two institutions closest
to my father's heart—Harvard University and the United States
Army. I first registered as a Republican myself, but soon I
switched to Independent and have remained so ever since, in
the belief that journalists should not be involved in partisan
politics.

I never had much use for Richard Milhous Nixon. Over the
years I saw him at close range perhaps a dozen times—at re-
ceptions, dinners, *Newsweek* lunches, on the campaign trail
for a day or so, now and then. In one dash to the Los Angeles
airport in 1962, during his gubernatorial campaign that year,
Nixon tried to persuade me to fire *Newsweek*'s San Francisco
bureau chief, Bill Flynn, on the ground that Flynn was too
close to Nixon's opponent, Governor Pat Brown. On another
campaign trip in 1968, I was admitted to the Nixonian presence for a private talk in a curtained-off compartment of his
plane. In what seemed to be well-rehearsed surprise, Nixon
looked up from his yellow legal pad and greeted me by nickname; he obviously had been well briefed. The "interview"
was scheduled so tightly that we had only five minutes before
the plane landed in Boston and Nixon was off and running.
That gave me little time for questions—but it gave *him* time
enough to let me know, pointedly, that he understood that
Newsweek's pollster, Lou Harris, was doing a lot of political
work for Democrats that year (which he wasn't). On another
occasion, at a dinner for a dozen or so editors in New York's
Links Club, Nixon put on a remarkable show. Just back from
a trip around the world, he talked for an hour—with great
articulateness and subtlety, and without a single note—about
the people and places he had seen.

My reactions to Nixon were not very original. He always
struck me as a man of indirection and cunning, with no real
center of gravity, no sense of humor, no human warmth. "The
real Richard Nixon," Stewart Alsop once wrote, "is a cold fish
—as cold a fish as de Gaulle or Woodrow Wilson, than whom
no fishes could be colder." Years before, in a conversation with
Herald Tribune editors, Walter Lippmann had put it more
ironically: "I'm not sure I understand Mr. Nixon. He's of a
different generation than mine. Certainly he is not of the gen-

eration that regards honesty as the best policy. However, he *does* regard it as a policy."

In 1961, I got an early whiff of what things might be like in a Nixon administration, although I could hardly have recognized the signal at the time. Soon after the appearance of *Newsweek's* "Thunder on the Right" cover story, which explored what was going on in the outer reaches of America's far right wing, our West Coast advertising chief, Bob Campbell, heard from H. R. ("Bob") Haldeman. Haldeman was then head of J. Walter Thompson's Los Angeles office. In protest against the magazine's cover story, adman Haldeman was threatening to cancel some $300,000 of *Newsweek* advertising by Douglas Aircraft. It was not quite in the old tradition of horsewhipping the editor, more in the newer twentieth-century vogue of putting the screws to the advertising department. Campbell, an Air Force general and friend of Barry Goldwater, managed to save the account.

The very next year, after Nixon had lost the California election to Pat Brown, the world had its first glimpse of the paranoia that would, one day, engulf the White House and bring a government crashing down. In his famous "last" news conference, the defeated candidate said to reporters: "For sixteen years, ever since the Hiss case, you've had a lot of fun—a lot of fun." But the fun was over—in the defeated candidate's now-immortal words, "You won't have Dick Nixon to kick around any more." Even after his amazing comeback in 1968, Nixon the president was still licking his wounds, real or imagined. "I have less . . . supporters in the press than any president," he complained in an interview with Howard K. Smith. NBC's John Chancellor summed it up: "Other administrations have had a love-hate relationship with the press. The Nixon administration has a hate-hate relationship."

Given the antipress animus of the Nixon White House, and the trouble vice-presidents traditionally have in finding a role to play, it came naturally to Spiro Agnew to be the administration's chief official critic of the media. Agnew seized his new megaphone gladly, and took off after that "effete corps of impudent snobs" for sniping at the president.

When, in November 1969, Nixon made a televised speech affirming his intention to hold the line in Vietnam, this surprised many people who had expected a more rapid and dramatic disengagement from the war in Southeast Asia. When the television commentators sounded critical, Spiro Agnew went on the attack again. He complained about network correspondents who engaged in "instant analysis" and who, "by the expressions on their faces, the tone of their questions, and the sarcasm of their responses, made clear their disapproval." (CBS later abandoned its "instant analyses.") Agnew was, as it turned out, only warming up. Still to come were his alliterative blasts against the "supersensitive, self-anointed, supercilious electronic barons of opinion," his attacks on the "nattering nabobs of negativism," his carping at the "professional pessimists" and "the hopeless hysterical hypochondriacs of history." In one speech, Agnew said that *Newsweek* and *The New York Times* were fit only to line the bottoms of bird cages—which inspired a friend of mine to give me a London street sign which I hung over my office door: "Bird Cage Walk." Everywhere he went, Agnew traveled with a platoon of speechwriters, an unabridged Webster's dictionary, and the unflagging support of his president. "There can be a mystique about a man," Nixon had said after he surprised the world by picking Spiro Agnew as his vice-presidential running mate in 1968. "You can look him in the eye and know he's got it. This guy has got it."

Whatever it was that Agnew had, he certainly couldn't lay claim to a thick skin. At Christmastime in 1969, he came to dinner one night with Kay Graham and a group of *Newsweek* editors, at the house of our Washington bureau chief, Mel

Elfin. The vice-president had just launched his first forays against the press, and we were curious as to what his motives really were. Agnew insisted he wasn't out to intimidate the media, all he wanted was some balance. Then he revealed what was obviously rankling him most—a *Washington Post* editorial that had appeared just after Agnew's nomination as Nixon's running mate, a year and a half before. "Given enough time," the *Post*'s 1968 editorial had said, "Nixon's decision . . . to name Agnew may come to be regarded as perhaps the most eccentric political appointment since the Roman Emperor Caligula named his horse a consul." Not the kindest editorial ever written, to be sure, but not the most inaccurate either, as events would ultimately prove. Spiro Agnew was still enraged when we had him to dinner—and for a surprising reason. "When you say something like that about me," he protested that night at Elfin's house, "you're endangering my livelihood!"

Much of the evening was spent in trying to persuade Agnew that the *Post* and *Newsweek* did not, as he had charged, "harken to one voice"—Kay Graham's; that each publication operated quite independently of the other. Toward the end of dinner, still unconvinced, the vice-president uttered what he clearly believed to be the *bon mot* of the evening, and roared with glee at his own high witticism. "I'm going to make a racy remark," he warned Mrs. Graham. "You people have an incestuous relationship with cross-pollination of ideas!"*

* It was the custom of *Newsweek* and *Time* to deliver advance copies of the magazines on Sunday night to a number of key Washington figures, from the president on down. A measure of the petty tensions that the vice-president liked to encourage, vis-à-vis the press, came when Spiro Agnew's name was added to *Newsweek*'s Sunday delivery list. His press secretary, Victor Gold, wrote bureau chief Elfin: ". . . Any promotional or advertising copy stating that Washington decision-makers, leaders, etc., read *Newsweek* before beginning their week would, at least in the case of the Vice President, be inaccurate."

So Spiro Agnew went his forensic way, flailing at the "radic-libs," the "Spock-marked" kids, the "troglodytic leftists," the "pusillanimous pussyfooting" on law and order—and finally found himself replacing Mickey Mouse on the face of a wrist-watch. Later, as the Watergate scandals grew, Agnew began to fade from the front pages. Then suddenly, in August 1973, there he was, front and center once again—but this time on the defensive. A federal grand jury was investigating him for brib-ery, extortion, tax fraud, and conspiracy. *Newsweek*'s story was headlined SCANDALS OF '73: ENTER AGNEW. The vice-president held a bristling press conference at which he denied all, and then flew off in high dudgeon to the Palm Springs home of his friend Frank Sinatra.

The next week, in a final display of bravado, Agnew show-ered subpoenas on writers, reporters, and editors (including me) . Before our lawyers even had a chance to move to quash the subpoenas, Mr. Law and Order was out. Only eleven days before, Agnew had announced to a cheering group of Republi-can women in Los Angeles: "I will not resign if indicted!" Now, on October 10, he pleaded no contest to a charge of tax evasion; he was sentenced to three years' probation and a $10,000 fine. And the U.S. government—the government of which he was vice-president—spread on the public record, for all the world to see, an "exposition of the evidence" picturing Agnew as having been on the take for all his ten years in public office.

· · ·

They say that even paranoids sometimes have real enemies, but the depths of suspicion within the Nixon administration were wondrous to behold. In the autumn of 1969, when opposition to the Vietnam war was on the rise, when inflation was billow-ing, and Nixon's nomination of Clement Haynsworth, Jr., to the Supreme Court was foundering, *Newsweek* ran a cover story headlined NIXON IN TROUBLE. The very same week, *Time*'s lead story said, "It did not take an alarmist of Chicken Little proportions to discern that bits of sky were falling on the Nixon administration." That moved William Safire, then a Nixon speechwriter, to accuse Mel Elfin of having conspired with *Time*'s Washington boss, Hugh Sidey, to concoct the two similar stories. Not so, said Elfin; he hadn't seen or talked to Sidey in months. In that case, said Safire, quite seriously, "Oz Elliott and Henry Grunwald [*Time*'s managing editor] must have cooked it up together in New York."*

In light of all the hostility and suspicion, it was fore-ordained that the Nixon administration would at some point come into full collision with the press. What was surprising was the issue upon which it chose to draw the line: a volumi-nous compendium of forty-seven typescript volumes drily en-titled "History of the United States Decision-Making Process on Vietnam Policy"—otherwise known as the Pentagon Papers. Defense Secretary Robert McNamara, disillusioned with the way the war was going, had commissioned the study in 1967, in the hope that such a historical record would help prevent similar mistakes in the future; dozens of government officials had labored for eighteen months on the project. And now, in

* The Nixon administration always suspected that the "Eastern-Establishment Press" was in a continual conspiracy to do it dirt. Actually, the only time I ever tried to conspire with *Time* was in an effort to persuade "Brand X" *not* to run the same cover picture as *Newsweek*. It was in the spring of 1975, and the last horrors of Vietnam were being played out. For the *Newsweek* cover, I had selected a tragic UPI photo of a woman carrying a bloody baby down a dusty Vietnamese road. A couple of days later, UPI called to tell me that *Time* was interested in the same picture for *its* cover. I called Henry Grunwald to say that our cover was already plated and practically on press. Grunwald gave no promises, but the next week *Time* used that dramatic UPI picture only as one part of a pictorial montage on its cover.

1971, one of those officials, Daniel Ellsberg, had taken it upon himself to leak most of the study to the press. His goal, he said later, was to show how "presidential assistants and other officials had virtually unlimited license to lie to the public." The very week the Pentagon Papers began to appear, Ellsberg told *Newsweek* in an exclusive interview: "Those responsible for the escalation of the war will be held to account for the papers they signed."

When Ellsberg slipped the seven-thousand-page collection of documents to Neil Sheehan of *The New York Times*, it didn't take long for Sheehan, an old and skilled Vietnam hand, to realize that he had a rich lode of fascinating material and a major behind-the-scenes story on Vietnam. His editors knew it, too; and so did Arthur Ochs ("Punch") Sulzberger, publisher of the *Times*, who went against the advice of the *Times* lawyer and decided to publish the documents—still stamped "Top Secret—Sensitive," even though their contents were from three to twenty-six years old. For six weeks, a task force of *Times* writers and editors worked secretly, almost around the clock, in two guarded suites of the New York Hilton Hotel. As their copy began to take form, type was set clandestinely in a special composing room down the hall from the paper's food-news department. And when the first installment appeared in the *Times*'s Sunday editions of June 11, 1971, it set off a classic conflict over the First Amendment.

The Pentagon Papers were a piecemeal history at best; their authors had been ordered not to interview any of the principals involved, and their research came almost entirely from Defense Department documents. Thus the views of such key Vietnam policymakers as Lyndon Johnson and Dean Rusk went almost unrepresented. But the documents contained enough to suggest strongly that the U.S. government had indulged in deceit and duplicity for years, and had hidden from the American people the truth about Vietnam and America's escalatory intentions there. The material went back as far as the Truman administration, and up through the reign of LBJ. In the papers, as *Newsweek* reported, "McNamara labors on as the war's most tireless technocrat even after he has begun to lose heart for the fight. Walt Whitman Rostow clings doggedly to the assumption that America is simply too powerful to be thwarted. Maxwell Taylor, the humanist general for whom Robert Kennedy named one of his sons, blusters like a pouty proconsul. And the Bundy brothers grind out options to order, while generals and admirals constantly promote the idea that more is better."

Sinners all—but almost all of the sinners committing almost all of their sins in Democratic administrations. So damaging to the Democrats did the revelations seem, in fact, that Henry Kissinger at first thought—or said he thought—that the release of the Pentagon Papers was a carefully planned Republican leak. Later, he counseled tactical silence. *"The New York Times* story," Kissinger said, "is an intraparty fight within the other party." But to others in the administration, it seemed a lot more than that; to them, the disclosures of the Pentagon Papers seemed an attack on the sanctity of the U.S. government itself. "There is only one establishment at a time," said one Republican, "and we're it."

After considerable research, Harrison Salisbury of *The New York Times* concluded—and so states in his book, *Without Fear or Favor,* that Kissinger was not so innocent as he has professed. In any case, the Nixon Administration decided to move against the *Times*. Thus began an epic, if sometimes comic, constitutional battle between the government and the press. No sooner had the government won an injunction against the *Times* than *The Washington Post* started spilling Pentagon Papers installments of its own—and these in turn were being carried via AP, UPI, and the *Los Angeles Times/Washington Post* News Service to practically every paper in the land. The *Times* lawyers argued, not without reason, that now only *their* readers were being denied the right to read what everyone else was publishing. When the government then got a court order that stopped the *Post* from publishing, other leaks began to spout in a raft of other papers, including *The Boston Globe* and the *St. Louis Post-Dispatch*. A Herblock cartoon depicted Attorney General John Mitchell as a Keystone Kop, trying to chase a veritable fleet of news trucks from a variety of papers, yelling: "Follow that car—and that one—and that one—"

In the end, the press won a split decision in the Supreme Court, but it was a Pyrrhic victory whose reverberations are still being felt. For the first time in history, however briefly, the government of the United States had succeeded in imposing prior restraint—that is, it was able to prevent the press from printing material to which the government took exception. Justice Hugo Black said: "I believe that every moment's continuance of the injunctions against these newspapers amounts to a flagrant, indefensible, and continuing violation of the First Amendment. . . . Now, for the first time . . . since the founding of the Republic, the federal courts are asked to hold that the First Amendment does not mean what it says, but rather means that the government can halt the publication of current news of vital importance to the people of this country."*

·   ·   ·

Dramatic as the Agnew case had been, and historic as was the confrontation with the press over the Pentagon Papers, these

---

* Eight years later, in 1979, the government was for a while successful in restraining the *Progressive* magazine from printing an article called "The H-Bomb Secret: How We Got It, Why We're Telling It"—even though the *Progressive* had apparently compiled the article from unclassified sources. Finally, the government dropped its case when other publications began printing essential details of the *Progressive* piece.

two eruptions faded into insignificance as the horror of Watergate accumulated during those mean Nixon years. Spiro Agnew's removal was quick and surgical; the Pentagon Papers case was resolved in a fortnight. But Watergate dragged painfully on and on—for more than two years from the clownish break-in at Democratic National Headquarters in June 1972 to the August morning in 1974 when Richard Nixon finally stepped to a waiting helicopter on the White House lawn to wave his last presidential farewell.

Hardly a week went by, in Nixon's final year, without some new disclosure of wrongdoing at the top; Watergate kept pushing other news aside. From April 1973 to the dramatic denouement sixteen months later, *Newsweek* ran no fewer than thirty-five cover stories on Watergate misdeeds—and another four on Spiro Agnew's disgrace. The first of these was headlined THE WATERGATE MESS; in May 1973, *Newsweek* already was picturing a worried Nixon, clinging to a life ring, under a headline that asked: CAN HE STAY AFLOAT? But Nixon stayed afloat, and stayed afloat, and stayed afloat, even as his Mitchells and Ehrlichmans and Haldemans and Colsons and smaller fry went under. It was an amazing exercise in political survival.

Nixon had started his second term, in January 1973, in what seemed a strangely subdued mood; we did not know then, of course, what Nixon already knew; perhaps he was already anticipating the end of his presidency. Mel Elfin wrote in some wonder about the sour atmosphere in the White House—"after an election in which [Nixon's] opponent [George McGovern] carried little more than Harlem, Harvard, and the Sans Souci Restaurant." Elfin noted that the White House inner circle was interpreting the election results as "a victory for 'our Washington'—those who enjoy the quiet buffet suppers at George Schultz's house in the Virginia suburbs—and a defeat for 'their Washington' and those who for so long have snickered at Mr. Nixon over the Porthault linen in the great houses of Georgetown." It was more than coincidence, Elfin went on to say, "that many of those in the first Nixon administration who best bridged the gap between the two Washingtons are precisely those who have not been invited to be a part of the 'team' for the second administration." "If you had one lunch too many with Art Buchwald," Elfin quoted an outgoing official as saying, "some of those people practically considered it a violation of the Alien and Sedition acts. It doesn't take much these days to get on Bob Haldeman's suspicious-persons list."

During the previous months, in the early days of the Watergate scandals, *The Washington Post*, with its Woodward-Bernstein team, was almost always in the lead with its revelations.* We at *Newsweek* found it galling to be so consistently scooped by our sister publication—which did indeed operate independently, Spiro Agnew's view to the contrary notwithstanding. Not many other papers seemed much interested. Press analyst Ben Bagdikian, in fact, estimated in the spring of 1973 that out of 2200 working reporters in Washington, no more than 14 had done substantial work on Watergate.

Not only was *Newsweek* being beaten by *The Washington Post*; for some time we had been taking our lumps from our arch-rival, *Time*, as well. At the beginning of almost every week in the early Watergate days, I was on the phone to our Washington bureau, demanding to know why the hell we had been scooped once again. Almost invariably, the answer was that *Time*'s sharp investigative reporter Sandy Smith, late of *Life*, had built up some excellent sources within the FBI over the years. Things got so competitive, and tensions ran so high, that when *Time* managed to get a jailhouse interview with

* The *Post*'s first story on the Watergate break-in, in its Sunday editions of June 18, 1972, carried the by-line of Alfred E. Lewis, a police reporter. At the end of the story there was an italicized note: "Contributing to this story were *Washington Post* Staff Writers Bob Woodward, Carl Bernstein . . ." and a list of six others.

E. Howard Hunt, *Newsweek* reporter Nicholas Horrock offered to resign.

But after a while, *Newsweek* began to hit its stride. The Washington bureau's John Lindsay scored a number of important beats, including the first revelation that John Dean would link Nixon directly to the Watergate coverup; and Horrock himself (who later joined *The New York Times*) came through with a number of notable scoops.

Newsweek's first Watergate cover story was triggered by James W. McCord's letter to Judge John J. Sirica, in which McCord offered to talk—and threatened to blow the lid off the whole affair. Within weeks came the next big Watergate break, with Jeb Stuart Magruder fingering Messrs. Dean and Mitchell as accomplices in the planning of various bugging schemes, including Watergate; Magruder added that they were "at least aware" of subsequent pay-off attempts. The president's press secretary, Ron Ziegler, now declared all previous statements on the Watergate mess to be "inoperative"—and apologized to *The Washington Post*. By May, the U.S. government was admitting that Howard Hunt and Gordon Liddy had burglarized the office of Daniel Ellsberg's psychiatrist, and a couple of weeks after that—not surprisingly—the Pentagon Papers case against Ellsberg was thrown out of court.

The tumble of events was incredible: Haldeman, Ehrlichman, and Dean fired from the White House staff; Mitchell and Maurice Stans indicted for influence-peddling and perjury (they were later acquitted in that particular case, which involved the financier Robert Vesco). *Newsweek* was reporting, by then, that "there were . . . mutterings about impeachment on Capitol Hill."

What is surprising is that Nixon's popularity rating in the Gallup Poll was still hanging in there in mid-1973 at about 45 percent—far above the 29 percent that would be registered by Jimmy Carter six years later, in the summer of 1979.

I was invited, in May 1973, to speak before the annual convention of the American Association of Advertising Agencies, at the Greenbrier Hotel—a golden opportunity to toot *Newsweek*'s horn before an important audience loaded with advertising dollars. But by then I was too angry merely to sing *Newsweek*'s praises; instead of my planned speech, "The Reader's Right to Know," I unloaded a talk called "The Citizen's Right to Outrage":

> . . . In order to communicate effectively . . . we must do it in a credible atmosphere, in a credible way. . . . For as long as this has been a Republic—which is to say, since the days of that old printer Ben Franklin—that enveloping, credible atmosphere has been provided by the printed page. More recently, of course, radio and television have provided their own particular environment of immediacy and credibility. . . .
>
> But what has happened is that this atmosphere began to disintegrate, for a variety of reasons, and then was deliberately pulverized by a variety of persons. . . .
>
> The news was bad—and in the great tradition of beheading the bearer of bad tidings, many people began to turn against the so-called media. . . . And into this atmosphere of growing suspicion leapt a happy band of politicians, their alliterations at the ready, their hyperbole in full sail. Instead of bringing us together, as they had promised, they sought to drive us apart. They chose to attack one of democracy's greatest institutions, the free press. . . .
>
> For the first time in the history of this country, the press was legally restrained from printing a story. . . . Reporters were subjected to a rainstorm of subpoenas, and some landed in jail for protecting the vital con-

fidentiality of their sources. Local television stations were put on guard with the warning that it should be their job to monitor and censor network offerings—and if they failed to meet some undefined set of governmental standards of fairness, the message was clear: their licenses would be in jeopardy.

It became a time when an American flag in the lapel was credential enough to establish the wearer as the possessor of some newer and higher morality that traveled under the misnomer of law and order. . . .

The Washington Post, I continued, had been accused of character assassination—but one had to wonder who the assassins really were. After all, it was the *government* that had been found guilty of burglary and conspiracy and of supplying the wigs and cameras and other accouterments of espionage aimed at assassinating the character of a defendant in a federal trial, Daniel Ellsberg.

The damage done to the media [I concluded] is as nothing compared with the damage these men have done to the machinery of government. . . . The Justice Department and the FBI have been suborned. The CIA, the SEC, and even the Marine Corps have been tarred. The State Department is revealed to have made possible the forging of diplomatic cables. The judicial process has been compromised. And even the electoral system, by which we choose who is to govern us, has been cast in shadow.

Under these conditions—which I enumerate in no partisan sense whatsoever—it seems to me a citizen has not only a right, but an obligation, to be outraged.

When I had scribbled out this talk the weekend before, I figured that it probably would not go over so well with all those admen, in their salmon-pink slacks and madras jackets, anxious to get out for the afternoon's assault on fairway, rough, and green. But as it turned out, there was prolonged and loud applause when I finished. Apparently Fairfield County, Connecticut, if not yet Middle America, had turned against Richard Nixon.

· · ·

So fast and furious did the Watergate news break from the spring of 1973 on, that we were hard-put to think up new headlines for our stories. A sampling: EXPOSING THE BIG COVER-UP; NIXON STATES HIS CASE; THE SEVENTH CRISIS HEATS UP; DEAN VS. NIXON; THE NIXON TAPES; EHRLICHMAN HANGS TOUGH; SHOW-DOWN!; THE HALDEMAN VARIATIONS. Sometimes the revelations were ludicrous. Jeb Magruder, for instance, testified that Gordon Liddy had once proposed that various radical leaders be "abducted and detained in a place like Mexico" for safekeeping during the Republican convention of 1972. Liddy had also suggested chartering a yacht for the Democratic convention in Miami Beach, wiring it for sound and film and putting a party of women aboard "to work with members of the Democratic National Committee [to] obtain information."

"And what would the women be doing at that time?" asked Samuel Dash, counsel for Sam Ervin's Senate committee.

"Well," said Magruder, "they would have been—I think you could consider them call girls."

And sometimes the flood of leaks seemed to have gone too far. Noting that Watergate had "distorted traditional liberal values," Stewart Alsop wrote a memorable column that asked: "Can those who respect this country's liberal tradition feel really happy about the way the Watergate mess has been surfaced?" Alsop went on:

The little-told story is that the entire Justice Department has been behaving for months like one huge
sieve, leaking secret information at every orifice. . . .
    Grand-jury proceedings are by law secret . . . to
protect both potential defendants and innocent people
who might be hurt by this kind of testimony. The
Watergate Federal grand-jury proceedings have been
about as secret as a three-ring circus. Yet this outrageous flouting of traditional legal safeguards has caused
no audible peep from the liberals. . . .

The time might well come, Alsop noted pointedly, "when
the ox to be gored is not the detested Mr. Nixon's, but a fine
liberal ox."

But the leaks continued, the case against Nixon mounted,
and his popularity finally tumbled to around 30 percent in the
polls. Things reached a climax on October 20, 1973, when the
president defied court orders to turn over a number of White
House tapes. He forthwith fired the special Watergate prose-
cutor, Archibald Cox, accepted the resignation of Attorney
General Elliot Richardson (who had refused to fire Cox, his
old law professor), and discharged Deputy Attorney General
William Ruckelshaus, who similarly refused to do the dirty
work. All of this came to be known as the Saturday Night
Massacre.

For me, that October Saturday had another special meaning.
As the government of the United States was falling apart, my
life was being put together; that was the day I married Inger.
That evening, she and I dined at a restaurant in New York
where by coincidence we were placed next to a table occupied
by Nixon's longtime friend and financial supporter Elmer
Bobst, who was loudly bewailing the fate of his beloved president. Next day, on the plane to Bermuda, Inger looked up
from the Judgment Day headlines of the Sunday *New York
Times* and said: "I think this is going to be the shortest honey-

moon on record." We were back in New York within two days —to find the Watergate pot boiling ever higher.

About this time Nick Horrock of *Newsweek*'s Washington bureau had discovered that investigators were looking into Nixon's Florida real-estate holdings, to see if he and his daughter Tricia (allegedly a joint owner) had paid sufficient capital-gains taxes on a sale of property. It was a complicated story, and it had taken Horrock most of the week to put it together; not until Saturday did he have enough facts with which to confront the White House. That Saturday night, Ron Ziegler called me at home; my stepson, Alec, then nine, answered the phone and announced bug-eyed: "It's the White House!" Ziegler was highly perturbed; he insisted that *Newsweek* should pull the story and give the White House a chance to reply fully. "Why didn't you come to us earlier in the week?" he asked. "We would have given you all the facts." For one thing, I said, we didn't have enough information early in the week—and for another; "our experience in checking facts with you people in recent months has not exactly bolstered our confidence in the results."*

CAN HE SURVIVE? was the question *Newsweek* asked about Nixon on its cover that week. His ability to do so, said the cover story, "was now open to the gravest doubt." But Nixon himself put on a display of strength. "The tougher it gets," he said in a news conference, "the cooler I get. I have what it takes."

But by then the president had surrendered the first of the

* The paranoia of the Nixon administration was catching. I came to assume that any call from the White House had to be bad news. Once Nixon's communications director, Herb Klein, called me, and I braced myself for the worst. It turned out he was calling to change the address of Julie Nixon's *Newsweek* subscription since she was moving to Florida.

White House tapes, and his fate was effectively sealed. It took another nine months for the end game to be played out. There was the case of the missing tapes. There was the mysterious eighteen-and-a-half-minute gap in one of them—perhaps caused, said Nixon's secretary Rose Mary Woods, by an incredible act of contortion on her part (ROSE MARY'S BOO-BOO was the *Newsweek* headline). There was the president telling the American people, incredibly: "I am not a crook." (I had watched this press conference on television with some of *Newsweek*'s editors, and the instant those words were out of his mouth we knew what that week's cover headline would be.)

On March 1, 1974, came the indictments of the president's men—Haldeman, Ehrlichman, Mitchell, Colson, and three others—and the naming, as it later turned out, of Nixon himself as an unindicted co-conspirator. Then came the tax charges, and the picture of Nixon, in *Newsweek*'s words, "as an angle-shooting, corner-cutting tax delinquent in arrears by a staggering half-million dollars." (One expense item he charged up to the government was $5391.43 for a masked ball honoring his daughter Tricia.)

And, at last, the edited transcripts of forty-six presidential conversations and phone calls about Watergate. Even in edited form, with all the "expletives deleted," these papers showed clearly enough the meanness of the Nixon administration and the cynicism that lay at its core—and exposed the president as a party to a criminal conspiracy to pay $75,000 in hush money to "keep the cap on" the scandals.

At times, in those melodramatic days, it seemed almost impossible that the nation could survive. But as the House Judiciary Committee started its work under the leadership of Peter Rodino, an almost unknown congressman from New Jersey, Americans were given a sense of their nationhood, and of the strength of their institutions. The committee members were just so many ordinary Americans, but somehow as they took up their solemn responsibility they projected a sense of grandeur into living rooms across the land. In the last week of July 1974, by a solid bipartisan majority (27 to 11), the committee voted to approve a first article of impeachment: "In his conduct of the office of President of the United States, Richard M. Nixon, in violation of his constitutional oath . . . has prevented, obstructed, and impeded the administration of justice. . . . Wherefore Richard M. Nixon, by such conduct, warrants impeachment and trial, and removal from office."

The next week, for its cover, *Newsweek* superimposed the hands of a clock on the face of Richard Nixon, under the headline THE ELEVENTH HOUR. We argued long among ourselves as to just how many minutes before midnight the minute hand should be placed, and finally put it at about seven minutes before the hour; even at that late date we did not want to be accused of overstating his peril. But as it turned out, we needn't have worried. A few days later, Peter Goldman, who had written so eloquently on the transfer of power from John Kennedy to Lyndon Johnson, was now called upon to describe a similarly dramatic presidential passage. Goldman ended his story on a somber note:

> Greatness in the end eluded Richard Nixon. It was left to history to judge whether his prodigies of peace-making would finally outweigh the moral ruin of his presidency. But his page in the record would forever be blotted by the crimes committed in his name and, as his own tape recordings now clearly show, at his direction. His presidency . . . died of what John Dean aptly called a cancer that grew and metastasized over two of the most dolorous years in the life of the American Republic. There were moments of high achievement for Richard Nixon in his 2000 days; the real tragedy of his passing last week was that nothing so honored his presidency as his leaving of it.

Week after week, month after month, the Watergate scandals had transfixed America and had consumed the energy and interest of almost everyone in the news business. By running so many cover stories on Watergate, *Newsweek* had, we thought, been functioning properly and responsibly. But it had also been forced to forgo or skimp on numerous other stories, serious and otherwise. On August 10, 1974, the day after Richard Nixon's resignation, I sent a Telex to the Washington bureau:

THAT WAS ONE SMASHING EPOCH. CONGRATULATIONS TO ALL. AND NOW, ON TO THE ALASKA COVER. . . .

•IX•
ON BEING
BOSS

Even bosses grow up being bossed—they have parents and teachers and senior officers and supervisors—and given this universal experience of being bossed, it's a wonder how many bosses turn out to be bad. In order to be any kind of a decent boss, perhaps it's a good thing to have had some awful ones yourself. Though I was only thirty-six when Phil Graham appointed me editor of *Newsweek,* I had had my share of good bosses and bad alike—at home, in school and college, in the Navy, at the *Journal of Commerce,* at *Time,* at *Newsweek.*

My parents were good bosses. Among other things, they encouraged my first journalistic stirrings in 1933, when I started a "newspaper" and sold it to them for a nickel a copy. I was eight years old, and my onion-skin sheet reported school events, as well as other news plagiarized from the *New York Daily News.*

School item: "The new craze is water pistols. The new pistols repeat six times. Mr. Jones is on the warpath and he has already taken about eight of them."

Local item: "Mrs. Belmont's jewels, valued at 3000 dollars, were stolen from her bedroom yesterday evening."

National item: "Peggy MacMath was kidnapped yesterday. . . . The kidnapper is thought to be possibly the kidnapper of the Lindbergh baby."

Cultural item: "Anderson's play [*Both Your Houses*] won the Pulitzer Prize. This is the second successive year that a play criticizing the Government has won the prize. *Of Thee I Sing* won last year."

At Browning School in New York, I had a few good teacher-bosses—Lyman Tobin, a gentle lover of the English language; Paul Dreisbach, who drilled grammar into us like a parade-ground sergeant; John Roberts, a wiry little man who taught French and who used to capture our attention at the beginning of every class by chinning himself on the transom of the door. He did it using only one arm.

And then there was the delightful Giles Alington, a rosy-cheeked young Englishman whose father had long been headmaster of Eton, and who taught me history at St. Paul's. Alington demanded—but never got—"absolute silence" in his classes. We boys called him "the Duke" to his face. "Hey, Duke," we would yell. Alington once selected a carpet for his room on the basis of its raspberry-jam, grape-jelly, and orange-marmalade colors—so "it won't show when little boys spill things on it at teatime." After one vacation, Duke Alington was driving me back to school in his rattletrap Buick, and we were stopped for speeding in Westport, Connecticut. My footlocker was on the backseat. "Whaddaya got inna trunk?" asked the cop. "The boy's mother," the Duke crisply replied.

After the war, Giles became dean of University College, Oxford, and I had sherry with him and the other dons one day. He had a burn hole in the breast pocket of his tweed jacket, where he had inadvertently stuck his lighted pipe. He loved his floppy flannel trousers. "Delicious," he would say. "They

never touch more than one part of the body at any given time."
Once he visited the Grand Canyon with a fellow Englishman,
and together they sat at the rim—in "absolute silence"—for
twenty minutes. Finally Alington spoke. "Fantastic," he mur-
mured. "Let's go." He died very young, when the only kidney
he had gave out. I wrote his mother that he had been a brother
to me.

Another, equally delightful boarding-school "boss" was
Henry Crocker Kittredge, acting rector of St. Paul's when I
arrived there, and a Harvard classmate of my father. Kittredge
was a big man with a striking voice that came from deep
within and rumbled from the back of his throat. We boys loved
to imitate that strange voice, and some of us developed it to a
fine art—particularly Pete Taylor and Stinky Sortwell. One day
Pete was bent over a water fountain, when he heard the unmistakable Kittredgesque voice of his friend: "Hallo, Pete,
how-ah-ya?" Without looking around, Taylor answered in his
own highly polished Kittredge style: "Fine, Stinky, and how
are *you?*" It was, of course, Kittredge himself, and his eyebrows
began bouncing up and down in the way they did when Henry
Kittredge was having a good laugh.

My brother, Jock, was, well, my big brother—and big brothers tend to be alternately both good and bad as bosses. On
occasion he used to beat me up, but he taught me how to high-
jump (not very high) and to race a sailboat. When I got out to
the South Pacific in World War II, I found that I had just
missed him—our ships had been in the same port only a few
weeks before, and he had come aboard the *Boston* and left a
letter for me. Jock's major advice to this green ensign was:
"Always look busy." I should have taken it to heart. Not long
after, when my ship was in Pearl Harbor for repairs, my top
boss, a lieutenant commander who was constantly nagging his
juniors and fearful of his superiors, told me that my *only* job
while in Pearl would be to patrol the forward superstructure

to make sure no noise was made around the captain's cabin while the captain was on board. I placed a chair in the sun and started to read a book, while cocking an ear for any undue commotion—not an ordinary assignment when a ship is in a clangorous Navy yard for repairs. My immediate boss, a lieutenant, was astonished to find me there. I explained my mission, which he could hardly believe. He went to the lieutenant commander and said: "Elliott tells me his only job in Pearl is to patrol the forward superstructure and keep the noise down. Is that right?" "I didn't say *only*," exploded the lieutenant commander idiotically, "I said *sole!*"

The Navy provided a rich supply of truly awful bosses. There was, for another example, the ship's captain himself, who thought nothing of keeping the entire crew waiting in the rain for half an hour or more until he showed up on the fantail and signaled for the nightly movie to begin. On at least one such drenching occasion, His Arrogance, having kept everyone waiting in a downpour, left ten minutes after the film started.

When I returned from the Pacific after the war, Jock was already out of the Marine Corps, and he was there to meet me at Grand Central Terminal. Up the ramp I came, loaded down with a Japanese rifle and a samurai sword (which I certainly had not "liberated" personally) and a glass-encased pair of Japanese dolls, acquired for a couple of cartons of cigarettes. There was my handsome, beaming father, himself a proud combat veteran of World War I. And there was my mother, pretty and teary. And there was Jock, in snap-brimmed gray fedora and (I swear) a gray flannel suit. He was a copywriter for Batten, Barton, Durstine & Osborn. Making $60 a week. Fantastic. And not only was the pay terrific, said Jock, you also have time to write at night and on weekends.

Good deal. An adman I would be.

And so, with my big brother's help, I started off on a round of interviews up and down Madison Avenue, hitting almost every ad agency in sight. Months went by without a nibble. Oh yes, there was one—"Vox Pop," a popular radio show of the day, needed someone to haul the refrigerators and other prizes on and off the stage, and was willing to pay the enormous sum of $85 a week. I didn't get the job. Finally, an advertising friend told Jock: "Your brother should *sell* himself in his interviews." So I thrust out my jaw, and looked purposeful, and boomed out my answers in subsequent job interviews. But the hard sell also resulted in no sale.

Jock, whose self-effacing, kindly, and conscience-directed personality has never evoked the image of your stereotyped adman, ultimately went on to become chairman of the giant Ogilvy & Mather advertising agency. But Madison Avenue never took to me. I got my first job through pull, in the form of a letter from Robert Moses, New York's master builder and long a close friend of my family. He wrote Joseph Ridder of the German-American publishing family. See this fellow, give him a chance, said Moses. And within a couple of weeks I was hired by the Ridders as a cub reporter on their *New York Journal of Commerce,* at $35 a week. The *Journal* then had a policy of taking on young veterans at $35 if they were single and $40 if they were married—which provided quite an incentive for a number of young reporters to head for the altar.

My boss at the *Journal* was the managing editor, Dr. Heinz Luedicke, a kindly German immigrant with a doctorate and a Kissingerian accent. My first assignment was to cover a conference in Newark on consumer credit, a big subject in those early postwar days. I had found my way across the Hudson River and back, through the gloom of a dark December afternoon, and now, as the deadline approached, I sat in the *Journal*'s Dickensian city room on Park Row, trying to figure out what the story was.

Our city editor, Arthur Kramer, was straight out of *The*

Front Page: He wore a green eyeshade and sleeve garters and had a rasping voice which at that moment was bellowing: "Where the hell's the Elliott story?" I hunched miserably over my notes, absolutely convinced that if I didn't produce "the Elliott story" on time, the paper could not possibly come out the next day.

Just then Dr. Luedicke wandered by, looked over my shoulder, and asked me to step aside. He plumped himself down, scanned my notes, asked a couple of questions, and banged out three short paragraphs on my ancient typewriter. "That's the vay it's done, Oss," Luedicke hissed pleasantly. The story appeared in the paper next day, a gloriously crisp bit of prose about the horrendously mundane consumer-credit conference, and I considered it mine. For years afterward, I proudly carried the clipping around in my wallet.

The New York Journal of Commerce was a great training ground for young reporters; we were thrown into journalistic battle on all fronts—reporting, writing, editing, making up the pages in the composing room. My mentor was Tom Waage, who taught me whatever I was able to absorb about the Federal Reserve System (Waage became a vice-president of the Federal Reserve Bank of New York). I shared a desk and phone with Paul Komisaruk, who simplified his name to Kolton and served for years as president of the American Stock Exchange. In fact, thirty years later, when I was a deputy mayor of New York, I found myself once again sitting across a desk from Kolton, offering arguments about why the Amex, then threatening to move out of the city, should stay put.

The *Journal* let me write a series of features on local New York businesses; soon my by-line was appearing on stories about garages, laundries, pet shops, pawnbrokers. I became the paper's nonferrous-metals editor, not knowing at first what a nonferrous metal was, and covered the markets in copper, lead, zinc, aluminum. I was given a column to write on municipal bonds, and chronicled the outpouring of school, sewer, and highway issues as America rebuilt itself after the war. I discovered, in those two years on the *Journal,* that for me almost any subject can become interesting as soon as I learn something about it.

I also discovered that in journalism, as in romance, faint heart ne'er wins fair lady. In those postwar years, the *Journal of Commerce,* with a circulation of 40,000, was competing quite successfully with *The Wall Street Journal,* whose circulation was 80,000. The *Journal of Commerce* had a much broader editorial base on which to build: authoritative coverage of commodities, textiles, petroleum, shipping, chemicals, insurance—even nonferrous metals—as well as the financial news that was *The Wall Street Journal's* particular forte. But Barney Kilgore, publisher of *The Wall Street Journal,* saw an opportunity for growth that the Ridders never spotted. Kilgore broadened his paper's coverage to appeal to a wider audience. He hired good writers and editors, sparked up his front-page "leaders," and promoted his bright new product with high professionalism. Success came soon, and *The Wall Street Journal* has been gaining momentum ever since. Thirty years later, it is a respected national institution, with a circulation of 1,614,000. At latest count, the circulation of *The New York Journal of Commerce* was around 25,000.

In two years my salary doubled, to $70 a week, which was about what my fiancée, Deirdre Spencer, was making in the personnel department of Time Inc.—so we decided to get married. Soon, at her suggestion, I was being interviewed for a writing job at *Time.* There was a session scheduled one afternoon with Otto Fuerbringer, then a *Time* senior editor and later to become managing editor; after that interview, I was to pick up Deirdre and take her home. Instead, I called her and said that Fuerbringer wanted me to see Dana Tasker, then assistant managing editor, so please wait. Sounded promising.

Tasker, in turn, wanted me to see Roy Alexander, then *Time*'s executive editor. Even better. And Alexander wanted me to see Thomas Matthews, the managing editor. Wow!

I stood at the door of Matthews' cavernous office and watched for a minute. Lean and hatchet-faced, *Time*'s "M.E." sat like a West Pointer at his desk, the wire of an old-fashioned hearing aid tumbling into his breast pocket. He held a pencil, with his pinky extended, about an inch above a piece of copy that he clearly found almost too distasteful to touch. I made a little noise in my throat, and Matthews waved me into a chair far below his eye level. "Well," he said, peering down at me, "why don't you start talking?"

"Where would you like me to start?"

"Most people start with where they went to school."

And so I started there—and just about finished there. I said I had gone to St. Paul's. Matthews stopped me cold. "Well, that's two strikes against you," he said. "I can't imagine a place that could *un*-learn you more about the English language than St. Paul's." I stuttered some mild protest, and went on about how I had studied Shakespeare at Harvard. I didn't know at the time that Matthews—the son of a bishop—was himself a graduate of St. Paul's.

After an endless ten minutes, I was sent back to Tasker. "Well," he said, "Matthews seems to think we should hire you. What do you think you ought to get paid?" I told him I was making $70 a week at the *Journal of Commerce*. I gulped, and asked for $100. Tasker looked at me in utter astonishment. "We don't hire people for as little as *that*," he said. He put me on the payroll at $125.

Thus began a mostly happy six and a half years of writing business news for *Time*—including fourteen cover stories and a bunch of year-end business reviews that ruined a number of Christmases for me.

My bosses at *Time* were a varied lot. The top man, Tom

Matthews, was cold and dour and distant. His No. 2, Roy Alexander, was always kind and concerned and jovial. "Alex" cared about his writers and used to wander the halls, poking his head into their offices to see how they were doing. Years later, after I had become editor of *Newsweek*, Alex asked me if I were finding time enough to spend with the writers. "Yes," I said, but I knew the answer was really no. When Alexander wanted to see you he called you direct; Matthews would get in touch through his secretary. Alexander was known as something of a steamroller on copy—although he could turn a phrase on occasion (he once described the hard-top convertible automobile as "that monument to planned frustration"). Matthews was a stylistic perfectionist. "This story reads all right in Choctaw," he wrote on one writer's copy. "Now try it in English." He transformed one writer's description of Churchill from "half-American, half-British," to "half-American, wholly British." He pulled together a cover story I wrote on Levittown by the simple insertion of two topic sentences: "Levittown's uniformity is more apparent than real"; and, a paragraph or two later: "Levittowners' isolation is more real than apparent."

After I'd been at *Time* for about a year, Alexander asked me to come to his office—he was sitting in for Matthews as managing editor while Matthews was on leave, trying to figure out how to make *Time* a better place to work. (Many writers found it better the instant Matthews left.) It was Christmastime, and Alexander had good news. I was to get a $1000 raise, to $7500 a year. I told him it couldn't have come at a better time: my wife was expecting our first child, and we were looking for a bigger apartment. I said I liked it at *Time*, and Alex said they liked me, and as for the raise, he was sure there would be "more where that came from." A very merry Christmas.

But a couple of weeks later, Matthews was back on the scene, and his secretary called to say he wanted to see me. I ran up the two flights to his office on the twenty-ninth floor and arrived at his door, gasping for breath. "I understand you were told you're going to get a raise," Matthews said. Yes indeed, I panted, and it couldn't have come at a better time: pregnant wife, new apartment—I went into my whole song and dance. "Well," said Matthews, "I'm sorry to have to tell you this. But there's been a mistake." You mean, I thought, my wife *isn't* pregnant? We're *not* getting a new apartment? Matthews continued: "I've just been talking to Gus Thomason, the business manager, and that raise of yours isn't going to be on your next paycheck." I was demolished. How could it have happened? How could we afford the baby now? Was this a warning that I was about to be fired? What on earth would I do? Slowly, Matthews went on: "There was a mixup in accounting. Your raise will be on the paycheck *following* the next one, and it will be retroactive."

In later years, I got to know and like and respect Matthews. Was his sadism real or had I imagined it? To whatever degree it was real, perhaps it was a reflection of the kind of strain Matthews himself had to endure at the hands of Henry Robinson Luce.

It will come as no news to anyone that back in those days, more than a quarter century ago, *Time* was a highly opinionated magazine, wedded to the cause of moderate Republicanism at home and American expansionism and the mystique of Chiang Kai-shek abroad. In the presidential campaign of 1952, tensions between the editorial staff and management reached a peak. Most of the editors were for Adlai Stevenson, but Harry Luce was determined to use *Time*'s influence to elect Dwight Eisenhower, and thus advance Luce's dream of "the American Century." Tom Matthews had been a classmate of Stevenson's at Princeton, and was equally determined to see his old friend treated fairly in the pages of *Time*. That cost Matthews his job. He was kicked upstairs to the newly created and almost powerless post of editor. "*Time* has never had an editor," Luce announced at a staff cocktail party. "I always thought *Time* deserved an editor. Well, now *Time* has an editor—Tom Matthews. Tom?" Whereupon Matthews said: "I gather from what some of you have been asking me that you rather expect me to become some sort of wizard. Well, I may turn out to be Dorothy, but I don't think I'll turn out to be a wizard." Matthews' weekly purview was sharply reduced—but he still had the right to "top-edit" cover stories.

And sure enough, one day a viciously anti-Stevenson cover story, written by Otto Fuerbringer, landed on Matthews' desk. For weeks, Matthews had been squirreling away quotes and clippings on Stevenson; now he took the cover story home to work it over. Next day, as *Time* writer Paul O'Neil said, "The fans were in the bleachers early, chewing peanuts by the peck" in anticipation of what was to come. When the Stevenson cover story finally emerged from Matthews' office, it looked like the raggedy tail of a kite, with newspaper clippings and handwritten inserts pinned to its margins. At least for that one week, Adlai Stevenson got a fair shake in the pages of *Time*.

But Adlai lost. When the election ended in a landslide for Ike, Luce invited *Time*'s entire New York editorial staff—perhaps 150 strong in those days—to a dinner at the Union Club on Park Avenue. The idea, so office rumor had it, was to heal the wounds of the campaign. Nobody knew what to expect. Nobody could have known. At the end of the dinner, Luce got up to speak in his uniquely nasal and staccato manner. It went pretty much like this:

"Lots of people ask me, why have party? Well, when you've lost for twenty years, then you win, you have party. Celebrate." You could almost hear the groans as Luce continued. "Lot of people in this room don't seem to know who I am. Well, I guess I'm boss. What's boss mean? I keep reading in *Fortune*

and *Time* business section that boss is fellow who keeps door
open, knows everyone by first name. Don't know many of you
even by last name. But door's open. Come see me—if you can
get by Miss Thrasher." Incredibly, Luce had a secretary whose
name really *was* Miss Thrasher. "What else is boss? Guess I
could fire anyone in this room. That's right, isn't it, Roy?"
Here Luce looked down at the gentlemanly Roy Larsen, president of the company, who was now shifting in his seat in embarrassment. "Nobody here has contract, do they, Roy?" Larsen mumbled no, that's right, Harry, nobody here has a contract.

Luce then launched into a disquisition on journalism and
morality and absolute truth, but for most of us the evening
had already ended—an incredibly inept attempt to bring staff
and management together, if that's what the intention was,
and I suppose it was. At the door of the Union Club, as people were leaving the party, Tom Matthews ran into Lester
Bernstein, then on home leave from his job as Rome bureau
chief. "Well, Lester," said Matthews, breathing a deep sigh,
"go back to the Piazza Navona and have a drink for me."*

It is impossible to leave the precincts of Time Inc. without
mention of two other bosses I had there. One was the business
editor, Joe Purtell, for whom I worked for most of my six
and a half years. Purtell was a survivor of what had come to
be known at *Time* as the "rat fuck." Not long before I arrived
on the scene, a number of *Time* writers were in competition
for some choice senior editorships. Five of them were told

* Not long afterward, Matthews was dispatched to London to study
the possibilities of bringing out an edition of *Time* edited in England and aimed strictly at the British market. After a few months,
he concluded that the idea was indeed viable and sent a lengthy
recommendation back to New York. But in the end the "numbers"
people at *Time* shot down the idea, thus inspiring a classic cable from
Matthews to Luce: WHY DID YOU KEEP ME STANDING ON TIPTOE SO
LONG IF YOU WEREN'T GOING TO KISS ME?

that they could compete for four plum jobs, and so the rat fuck had begun. I don't know who was the poor fellow who lost, but Purtell was one of the winners.

He was a newspaperman from Detroit, and he had learned a lot of the tricks of the newsmagazine trade. The snappy lead ("Edward J. Noble, who made a mint out of Life Savers . . ."). The sentences that march in tight formation, one leading inexorably into the next, with no seams showing. The matter of structure—a story must have a beginning, a middle, and an end. The use of clever, popular language—that was the style of *Time* in those days ("When in doubt," said Allan Ecker, a *Time* writer, "always use a cliché—because if *you* don't, your senior editor *will*"). The slower pacing of more difficult sections of a story, where the reader must be led by the hand through a thicket of scientific or technical material. The crisp ending—you can always use a pertinent quotation if you can't think of anything conclusive to say yourself. In my first weeks at *Time,* Purtell would assign me six and seven and eight stories a week, an impossible load for even the most experienced hand. I rewrote frequently, and most of those early stories never made it into print. But slowly, painfully, mostly by osmosis, I learned.

Purtell's weakness was that he was unsure of what he (or *his* editors) wanted in a story; he could never decide until he had seen something in writing—sometimes two or three or four versions. In one memorable week, after I'd been on *Time* for a couple of years, I was writing a cover story on Studebaker and its new, double-ended Raymond Loewy car. I handed in the first draft on Wednesday. Purtell didn't like it. He marched me through the piece, suggesting both structural and substantive changes. I stayed up most of that night rewriting, and had the new version on his desk by midday Thursday. He liked this effort even less. Once again, we went through the thing, and once again I rewrote it. Friday was yet another replay, and I put the piece through my typewriter for a fourth time. I handed it in at lunchtime Saturday, and stumbled out to the New Weston for a couple of martinis and a sandwich. When I got back from lunch, I found the fourth version of my cover story stuck in my typewriter, with a typed note attached: "This story is very poor." (The "very" had been inserted in longhand.) "Let's pull up our socks and write a story. Joe."

That did it. I marched into Purtell's office, told him I'd been around long enough not to have to take that kind of crap from him. And from then on, working relations improved.

While I learned structure and technique from Purtell, I had a lesson in decency from Tom Griffith. Early on in my stay at *Time,* I was loaned for one week to the National Affairs section, which was short of writers. Griffith, the "N.A." editor, assigned me four or five stories. One by one I ground them out, and one by one they were killed as the week progressed— except for a piece that was totally rewritten by the old pro Paul O'Neil. I was miserable. Obviously I could never be a *Time* writer. No doubt the whole staff, including my own boss, Purtell, would soon hear of my disastrous performance in the National Affairs section. At the end of the week I poked my head into Griffith's office and asked if he needed me for anything else. The very question seemed absurd. Griffith was busy editing copy; he hardly looked up as he waved a small goodnight. I made my way to the elevators. A failure at twenty-four. I didn't know what to say to my wife.

Suddenly Tom Griffith came trotting to the elevator hall. "Say," he said, "I'm sorry I was busy in there just now. I just wanted to thank you for all your help this week." A nice man. But a liar.

As the months passed, I began to get the hang of producing that highly compressed, highly structured prose that is the essence of newsmagazine writing, and I began to savor some of the pleasures of working for a national magazine. In those days, most of the reporting was done by *Time*'s correspondents in the field. But on occasion we writers in New York were allowed to go out and get at least a glimpse of our subjects. For a cover story on oil millionaires, I went to Texas and spent a few days hobnobbing with the rich. I was to meet Clint Murchison and Sid Richardson at six o'clock one morning in their hometown of Athens, at a simple fishing camp called—and appropriately spelled—the Koon Kreek Klub. I arrived on time, with *Time*'s Dallas bureau chief, Bill Johnson, and found half a dozen millionaire fishermen gathered in the kitchen of a simple cabin, drinking coffee. "Is Mr. Murchison here?" I asked, Eastern Establishment marbles in my mouth. Sid Richardson answered: "Why, that sumbitch was supposed to be here to cook us our coffee, but he ain't showed yet. Set down, son, have a cup."

In a few minutes Murchison arrived; when he wasn't looking, one of his friends snitched Clint's ten-gallon hat and hid it in the refrigerator (this group was blessed with an appreciation for the higher forms of comedy). The fishing turned out to be an exercise in guaranteed success—two men and a guide in each boat, put-putting around a lake stocked with thousands of starving bream (pronounced "brim"). Every time there was a tug on your line, you pulled it up, and there, sure enough, was a little fish wriggling limply on the hook; you'd swing it to the stern of the boat until it hit the guide in the face, and he would replace the tiny fish with another worm. We must have caught thirty fish apiece in less than an hour. "You know," said Murchison at breakfast later, "I've been trout fishin' in France, and salmon fishin' in Canada, and deep-sea fishin' in the Gulf, and there ain't nothin' that'll beat brim fishin' right here in Athens, Texas!"

Richardson, reflecting on the state of the U.S. economy,

waxed even more philosophical. The trouble with the country, he said, was that it was too conservative—and the reason for that was that the women controlled 80 percent of the money. "Of course, they control a hundred percent of the pussy, and the way I figure it that hundred percent of the pussy, sooner or later, is gonna get the other twenty percent of the money."

It was 1954, and my Texas trip happened to coincide with the televised Army-McCarthy hearings which were to be Senator Joseph McCarthy's undoing. In Houston to interview some other oilmen for background on my story, I went to see Hugh Roy Cullen, a fabled wildcatter. He invited me to join him in his boardroom to watch that morning's televised hearings with a few of his colleagues. Every time Roy Cohn's face appeared on the screen, Cullen would slap his thigh approvingly and say: "You watch that little Jew-boy, he's gonna get 'em now!" I learned nothing of political or social significance from Cullen, but I did learn a little about how he had discovered all his millions of barrels of oil. "I rely on creekology," said Cullen as he drew two wavy, parallel lines on a piece of paper. "Take an old riverbed like this," he said. "Now over here"—his pencil stabbed the paper—"there's a rise in the ground, a kind of mound. There's a reason for the ground to be higher there, and so that's where I drill. And *that's* what I call creekology."

I asked Cullen if he knew the famous oilman H. L. Hunt, who had taken it upon himself to save America from Communism by sponsoring far-right-wing radio broadcasts and other propaganda. Cullen told me: "I wouldn't have any truck with a man of that sort. Why, I was doin' a little tradin' with one of his associates one day, right here at this desk, and I had a gold lighter on the desk to light my cigars. You realize that when *he* left, my lighter was gone?" "Tradin' " was how these Texas individualists referred to doing business. They seldom made formal contracts with one another; a handshake was all that was needed—that and a reading on a man's credit rating. "Down here," said Murchison, "we have a saying—a man is worth twice what he owes."

Sometimes their tricks went beyond hiding hats in refrigerators. One day, Sid Richardson told me, he had got a tip from his partner Murchison on a hot new stock issue. Richardson called his broker and told him to buy all he could lay his hands on. A week later, the broker called and asked him if he should keep buying. "How much I got now?" asked Richardson. Oh, half a million or so, said the broker. It wasn't until days later that Richardson discovered that "that sumbitch Clint was unloading." Unknowingly, Ole Sid had been buying all of his stock from his friend, Ole Clint.

Time's cover stories in those days, at least its cover stories on business leaders, tended to be circumspect and reverential. Looking back now, in these post-Watergate times, it's amazing what we didn't report. My cover story on Chrysler boss Lester Lum ("Tex") Colbert was a case in point. Colbert was widely known in Detroit as a big drinker and ladies' man, and endless stories were making the rounds about his peccadilloes. Colbert was relieved that none of them had found its way into the pages of *Time,* and after my article appeared he invited a group of us to a celebratory lunch at the "21" Club. Howard Black, Time Inc.'s chief guru of advertising sales, was there, and so were *Time*'s publisher, Jim Linen, and various of my editorial bosses. I was the junior officer present. We had a couple of drinks at the bar, then adjourned to a private dining room upstairs, and had a few more drinks before lunch. At one point, Colbert turned to me and announced to the group: "I'll be everlastingly grateful to you, Oz, for not printing all those stories you must've heard about me in Dee-troit—including the one about how I was supposed to be fuckin' another man's wife. There wasn't any truth to that one anyway."

Colbert went on to tell exactly what *had* happened. "I had

a few drinks one night, and went around to call on this lady I had known, and I called on the house phone and her husband answered and he was very cordial and invited me up. Then he had a drink, and I had a drink, ·and we had some more, and before I knew it he was accusin' *me* of fuckin' *his* wife. Not a word of truth to it. She's dead now, God rest her soul."

Howard Black said: "The way we heard the story, Tex, was that you sent the husband out to get some pistachio ice cream, and when he came back you wouldn't even let him have any ice cream."

· · ·

Even though I was only in my mid-thirties when I became editor of *Newsweek,* I had already spent a number of years working for a lot of bosses. What had I learned? What I *hope* I learned was: The importance of kindness. The idiocy of arrogance. The virtues of boldness. The pettiness of cruelty. The need for self-assurance. And, above all, the uses of humor.

There were, of course, a lot of things I was yet to learn, including the intricacies of trying to manage a group of creative people—particularly in the emotion-charged sixties. The problem was not just the divisions caused by the Vietnam war; the general unrest in the nation, in those years, engendered a rebellion against authority of every kind.

In a quite absurd manner, this was crystallized at *Newsweek* by the Great Bicycle Affair. One Friday night, enforcing a sudden ordinance by the *Newsweek* building's management, the elevator starter had tried to prevent a proofreader from bringing her bicycle up in the elevator. Everyone who had ever ridden a bike to work, or had ever *thought* of doing so, was up in arms. After dinner that night, our martinis not yet fully absorbed into the bloodstream, John Jay Iselin, the National Affairs editor, bustled angrily into my office. A professed bike buff, Jay was outraged by this inhuman and inflammatory and unreasonable attack upon the rights of citizens. He had a plan to strike back. Those were the days of "sit-ins" and "teach-ins" and "pray-ins." The next morning, Iselin said, all the bike riders of *Newsweek* were going to cycle through Central Park, round up all the sympathetic bicyclists they could find, and stage "the biggest goddamn bike-in you've ever seen."

I was aghast. "Jay," I said, "instead of a mass bike-in tomorrow morning, how about a single, symbolic bike ride—by me?" Iselin thought that would be nifty. Real, honest-to-God leadership. And so, early that Saturday morning, I wobbled down Lexington Avenue on a borrowed bicycle, and puffed up to the *Newsweek* building, to loud cheers from the staff.

"Good morning, Peter," I said to the elevator starter. "As you can see, I've decided to bring my bicycle to work today. Where would you suggest I park it?"

"Why don't you just bring it right upstairs?" said Peter, waving me into a waiting elevator.

·   ·   ·

I learned that it was not always easy for an editor to retain friendships, especially among those who are criticized by your magazine. There was the time, for example, when *Newsweek* ran a review of a book by Robert Moses, the man who got me started in journalism. The piece was critical, but I thought fair. I removed what I considered to be a gratuitously nasty phrase, specified that the Moses review should have top billing in the Books section, and ordered up a particularly attractive picture that Bob had given to my parents years before. An excerpt from the review: "His book is too rancorous; it is too much the pastime of a man who delights in first confounding his enemies and then thumbing his nose at them. But it is also the record of an overwhelming life of work, a life spent tearing apart and building. . . ."

I set off on a trip to the Far East before the review appeared, and when I returned a few weeks later, I found that all hell had broken loose. It was just before my parents' fiftieth wedding anniversary, and my brother and I were giving a dinner dance for them. At the top of the list of invitees, of course, were Bob Moses and his wife. But they had regretted the invitation—because of the *Newsweek* review. Moses wrote my brother:

> . . . Nothing pains me more than to strain a long and cherished friendship with your parents especially on such a notable occasion. I have no quarrel with you and Elly. I shall not however accept an invitation from Osborn. What he did was inexcusable and no one with the slightest self-respect would put up with it. . . . [He] adds a gross vicious personal insult in the nasty sadistic tradition which is more and more the hallmark of American journalism. I realize that Osborn has become a publishing tycoon too busy for trivial comments by his staff. By the same token he need not worry about friendships. . . .

What particularly bothered Moses was the reviewer's allusion to Thersites, described in *Troilus and Cressida* as "A slave whose gall coins slanders like a mint."

All this became known to me on my return from the Orient, just two days before the Golden Wedding party for my parents. My wife had already visited Moses, begging him to change his mind and to come. My brother had written him.

Now I wrote a letter expressing my "utter dismay" and sent it off by messenger:

> . . . I have read your letter to Jock, and understand that you feel personally betrayed by an old friend who owes you much. . . . Perhaps it is too much to expect you to change your mind on this, but for the sake of the family . . . I implore you to do so. . . . I found the review, though critical, fairly so—describing you, as it did, in both headline and text, as "master builder." . . . Having now looked up the classical references [to Thersites], I very much regret the analogy, and I want to apologize to you. . . .

In short, I crawled. But Moses never came to the party. It was several years before I saw him again.

A similar problem, with happier denouement, presented itself with the publication of Theodore H. White's *The Making of the President, 1968.* I had just hired Geoffrey Wolff away from *The Washington Post* as *Newsweek*'s chief book reviewer, with all sorts of promises that his copy and critical comments would not be tampered with. As it happened, the very first Wolff review to come across my desk was a sharply critical piece on this new book by my good friend Teddy White. I took the book home over the weekend and concluded that, while I might not agree with the reviewer's conclusions, they were fair comment. So I let the review run as was, and wrote a letter to White, who was then on the West Coast, to warn him what was coming.

"My problem," I wrote, "is that I have an old friend who I think is very good, and a new book reviewer who I think is very good, and the new book reviewer doesn't think that the old friend's new book is as good as the old friend's old books. . . ." Teddy, being the pro that he is, understood my dilemma. Our friendship survived.

·   ·   ·

Hiring the talented and promoting the worthy are always happy occasions for a boss, and I rejoiced in the acquisition of such columnists as Walter Lippmann, Stewart Alsop, Bill Moyers, Shana Alexander, Milton Friedman, Paul Samuelson, Henry Wallich, George Ball, Zbigniew Brzezinski, William Bundy, and later Meg Greenfield and George Will. I always made a point of greeting new staffers on their arrival. When the talented Southerner, Frank Trippett, came into my office for the official "welcome aboard," I got up from my desk, stuck out my hand and, by way of introduction, said: "Oz Elliott." "Ah's Trippett," Frank drawled.

Not every effort at hiring was successful—the elusive Tom Wolfe being one early example, and Time Inc.'s Hugh Sidey another. When Ben Bradlee left *Newsweek* to join *The Washington Post* in 1965, I had long discussions with the top editors about who should succeed him in the key job of Washington bureau chief. At last I called Sidey, then in *Time*'s Washington bureau and—so we had heard—looking for a change. Would he like to join *Newsweek*? Sidey seemed interested. He would call back. That weekend I was on Long Island, visiting my friend Dick Clurman, who as Time-Life's chief of correspondents was Sidey's boss. When we came in from blue-fishing on Saturday, there was a message for Clurman to call Sidey. Even though we worked for competing magazines, I always considered Dick Clurman a valued adviser, and never hesitated to ask him for ethical counsel; now, I thought, my ethics were a little wanting. I cleared my throat and said: "Dick, there's something I think I ought to tell you. . . ." Clurman returned Sidey's call, and within a few days Hugh turned down my job offer. Soon after that, Sidey began appearing as a regular columnist for *Life*.

Things turned out all right for *Newsweek,* too. We appointed Mel Elfin to the Washington job, and for the past fifteen years he has served as bureau chief with energy and effectiveness.

I made plenty of mistakes, both in hiring and promoting. My most egregious error was when we were about to reshuffle the top editorial management, and I assured one of the senior editors that if any promotions were involved, he would certainly be among those moved up. The man was able, tireless, and full of ideas. But people who worked for him found him unpredictable and difficult. As word of his impending promotion got out, a firestorm of protest swept the staff. I reneged on my promise. I didn't blame him at all when the disappointed senior editor angrily quit.

On the hiring front, after years of hits and misses, I have come to the conclusion that there is no sure way of determining who will make a competent newsmagazine writer. Sometimes a person with no journalistic experience whatever would come in, sit down at a typewriter, and start writing finished *Newsweek* pieces in the very first week. Ken Auchincloss, who went on to become managing editor, was a case in point—but he may have had a genetic advantage, with a father who wrote for *Time* for years. Often people with long experience on wire services, newspapers, even other magazines would strike out— as I very nearly did myself when I first joined *Time*—lacking the knack for story structure and compression. There are those who allege to this day that, after a lunch with a prospective writer, I refused to hire the man because he had put his pipe in my butter plate. That may be as good a criterion as any.

Once you have hired a writer or a correspondent, you must tend to his care and feeding, a tricky undertaking on which there can be no experts. It is easy enough to read copy before it goes to press, and to call for a new "lead" or to write questions ("Huh?") and comments ("Pls say better") in the margin—or to kill stories outright and order up new ones. But what is difficult to remember, especially under a newsmagazine's deadline pressure, is the sensitivity of the writer who has worked hard and long, and has probably already done battle with his senior editor before his story ever crosses your desk.

An editor has a lot of power over his people and his "product," and it's not a bad idea to admit fallibility now and then. On one occasion, our theater critic, Leslie Hanscom, was reviewing a Judy Garland performance at the Palace; he commented critically on a juggling act that was part of the show. I wrote in the margin of his review that the *Times* had praised the jugglers. A note came back from Hanscom: "If you don't trust me to judge a juggling act, how can you set me loose on Shakespeare?" I scribbled back: "You win. Guess I had too many balls in the air at the time."

I used to make a conscious effort to involve people in decisions, and encouraged them to come up with new ideas; one of our most successful endeavors was a special issue, in 1973, on The Arts in America. It happened to be my idea, but that issue was distinguished because it was executed entirely under the direction of our brilliant cultural editor, Jack Kroll.

At the beginning of each week, we tried to keep the story conferences light and airy—there would be enough tensions around as deadline approached. On occasion, I would take the senior editors for a few days to Puerto Rico or some other pleasant retreat to "rethink" the magazine. We would actually work hard at round-table sessions in the mornings, and play in the afternoons and evenings. But the collegiality that grew from these meetings was as important as any decisions made.*

We top editors, we "Wallendas," used to socialize with one

* At one of these sessions, at Dorado Beach, Jack Kroll went off to get a haircut. The Puerto Rican barber asked him, in heavily accented English, if he was from New York. Yes, said Kroll. "Then you must be hoo-ish?" "Jalf and jalf," Jack replied.

another, and with the senior editors. Soon after I had persuaded Bill Emerson, our Atlanta bureau chief, to become a
senior editor in New York in 1961, I invited him to spend a
day with me on Long Island. I had my little Chris-Craft
loaded with food and drink and ready to cross the Great South
Bay for Fire Island, where we planned to swim and picnic.
Emerson and his wife, "Miss Lucy," and children were a
couple of hours late, and when we finally reached Fire Island
my tiny mother was coming down the boardwalk, heading for
the ferry to go home for lunch. I introduced her to the towering Southerner.

"Yew Ahz Aillyitt's mothah?" Emerson drawled. "Fantastic!
Whah, do yew realize Ah got up at dawn this mornin', and
drove over the hah-ways and bah-ways of Westchester County,
and got lost umpteen times, and came across the *Frog's* Neck
Bridge and got lost again and wound mah way to this tiny
hamlet of Bellport and crossed this vast expanse of water,
and heah on this desert strip, whom should Ah meet but Ahz
Aillyitt's mothah! Fantastic! Ah'm delighted to meet yew,
ma'am."

But for all the efforts I made, or *thought* I was making, to
get to know the staff, and involve them in the "decision-
making process," I often fell short. Because the final decisions
were mine to make, I sometimes gave short shrift to the opinions of senior editors—and too often we Wallendas simply
ignored what the writers had to say. In the spring of 1969,
word reached me of "the colonels' revolt," a move on the
part of senior writers of the magazine to get more impor-
tantly involved in story planning and editorial policy. I sent
a memo to the rebellious "colonels": "I hear that you are
unhappy, and that you may be drawing up a list of suggestions
on how to improve things around this place. . . . There is
no question in my mind that you have some legitimate complaints, and that your interest is professional as much as it

is personal. I think you all agree—in fact I should think it may well be your major point—that this is a delicate mechanism we're dealing with. . . ."

We Wallendas talked with the "colonels," and let them know we cared. Perhaps those talks led to the writers having more influence on the magazine—or perhaps it was all illusion. Whatever the case, the "colonels" *felt* better as a result.

If the pressures of deadlines made it difficult to communicate adequately with the staff in New York, the awkwardness of time zones and geography made it almost impossible to do so with the correspondents in *Newsweek*'s foreign bureaus. The foreign correspondent leads a dashing life, even in these days when the news tends to be dominated by trade balances, monetary crises, inflation, and the energy crunch. But it can be a lonely life, as well—sporadic and incomplete communication with the home office and long hours available to develop simple self-doubt into the raging heebie-jeebies. At the cablehead, the voice of the home office can sound terribly impersonal and demanding—"How many Seabees in Khe San?" was one notable "query" from *Newsweek* New York. The editors never seem to have any grasp of the logistical, linguistic, and bureaucratic problems faced in the field, with the result that the foreign correspondent often becomes cantankerous—and it is all too easy to respond in kind.

My letters to *Newsweek* correspondents ranged from the sarcastic to the honeyed, and even in the most straightforward messages the recipients no doubt read things that were not there. A few excerpts:

Dear Winded and Sad:
The one thing I cannot stand is the kind of back-biting vendetta that you describe in your letter—and which, I may say, was not exactly diminished by your letter.
. . . Things look different through different prisms; maybe what we all need is a little more good old-

fashioned plate glass. I'm ordering up some for myself, in any case. . . .

Dear _____:
The long arm of New York is about to reach out to embrace you, and to confer new honors upon you. In short, I want you to come back here . . . as a senior editor.

Dear _____:
I have spent a large part of the last three days thinking about your letter. . . . My thinking has been in a broader context than the simple matter of whether or not you should have a leave of absence. . . .

Dear _____:
After going through a considerable period of ups and downs—too many of which, as you know, we considered downs—I feel that you have really hit your stride. . . .

Dear _____:
I'm embarrassed by your acute embarrassment but honestly feel that we're saving you from more acute embarrassment by killing [your] story in its present form. . . .

Dear _____:
Without going into specifics . . . I would say that in general your bureau has been too predictable; too seldom have there been stories, or angles to stories, that some of us, or all of us, have not already read in the foreign press. Too seldom have I seen the burbling up of imagination that should be the hallmark of each and every *Newsweek* bureau. . . .

Dear _____:
Much as I love you, you can sometimes be an incredible pain in the ass—and that's what you are being right now. . . .

Dealing with opinion columnists is another art unto itself. For one thing, they are smarter than the rest of us—how else would they be able to persuade us editors to run their material? For another, by definition, the columnists have an independence denied the regular staff and are even at liberty —at least under the *Newsweek* rules—to attack the very publication that gives them their voice.

Mostly, my dealings with columnists were pleasant, civil, and mutually respectful. Often I would suggest topics to them; almost as often my suggestions would be ignored. Sometimes we editors would straighten out the columnar prose, and usually the changes would be accepted gracefully. But mostly my advice would be technical, as in this memo to Messrs. Friedman, Samuelson, and Wallich, our three economists: "I have noticed that in recent weeks a clear majority of you have promised readers, in effect, 'more to come' on such-and-such a subject in your next column. Running on the tri-weekly cycle (tricycle?) that you do, I think it's asking a bit much to expect readers to pick up where you left off three weeks ago. And so, I urge you all to stick to the unicycle as much as possible."

In 1967, after *Newsweek*'s special issue on "The Negro in America," Milton Friedman weighed in with a column attacking the magazine's whole approach to the racial issue: "Many of the problems that the Negro faces in America today were produced or aggravated by governmental measures proposed, supported, and executed by liberals holding the views that dominate the *Newsweek* story. . . ." Friedman wrote to me in an accompanying letter: "I had been optimistically supposing that sophistication had been spreading among liberals.

. . . But I guess I was making the mistake of confusing Moynihan with a trend!" My answering letter said: "I was dismayed to hear that you consider us all a bunch of lily-livered liberals—a judgment that may be confirmed in your mind by our willingness to run your editorial attack on our program. . . ."

As usual, "Uncle Miltie" had the last word: "What bothers me is not the color of your liver but the blinders on your eyes."

There was at least one incident when one of our columnists —and his wife—got too big for their breeches. A letter arrived one day from Walter Lippmann's wife, Helen, just back from a European trip, complaining about their treatment at the hands of *Newsweek*'s Paris bureau: ". . .No one seemed to wish to be of any assistance. In fact, no one seemed to know who Mr. Lippmann was. . . . The Paris *Newsweek* bureau was as unhelpful as it is possible to be. . . . I shall, of course, never expect anything from the Paris bureau in future but, in a way, am somewhat curious to know why they were so outstandingly unhelpful. . . ."

So was I, and so I sent Mrs. Lippmann's letter off to Ed Behr, our Paris bureau chief, for comment. His response:

> Shortly after I had been hired by *Newsweek*, Joel Blocker asked me to meet the Lippmanns at Orly Airport, which I gladly did. Unfortunately, Mr. Lippmann's secretary got their time of arrival all wrong. . . .
>
> I raced round to the Ritz, Place Vendôme, where we had booked a suite for them, and caught up with them just as they were checking in. I tried to apologize . . . but never managed to make myself clear. For both of them (but especially Mrs. L) turned on me with a savagery and rudeness which, to this very day, makes me break out in cold rage. . . . To each other, they referred, over my head, to my stupidity, laziness, and incompetence and inferentially to the incompetence of that wretched magazine, *Newsweek*,

which was unable to get the slightest instruction straight. . . .

A few days later Walter Lippmann phoned me from London, and, with the amenity of a Marine drill sergeant, asked me, or rather told me, to get him an appointment with Pompidou [who was then Prime Minister]. . . .

I . . . was finally able to phone [Lippmann] and tell him that the appointment had been fixed for 10:00 a.m. the following Friday. . . . I didn't expect any thanks, but I must say I didn't expect what followed. For all Lippmann said was: "Tell him that's too early in the morning. Tell him to find another time"—and hung up. . . .

Stewart Alsop started writing weekly back-of-the-book pieces for *Newsweek* in the summer of 1968. By common agreement among journalists, Stew was the quintessential commentator —and a wonderful human being. When he was confronted with a mysterious blood disease, Alsop refused to believe that it was leukemia, which it finally turned out to be. In a memo to himself, after a bone-marrow test that strongly suggested remission, he wrote: "I am tempted to murmur, 'Fuck you, Dr. Clarkson, you and your lymphoproliferative disorders.' " And to one of his doctors, Stew said: "Would you like to hear Dr. Alsop's theory? I think God was wrestling with the Devil every night, and finally threw him out of my body."

Sadly, the Devil finally won—but not for another two years or so. And that gave Alsop time to write a number of columns, and a book called *A Stay of Execution: A Sort of Memoir,* which gave the world a view of his nobility as he faced the ever-increasing inevitability of an early death. On occasion, Stew shared health information with me, as in this April 1973 memo about his "peculiar medical situation":

A plus: The proportion of abnormal cells in my marrow is [now] less than 30 per cent. . . . Conclusion:

whatever it is that fights the proliferation of malig-
nant cells (whoever identifies this Factor X is a sure
winner of the Nobel Prize) is still in there
fighting. . . .

A minus: I am beginning to reject transfusions.
. . . The last couple of times I had very violent chills-
and-fever rejection. . . . In a couple of days I'm getting a platelet transfusion from brother Joe, the poor
old sonofabitch. I say that advisedly, since [Dr.] Glick
insists Joe has to go on the wagon—alcohol has a bad
effect on platelets. I wrote Joe a paraphrase of the
Bible: "No greater love hath any man than this, than
that he will go on the wagon for his brother." . . .

Anything might happen—my leukemia . . . is unlike any classic leukemia. So don't count me out. . . .
But I'm tired, and running short, so I may stop writing for a couple of weeks. In that case, I expect *no*
pay for what I don't write. . . .

This, in my experience, was unique—a writer actually demanding that he *not* be paid! And on December 7, 1973, four
months before he died, this brave gentleman returned to the
theme:

Just after you called, my doctor came in with the
happy news that the X-rays showed that a pain in my
chest I'd been gently complaining about had been
caused by a pulmonary embolism. . . . This one
turns out to be no worse than a bad cold—it only
hurts when I laugh. So I still expect one of these days
to be up and about and tapping away on my typewriter. But for the moment, I feel as weak as a baby
and as flaccid as a wet towel.

That brings me to a subject which I have brought
up before. . . . According to our contract, you pay
me $800 per column (well worth the price when I'm
in the groove) and nothing for no column, which is
fair enough. . . . You can't (or I can't) produce consistently a respectable column if you're really sick.

. . . But you've also paid me in the past when I was not really sick, and on those occasions, my New England conscience gave me a sharp twinge. The purpose of this letter is to ask you *not* to pay me on this sort of occasion. . . .

Finally, a good deal of the time I do not feel very sprightly. . . . All this is to try to explain why I want to be in a position to say from time to time: "The hell with it. I haven't got a good enough column this week, so I'll skip it." I want to be able to say this even when I'm not hospitalized and wholly operational. But I can only do so in good conscience if it's understood between us that when I skip a column under such circumstances, there will be no check for $800 for S. Alsop.

I scribbled a note back to Stew:

"Entendu.

"Far be it from me to prick the conscience of a good Puritan. And so . . . we'll agree not to pay you for goof-off weeks.

"We will, however, continue to pay you whenever you are in the hospital or flat on your back—and, of course, whenever you are goofing *on*!"

Stewart Alsop died on May 26, 1974. He was sixty years old. A couple of years before, he had written his own epitaph:

"When I first got sick, I came across a sentence in an old piece by Winston Churchill: 'For the rest, live dangerously, take life as it comes; dread naught, all will be well.' "

· · ·

An important, and usually enjoyable, part of the editor's job at *Newsweek* was representational—entertaining visiting dignitaries at editorial lunches, appearing at dinners, running panel shows, speaking before business groups and advertisers, and intervening, on occasion, at the highest level to help open doors for correspondents and reporters. All this, I thought, was both good for the magazine and for me, affording me some contact outside the tight little world of journalism.

My files are full of fawning letters and cables to the high, the mighty, and the merely glittering. "Dear Mr. and Mrs. Onassis," I wrote in one 1969 letter . . .

> . . . It is my understanding that Prince Radziwill has informed you in general terms of *Newsweek*'s desire to publish a long, thoughtful article on the remarkable new life that you have made together, and the important role which you, as a couple, play on the current world scene.
>   . . . Accordingly, I have chosen to report and write the story—assuming that you agree—Mr. Arnaud de Borchgrave, a senior editor of *Newsweek* in whom I place implicit trust. (Mr. de Borchgrave, as you may know, is a former Royal Navy officer who renounced a Belgian title in order to become a U.S. citizen.) . . .

I never got an answer.

In March of 1969, Clark Clifford appeared one evening before the Council on Foreign Relations in New York, and proceeded to unburden himself to the foreign-policy establishment about how, beginning a year before when he was Secretary of Defense, he had become a dove on Vietnam. "A suspicion became a belief," he said, "the belief became a conviction, and the conviction became an obsession—that we must disengage." I was at the council that night, and found his talk extraordinarily interesting. But when I asked Clifford if we could adapt it for *Newsweek*, he said he had already been talking with Hamilton Fish Armstrong, editor of the council's own publication, *Foreign Affairs*. I wasn't about to be scooped by the seventy-five-year-old Ham Armstrong. I dispatched a tearjerker of a letter to Clifford stating that he could honor both his tentative commitment to *Foreign Affairs* and serve the national interest by submitting to an interview by *Newsweek*.

This stirring plea—which really did express my views—had no more effect than the letter to Jackie and Ari. Clifford called me a few days later to say that he thought he could be more effective in swinging the new Nixon administration to disengagement by talking privately on the inside, and not going public in the pages of *Newsweek*. History strongly suggests that, in this judgment at least, Clifford was wrong.

I would go to almost any epistolary lengths to get a story, secure an interview, or acquire a visa for a correspondent—as suggested by this cable to North Korea's dictator Kim Il Sung in the summer of 1972:

AS YOU KNOW, THE AMERICAN PEOPLE HAVE WATCHED YOUR EFFORTS TO RESTORE THE UNITY OF THE KOREAN PEOPLE WITH EXTRAORDINARY INTEREST AND ENTHUSIASM. FOR THAT REASON, I WOULD APPRECIATE ANY ASSISTANCE YOU MIGHT BE ABLE TO GIVE IN GRANTING A VISA TO A REPRESENTATIVE FROM NEWSWEEK TO THE OPENING OF THE NORTH-SOUTH TALKS IN PYONGYANG ON AUGUST 30. I MIGHT RESPECTFULLY POINT OUT THAT NEWSWEEK IS ONE OF AMERICA'S LEADING WEEKLY MAGAZINES WITH 15 MILLION READERS IN INFLUENTIAL POSITIONS IN THE UNITED STATES AS WELL AS IN EUROPE, ASIA AND AUSTRALIA.

Quite a number of influentials. But we never got the visa.

Often, of course, an editor must defend his writers and reporters against people who think they or their organizations have been mistreated by the magazine. A case in point arose from a critical story we ran on Marshall Field's Chicago papers, the *Sun-Times* and the *Daily News*, which elicited an angry letter from editorial director Emmett Dedmon of the *Sun-Times*. He found our story inaccurate, incomplete, and unfair. I responded that I had asked the *Newsweek* people to retrace their tracks on this story, and that, in turn, I had retraced theirs. The upshot was that our Chicago bureau stood by the essential thrust of the story, and so did *Newsweek*, and so did I. "After all," I wrote to Dedmon, "you and I both know that this is an inexact science."

·   ·   ·

There was a weekly parade of visitors to *Newsweek*'s executive dining room, Top of the Week—the sprightly Shirley Mac-Laine, the bubbling Beverly Sills, the intelligent (that's right) Raquel Welch, the sinister Madame Nhu, the beauteous Faye Dunaway, the enchanting Liv Ullmann, the tough Golda Meir, just to name some of the female contingent.

Mostly, we would invite who we wanted—sometimes with a nudge from our correspondents or from a press agent advancing a person or a cause. Bobby Kennedy came more than once; he arrived a couple of hours late for dinner one night, and by the time he got there the distinguished editors of *Newsweek* were so deep in their cups that nobody could remember later much of what was said. Usually, however, we were skeptical and closely questioning. Jimmy Carter was among the battalion of presidential aspirants who came to lunch in the winter and spring of 1976, but he was such a soft-spoken long shot that no one paid much attention to what he had to say. Sometimes we looked forward to a good time, and were disappointed. Hubert Humphrey, the normally ebullient Hubert, came to see us in the midst of his 1968 presidential campaign—and was so apprehensive of being misquoted that he ordered the proceedings to be taped, with a back-up stenographer doing a transcription in case the tape recorder failed. About a dozen of us sat around a big table, with a microphone at every place. "Mr. Vice-President," I said, "some of us here have mike fright. What ground rules would you like to set for this session—on the record, off the record, or not-for-attribution?"*

"What ground rules would *you* like?" asked Humphrey.

"I'd like you to talk to us *on* the record as if you were talking to us *off* the record," I said. Humphrey laughed.

Nelson Rockefeller came for lunch while he was governor, and ordered his usual Dubonnet-on-the-rocks. His press secretary, the witty Les Sloate, stage-whispered to the waiter: "Bring me a Bloody Mary, but make it look like a Dubonnet." At the time, George Christian was Lyndon Johnson's press secretary; Sloate vowed that if ever Rockefeller became president, and he was press secretary in the White House, he would change his name to "Les Jew."

Sir Seretse Khama, president of Botswana, President Mobutu Sese Seko of Zaire, and liberal Helen Suzman of South Africa all broke bread at the *Newsweek* table—as did Henry Ford II, Irving Shapiro of Du Pont, and many other presidents and chairmen of Fortune's 500 top companies. Heads of countries and heads of corporations were flattered to be invited. It was an inside joke that Pete Callaway, *Newsweek*'s publisher and the man responsible for gleaning advertising dollars from the tycoons, would invariably open each of the business lunches by announcing to the honored chief executive: "Well, I just read your annual report, and it's the finest annual report I've ever seen." Editors are not the only ones capable of buttering up people who are important to them.

---

* These terms are often confused even in politicians' minds, but to responsible journalists they have the quite specific and differentiated meanings conveyed by the words.

When the mountain wouldn't come to Mohammed, Mohammed would frequently go to the mountain. Over the years, I had sessions with three Japanese prime ministers, three British P.M.'s—the chilly Edward Heath, the old-school-tied Alec Douglas-Home, the shifty-eyed Harold Wilson (who struck me as the Richard Nixon of Britain)—and with France's suave and elegant Valéry Giscard d'Estaing. Britain's Reginald Maudling came for drinks at my house one night and confessed he hadn't the slightest idea where Vietnam was.

Once a group of us were in Australia to celebrate the start-up of a *Newsweek* printing operation Down Under—complementing our Asian plants in Tokyo and Hong Kong to speed delivery of the magazine in the South Pacific. In Canberra, Lyndon Johnson's ambassador and Texas crony Edward ("Big Ed") Clark invited us to dinner with Prime Minister Harold Holt. At the door of the embassy, a butler pinned us each with a yellow rose of Texas, and as Holt was introduced around, he eyed our group and said: "Well, this seems to be quite a *Newsweek* evening. I must take this opportunity to inform you that twice in recent months your magazine has described me in the most unfortunately inaccurate manner." Oh God, I thought, what have we done this time? "In the first instance," continued Holt, "you called me a teetotaler"—here he swept a martini from a passing tray. "Well, gentlemen, here's to you"—and the drink vanished down his throat. "In the second instance," Holt went on, "you described me as taciturn. Before the evening is over, you will have discovered how wrong you were on that score, as well!"

At various times in Germany, I called on Konrad Adenauer —"Der Alte," stiff and ancient and formal; dined with Kurt Georg Kiesinger, and interviewed Willy Brandt—a session made memorable by a notable bit of one-upmanship on the part of *Newsweek*'s correspondent Bob Elegant, recently transplanted from the Far East, who sat there ostentatiously taking notes in Chinese characters.

On a few occasions, we editors were invited to the White House—by Eisenhower, Kennedy, Johnson, Ford—but never by Nixon. A magnificent white-tie state dinner in the Kennedy years, complete with the Air Force's "strolling strings"—on the very day that John Glenn first orbited the earth—contrasted sharply with a lunch with Lyndon Johnson a few years later. At LBJ's table we were served flat, square, overdone hamburgers, as a butler passed around a ketchup bottle on a silver tray. Gerald Ford gave *Newsweek* his first interview as president, on Thanksgiving Eve, 1974, fifteen weeks after he had moved into the White House. It was snowing, and canceled trains and planes ruined that Thanksgiving for me; Ford left us with an impression of a man far more in command than his public image suggested at the time.

There were audiences with Pope John XXIII and Pope Paul VI—who advised me always to tell the truth. The session with Pope John, in 1962, was memorable for the journalistic tenacity of Bill Pepper, *Newsweek*'s Rome bureau chief. Pepper, under orders from the Vatican to ask "no journalistic questions today," had somehow become convinced that the pope would soon be coming to America, and was determined to pin the story down. "Oz," said Bill, "when the pope comes by, he's bound to talk to you—editor of *Newsweek* and all that stuff. Do me a favor and ask him when he's coming to America, will you?" I said, "Look, Bill, they know we're here together, and if I ask that kind of a question, they'll never let you back in the Vatican."

Pepper is not one to give up easily. He turned to my wife, and asked her to do the job for him—"Tell him you've got three little Catholic daughters at home." Deirdre said she was so scared she could hardly open her mouth, much less ask any questions. In fact, she was distressed because she had mislaid a package containing rosaries and religious medals, which she had planned to have blessed by the pope and distribute among Catholic friends and relatives at home. "Not to worry," said Pepper. "This stuff works like X-ray."

At last, we found ourselves sitting on a bench next to three Franciscan brothers, all in brown robes and sandals and, from their whispered conversation, quite obviously Americans. Two of them were barefoot, the third was wearing socks. Pepper turned to Franciscan No. 3, gazed at his stockinged feet, and said: "Father, how come you're out of uniform?"

That broke the ice, and within a few seconds I heard Pepper's inevitable question: "Look, Father, when the pope comes by, he's bound to talk to you three Franciscans from St. Louis. Do me a favor, will you, and ask him if he's coming to America?" "Jack Kennedy," said Franciscan No. 3, "has enough problems without *that!*"

When Pope John finally showed up, he talked to no individual. He smiled at us all beatifically and said a prayer "for the very young, the very sick, and"—motioning to himself—"the very old."

There were other memorable moments in these travels—the time in New Delhi, for example, when Kay Graham and I went to interview India's chief birth-control bureaucrat. We met him in his dingy, dusty office, and he had an array of white, wiggly intrauterine devices laid out on his dirty desk for our inspection. Had there been much progress, we asked, in persuading Indian women to use the IUD?

"Oh, yes, there has been very much progress," he chanted. "But some of the ladies complain about rejection of the device, and some complain of headaches. Of course, I do not think the headaches come from the IUD. I think they come from the in-laws." By now, India's chief birth controller was idly sucking on an IUD injector, as he contemplated the plight of the subcontinent's female masses.

On my first trip to Russia, in the winter of 1967, I was fortunate to have some letters from John Steinbeck to a few of his Soviet friends. I had come to know Steinbeck as a warm and sentimental person when I had bought a brownstone house on East Seventy-second Street from him a few years before. His letters to his Russian friends were wonders of literacy and good humor, each carefully handcrafted for the particular recipient.

To the poet Yevgeny Yevtushenko:

> My dear Siberian Pine Nut:
> Please permit me to introduce to you and to Galya our friends Mr. and Mrs. Osborn Elliott. He is a very important editor and she is very pretty, and both of them overcome these hazards by a curious empathy and entropy (which used to be called the music of the spheres).
>
> You would please me very much, Zhenya, if you would show my friends your Potemkin villages, your brutal Cossack soldiery, your harsh and bitter country- side, and, if there is any time left over, a little, little pinch of the loveliness of Russia and the warmth of your comradeship. I could wish that you might also tell them a few lies without which no foreigner feels safe. Oh! yes and pickled mushrooms and vodka still warm from the cow. . . .

To the writer Konstantin Simonov:

> May I introduce to you friends of Elaine and mine. . . . Let not the fact that he is an editor of one of our more important magazines make you think ill of him. I know that he represents the *enemy* to us as writers, but just as you and I sometimes drink rather than

write, so does he pause in his editing to let a little
alcohol soften his icy veins.

If you can find the time, please show our friends
what a Russian birch tree looks like in the moonlight
as you did for us. . . .

And to the editor of *Novy Mir*, Aleksandr Tvardovsky:

Permit me, my friend, to introduce my friend. . . .
I send him to you because he, like you, is an editor
of courage and imagination. I hope you will be able
to show him how you do the thing in Moscow.

My best greetings. I am now off to Vietnam to
slaughter little babies and old and helpless women,
as my savage nature requires. . . .

Tvardovsky we never saw; but Yevtushenko spent a day
with us, taking us to a Moscow film studio for a preview,
and to a lunch that featured endless Georgian toasts and
creamed cocks' combs, which I happily mistook for ravioli;
and the Simonovs had us to lunch one Sunday at their dacha
outside Moscow, deep in a birch forest. Over three kinds of
vodka—with mountain-ash berries, pickled onions, and
lemon peels—and a "Russian daiquiri" chilled with a fistful
of Soviet snow—we talked about Vietnam.

Most of my visits with world leaders, over the years, were
interesting as much for the atmospherics and the personalities
involved as for the actual content of what often turned out
to be rather stilted, formal conversations. It would be easy
to parody an audience with the emperor of Japan—who sat
awkwardly bouncing in his chair and wringing his hands as
he finally thought of a question to open a conversation with
Kay Graham: "Is this your first trip to Japan, Mrs. Graham?"
And in retrospect, the gentle John D. Rockefeller 3d looks
almost comical, trying to persuade King Mahendra of Nepal
to show his people a birth-control film narrated by—Donald

Duck ("But, Mr. Rockefeller, we have no cinemas in Nepal in which to show such a film"). But of such minutiae is the human comedy constructed.

· · ·

My friend Arthur Houghton, who ran Steuben Glass for years, thinks he knows how to fire a person. You simply call him in and say, "Harry, I've been watching you for some time now, and I can see you're not happy here." Oh yes, says Harry, he's very happy right where he is. "No you're not, Harry," you insist. "And I'm not the only one who's noticed it. In fact, it's practically the talk of the office." In time, says Houghton, hapless Harry is sure to agree, and leave quietly.

Maybe so. But I can't think of a more difficult or unpleasant task. I had to fire a close friend once, and did it in my library at home with another editor there to give me support. I fired a correspondent in the rooftop bar of a European hotel, as Fritz Beebe, chairman of the company, sat with us humming little tunes to himself in embarrassment. I had to fire a senior executive of *Newsweek*, and blamed some management consultants for the decision. When I first took over the editorship, I had to fire a number of longtime employees and at least one of them I thought was going to punch me in the nose. The most dramatic firing, and the easiest, was the discharge of a correspondent who, in a drunken brawl on the street, had run afoul of the constabulary of a Communist state. The State Department advised us to get him the hell out of that country as fast as possible. The firing, which took place in my office, was the civilian equivalent of a court-martial. Instead of epaulets and buttons, I stripped the man of his credit cards, and he dropped them on my desk, one by one.

The most interesting firing was my own. It was July 1975, and I was vacationing at our place in Stonington on the

Connecticut shore. A beautiful summer day; my wife, Inger, and I had taken our little Boston Whaler to the spit of sand where we swim. Disaster. Somehow the inside of the Thermos had broken, and our Bloody Marys were laced with shards of golden glass. I hopped into the Whaler and zipped back to the mainland. Judi, our Chinese amah, was jumping up and down in her black pajamas on the steps of our remodeled church. "Missy call," she said. I looked at the telephone number Judi had managed to scrawl, recognized it as *The Washington Post*'s exchange, and knew it must be Kay Graham calling from Washington.

Kay's voice was tight when I reached her. "They've done it to us again," she said. "We've got to talk." "Who's done what?" I asked. It was *Time*, with a cover story called "Can Capitalism Survive?" which Kay thought *Newsweek* should have done. "I've got to see you," she said stiffly. I had another week of vacation left, and suggested we get together after that. Then I mixed a new batch of Bloody Marys and headed back to the beach. The end, I told Inger, was at hand.

And that was fine by me. Back in 1969, after having edited the magazine for more than eight years, I had become stale and bored, and persuaded Kay and Fritz Beebe to relieve me of the weekly editing grind. Then, in 1972, I had agreed to step back in for a year or so; that year or so had stretched to three and I was bored again. From time to time, in those three years, Kay and Fritz and I had talked about my stepping down again, but we had never done anything about it.

The night before my date with Kay, I took Ed Kosner, by then my No. 2, to a Chinese restaurant for dinner. "I gather Our Lady of the Potomac is upset," I said. Whereupon Kosner revealed to me the degree of her dismay and the urgency of her desire to replace me. In her view, as related by Kosner, I had become uninterested, selfish, self-centered, not committed anymore, and a lot of other things as well, most of them true. Clearly, time for a change.

Next morning, in Washington, I said to Kay, "I guess we have a problem." I reminded her that once before, she and Fritz Beebe had kindly accommodated my desire to step down; it was certainly her prerogative, I said, to initiate my removal now, and I was more than prepared to move aside. "But to get this word from my Number Two, and not from you," I said, "is just not the way you do things. One thing I learned in the Navy is that there is such a thing as loyalty *down* as well as up." Kay was bathed in remorse. She knew she had been wrong. She apologized for having said those things to Kosner. How could she have done such a thing? It was awful, and she was sorry.

Then we talked for a while about who the next editor should be. We agreed that Kosner was the best qualified—a decision that she had perhaps already reached. A moment of silent embarrassment. And then I blurted out, good-naturedly: "Kay, why don't you go fuck yourself?" Kay said: "I would if I could." Then suddenly—and this can best be described in pulp-fiction prose—I was in her arms. We kissed warmly and a bit tearily. Breaking off the mouth-to-mouth resuscitation, which was obviously too late to work, I said: "Say, I'm beginning to enjoy this."

That's the way it happened.

I swear to God.

·X·
CITY
LIGHTS

So that was that; Katharine Graham knew it, and I knew it. But we both also knew that that couldn't be that, just like *that*, not after twenty-one years. What neither of us could anticipate, that summer day in 1975, was that within a year or so I would be gone from the *Newsweek* scene for good—and that in my next job I would be a source of the news, rather than a seeker of the news, for the first time in my life.

On Kay's side, I am sure, there was some real affection and a feeling that I had served *Newsweek* well and could continue to be useful for a while. On my part, despite what I considered to be a rather graceless *coup de grâce,* there was real affection too, and admiration for this woman who had assumed such enormous responsibilities under such difficult circumstances. *Newsweek* had long been a large part of my life. I had done just about every job there was to do at the magazine—as senior editor, managing editor, editor-in-chief, president, chairman of the board—and editor a second time around. What on earth might I do anywhere else? Teach? Write? Become an ambassador? Go on the stage? The Walter Mitty juices were running pretty strong at times, but I felt almost as ill-prepared as when I had left the Navy back in 1946.

Kay and I agreed that I would once again assume the largely ceremonial role of editor-in-chief as Ed Kosner took over as *Newsweek*'s editor (he was summarily fired less than four years later).

A strong case can be made against an editor getting involved in almost any activity other than his job as a journalist —lest he expose himself to conflicts of interest of the type I faced, and dodged, when I was a Harvard Overseer and *Newsweek* was covering the revolt at University Hall. But over the years, I had become involved in a number of extrajournalistic activities—as trustee of the New York Public Library, the American Museum of Natural History, and the Asia Society, to name a few. I found these civic activities interesting, and figured they might be of some benefit to *Newsweek*, as well.

In the end, they turned out to be useful to me. In late 1975, as I was leaving the *Newsweek* editorship, New York City was in the throes of its financial crisis. No bank would buy its bonds, the city teetered on the edge of bankruptcy; there was the scent of doom in the air. New York's senior senator, Jacob Javits, sensing that many New Yorkers wanted to help their city in its time of need, devised a scheme to give them an outlet for their energies. Bringing together an initial group of fifty business, labor, church, academic, and community leaders, Javits formed the Citizens Committee for New York City. Nobody knew what the new group might accomplish, or what its precise goals should be. But when our mutual friend Dick Clurman asked me, for Javits, if I would like to become the new committee's chairman, I said yes. After all, I suddenly had some extra time on my hands and—who knew—the Citizens Committee might ultimately lead to something outside *Newsweek*.

Beyond that, I had a special feeling for New York City, or at least that part of it, mostly Manhattan, that I knew. I had been born there, and so had my parents and all my grandparents; my father, then eighty-five, treasured a New York City Directory of 1856, in which his two grandfathers were listed. At the age of twelve, I had been mugged in Central Park; forty years later my stepdaughter Kari, also twelve, had been mugged in Carl Schurz Park. But I remained a romantic about New York; I thrived on its tempo and excitement and variety, and it had been good to me. So I went to work as chairman of the Citizens Committee.

Early on, help came from an old and friendly source. Brooke Astor—whose sale of *Newsweek* to Phil Graham had propelled me into the editorship fifteen years before—put up an initial $50,000 from the Vincent Astor Foundation. John D. Rockefeller 3d and his wife, Blanchette, came in for $35,000 more, and a number of banks, foundations, corporations, and other individuals helped put us in business.

As the committee's first task, we took on the job of recruiting volunteers to help fill personnel gaps in city agencies that had been caused by the budgetary crunch. Not long before, someone had spoken of New Yorkers as a "greedy, heartless" lot. With the help of Madison Avenue's Bill Bernbach, we put together a full-page ad for *The New York Times* inviting "10,000 greedy, heartless New Yorkers" to help their city. An army of New Yorkers responded, and we managed to place thousands of them in volunteer jobs which our executive director, Dennis Allee, caused to be made available in every major city agency.

Allee, a lawyer who is now deputy attorney general of New York State, had a sense of the vigor of New York's neighborhoods, and it was at this grass-roots vitality that he next aimed the Citizens Committee's programs.

There are, in New York, a total of some ten thousand block

associations aimed at improving the quality of life in the five boroughs. They run clean-up drives, plant trees, paint park benches, supply shopping escorts for the elderly, run after-school programs for the young; they provide block watchers and security patrols and auxiliary police; they run block parties in the streets, put sprinklers on the hydrants to cool city kids in hot weather. In short, they care. The Citizens Committee set about mobilizing this great urban force. We held conferences, printed brochures, handed out thousands of street-cleaning brooms, and gave cash awards to exemplary groups. There had never been anything quite like the committee in all the history of New York. And it worked.

The result, a year later, was that when Mayor Abe Beame was looking for someone to head up the city's economic development activities, somebody mentioned my name. The job sounded interesting—particularly since Beame was willing to elevate it to a deputy mayorship, and to double the economic development budget to $7 million. But first I had to persuade stepdaughter Molly, then nine years old. "I don't think you should take the job with the city, Oz," she said. Why not? "Well," said Molly, "I think you're climbing the ladder very nicely at *Newsweek*." I explained that I had just about run out of rungs on the *Newsweek* ladder.

My retirement agreement with *Newsweek* enabled me to serve the city without pay for a year—but should I do that, or should I take the $49,000 that went with a deputy mayorship? I asked two old political friends and got totally contradictory opinions. Jack Javits said: "If you can possibly afford to do the job without pay, do so—that way you'll be putting distance between yourself and the political process. And your credibility will be much greater both in City Hall and in the business community." John Lindsay, New York's former mayor and an old schoolmate, had a different and equally persuasive view. "Take the money," he said. "If you don't, you'll be viewed as a dilettante—you won't be taken seriously." They were probably both right. I finally decided to forgo the city salary for the pragmatic reason that if I took the $49,000, and my deal with *Newsweek* were revealed, it would look as if I were ripping off a nearly bankrupt city. Which would have been the case.

And so I started as a deputy mayor, at $1 a year.

As I moved from the press world into public office, I remembered a conversation I had had with a *Newsweek* colleague years before. My friend Jim Cannon had left the magazine to work for Nelson Rockefeller, and after Cannon had been in his new job for a few months, I asked him, from his new vantage point as a public servant, how much he figured he had actually known about any given story when he was a working journalist. "About fifteen percent," was Cannon's rather insulting reply. I wondered if this was true—and figured that fifteen percent was about all I knew about economic development, in any case.

But in my new job, I had a couple of things going for me. Because of my many years in journalism and my position at the top of a major national magazine, I had access to the business community, and a good rapport with the press. By and large, both of these advantages served me well—although there were twists and turns along the way, and I came to view the press with a somewhat less reverential eye than I had for so many years until then. My particular beef was with the local television-news programs, which in New York, as elsewhere, tend to front-load their shows with murder, rape, arson, and general mayhem—anything to get the suckers under the tent and thus improve their ratings. I couldn't help thinking of the visiting businessman from Chillicothe, returning to his hotel room at the end of a hard day, flicking on the television and looking through this lurid lens at our city's life. I did not endear myself to the local television media when I made a speech to them along these lines at a Waldorf-Astoria lunch one day. The manager of a big local station came up to me afterward and said: "Well, Oz, I still like you personally."

In general, the *Times* and the *News* treated me kindly, each of them starting me off with pleasantly complimentary editorials. But I had my problems with print journalism, too—some of them amusing. There was, for example, my transmogrification at the hands of a *Times* reporter—the diligent and, in the end, far too accurate Michael Sterne. On the day it first became known that I was in line for a city job, this masterful word mechanic described me as "slim, elegant, personable and patrician in manner." Then we met for an interview, and soon the churl was writing about a "substantial figure in a navy-blue pin-stripe suit cut along slimming lines," and finally —unslimmingest cut of all—about a person "slightly above medium height, baldish and chunky in build." It just shows that certain things shouldn't be checked too hard.

On one occasion I tangled seriously with the *Times*—over a story that demonstrated journalism's power to convert a perception, or even an anticipation, into "fact." In the spring of 1977, six months into my brief tenure as deputy mayor, a group of us economic developers decided that it would be a good idea to bring Mayor Beame to Houston to make love to the offshore oil industry, then in convention assembled, sixty-seven thousand strong. The oil industry had bet $1 billion that there was oil in the Atlantic, off the coast of New York and New Jersey, and was about to start drilling. If they found substantial amounts of oil and gas it could mean thousands of jobs for the city.

And so we put together a little film on the wonders of New York's magnificent harbor—voice-over, Liza Minnelli, belting out "New York, New York"—and we invited a few hundred oilmen to a reception at the Houston Museum of Natural Science. The money for the expedition was put up by New

York real-estate man Lewis Rudin and other businessmen, and we took a couple of dozen of the city's business and labor leaders to Texas to help make the pitch. The reception was a great success; the oilmen were flabbergasted that the mayor of New York had actually traveled all the way to Houston to show them he cared. Next day, a friend called me from New York and read the *Times* story on the event. Borrowing a famous headline from the rival *News*, the *Times* story began: "Mayor Beame to oil companies: Please come home. Oil companies to Mayor Beame: Drop dead." I was stunned. Several days before, I had alerted my friends at the *Times* to what might be a nice, upbeat story, and they had sent their Houston reporter to our reception: in fact, he had personally complimented me on how well it seemed to have gone. Then it dawned on me that the *Times* man had written his story *before* the event—before Beame's arrival in Houston, before the reception, before the Houston papers reported on this remarkable pilgrimage.

So I called up the *Times* in a rage. To Punch Sulzberger, the publisher, I said: "You ought to get your people together and tell them to give the city some kind of a break every now and then, particularly when some of us are knocking ourselves out to save it." Punch said he had seen "that funny little story —but I guess you didn't think it was so funny." To Seymour Topping, the managing editor, I said: "What the hell are you people doing? Pissing on the very city that is your bread and butter?" Topping said, apologetically: "That story got by me. All I can say is that quite another kind of piece is going to be running tomorrow." And sure enough, there, the next day, starting on Page One, was the longest retraction I have ever read in *The New York Times*. They didn't call it that, of course, but the headline said: OILMEN URGE "SECOND LOOK" AT CITY AFTER BEAME VOWS "NEW ATTITUDE." That made me feel a little better. But it also made

me think of all those people who are wronged by the press
(*Newsweek* included) who don't know the publisher or the
editor and can never hope for that kind of a retraction.

The most egregious wrong committed by the press during my
deputy mayorship was the *New York Post*'s coverage of the
blackout of 1977, and the looting that took place in scattered
parts of the city. In a screaming headline, the *Post* announced
on Page One: 24 HOURS OF TERROR; inside, a special
section was captioned: A CITY RAVAGED. Dining alone
that night at P. J. Moriarty's on Third Avenue, I scribbled a
letter to the *Post*'s Australian publisher, Rupert Murdoch, and
released it to the press the next day:

> Dear Rupert:
> So your *New York Post* has now covered New York
> City's first big crisis since you took over. Are you proud
> of what your headlines produced?
> After reading your Friday editions, my conclusion—
> as a lifelong journalist—is that the disaster may turn
> out to be yours, not the City's. . . .
> Perhaps you wouldn't have got so many people to
> buy your papers—for that one Friday—if you had been
> more responsible. But in the long run, you might
> better have helped the *Post*'s recovery—the kind of
> goal to which I am pledged for all New York busi-
> nesses—if you had given a more balanced view of
> things.
> The ostrich—not common to Australia—is usually ac-
> cused of hiding its head to avoid bad news. There also
> seems to be an ostrich (genus Australis) that refuses
> to poke its head up to recognize the good.

Murdoch was not amused; he responded with a full-column
editorial labeled OSTRICH OS FOOLS NOBODY: "While
Mayor Beame and Elliott spent last Wednesday night and
Thursday producing a spate of utterly irrelevant press conferences . . . the *Post*'s great team . . . was out on the streets.

. . . It is the responsibility of the press to report events as they occur, no matter how distasteful or how the chips fall. As a former editor, Elliott may once long ago have understood this. Now he merely shows how dangerous out-of-work editors can be when they become political flacks. . . ."

I have to grant Murdoch one point: there were indeed a number of mayoral press conferences on the sweltering day after the blackout; it was in the midst of the mayoral campaign, and Abe Beame's political advisers were determined that he should dump as much as he could on Con Edison, the much-unloved local utility. Because electric power was out in City Hall, the municipal government spent a fair amount of the day shuttling back and forth to police headquarters, a couple of blocks away, where emergency generators were providing enough juice to feed the television lights and cameras.

Just before one of these press conferences, one of Beame's pols cast an eye at the tiny frame of the dapper mayor and said: "Say, May-ah, for this one, I think ya better have the coat and tie off." Abe Beame dutifully obliged, stripping down for action. But just before he went into the news conference another aide recalled that a few members of the press had walked over from City Hall with the fully clothed mayor; surely it would look strange to them if he suddenly appeared tieless and coatless now. Back on went the mayoral tie and jacket.

Most politicians are a likable lot. But some of them can be laughable in their compulsiveness. A couple of months after I took office, on the day after Christmas 1976, I appeared on a local CBS-TV interview show. Because the day after Christmas is the most newless day in the year—especially if it is a Sunday, as was the case that year—what I had to say was front-page "news" in both the *Times* and the *News*. I said that Westway, the controversial new highway proposed for Manhattan's West Side, would trigger billions of dollars of

private investment if it were approved. Suddenly, the ferocious
Bella Abzug was on the phone, steaming. A vociferous opponent of Westway, she yelled at me for better than twenty
minutes. "I know your type," she said, without further explanation. "And I know yours," I said finally, before I hung up.

When St. Patrick's Day rolled around, I figured I might as
well have a little fun and join the line of march up Fifth
Avenue. I dashed to the starting point, and found the parade
already under way. "Where are the deputy mayors?" I asked
a cop. He said they were already a couple of blocks north, and
so I huffed and puffed my way to the head of the parade and
fell in with a line of politicians making up the third rank. I
placed myself between City Council President Paul O'Dwyer
and Manhattan Borough President Percy Sutton, figuring
that they would be among those most photographed. Just
ahead of us, making up a file of one, was City Comptroller
Jay Goldin; and ahead of him, leading the parade, was the
Mutt-and-Jeff combination of Police Commissioner Mike
Codd and Mayor Beame.

O'Dwyer was furious at Goldin for having insinuated himself into so prominent a position in the parade. In a marvelously inventive blend of New York's mixed argot, O'Dwyer
grumbled in his thickest Irish brogue: "Have ya' ever seen the
likes of such chutzpah?"

Often it was not what the press said, but what it didn't say,
that bothered me when I was deputy mayor; what so many
New Yorkers were doing for their city was simply ignored by
print and electronic media alike. One beautiful spring Saturday, for example, the Citizens Committee—which I continued
to chair—sponsored a daylong conference at Hunter College to
help community leaders learn how to make their neighborhoods better places to live. More than a thousand New Yorkers came to this conference, from all five boroughs, a wonderful

cross-section of the city—young and old, rich and poor, black, white, Oriental, Hispanic. The papers and television stations had been alerted, and follow-up calls were made. The lieutenant governor came and stayed all day. The mayor was there, and so was Senator Javits. The participants attended thirty-eight workshops on block association activities of every kind. But not one line about this conference appeared in any major newspaper the next day, nor a single picture on any television screen. An echo of the charges so often hurled at me —and rejected by me—in the past: the press reports only the bad news!

Government work was not as different from journalism as I had expected. I had spent much of my journalistic career as an administrator as well as a worker with words and pictures, and that kind of work with people is much the same no matter what your field. I also found that journalism's extraordinary variety of experiences was matched by government. In any given day, I might be immersed in the prospects for offshore oil; or the economic implications of a downtown parking ban; or the importance of the arts in promoting New York; or the latest tax actions by the state legislature; or the expansion of a kosher meat plant in the Bronx; or the need for some business education in the schools; or visiting small businesses that were ransacked and looted after the blackout; or talking with out-of-town executives thinking of moving their company to New York—or some other group threatening to move out.

I figured from the beginning that economic development— a somewhat fancy term for creating jobs—had as much to do with psychology as anything else. And so at my swearing-in at City Hall I invited Betty Comden and Adolph Green to sing a few verses from their 1944 show *On the Town*. "New York, New York," they sang—"it's a helluva town!" These two lovers of New York have never said no when asked to help their city.

My first move as deputy mayor had been to persuade Dennis

Allee to come into the Office of Economic Development as my
No. 2; then I took a look at OED's existing staff—and was
pleased by what I found. Encrusted, as I was, with thirty-one
years of journalistic cynicism, I had expected every city agency
to be staffed by political hacks—and had been told that this one,
in particular, was renowned as a political dumping ground.
But I discovered that OED, despite a recent cut of 40 percent
in personnel, still had a cadre of hardworking and highly intelligent public servants at the top: research and technical people, a few industry experts, a good speechwriter and PR man
in the person of Frank Corbin, and a towering Irishman from
the Bronx, Hank Gavan, as the agency's able chief counsel.

I also discovered that not every city employee is a paragon
of productivity and diligence. My first day on the job, my
driver—or "motor-vehicle operator," as the municipal jargon
will have it—simply refused to work after 4:30 p.m. As I was
heading for a late-afternoon appointment, some angry sentiments came floating from the front seat: "Sonofabitch-fuckin-
executive-driving-eighthours-goddamnshit-that's it!"

"You don't seem to be very happy in your work," I said.

It turned out that, because of the financial squeeze, the city
was paying no overtime to "motor vehicle operators." I told
my "M.V.O." I would see what could be done, and within a day
or two was on the phone to the city's budget director, Don
Kummerfeld.* "Why don't you have one of your guys see one
of my guys," said Kummerfeld, "and we'll see what can be
done." So one of my guys saw one of his guys, and it was arranged that my driver would get overtime. A week or so later,
I thanked Kummerfeld's guy for his help and he said okay, but
this of course couldn't be a permanent arrangement—can't set
a precedent like that. The upshot was that I was given *two*

* Later to become a top executive in Rupert Murdoch's publishing
empire.

drivers, each earning full pay but working on shifts so that neither got overtime—and together, of course, costing the city more than would *one* driver *with* overtime.

I was lucky in the timing of my appointment as deputy mayor. The dimensions of the city's economic woes were staggering: New York had lost 650,000 jobs in the previous nine years. But that meant that, by 1976, even the politicians of Gotham had come to realize that they had to pay some attention to the private sector if any of those lost jobs were ever to be reclaimed. They knew, at last, that the jobs would not come from the feds or the state or the city—and so when Allee and I and our staff at OED, and others in City Hall produced a package of legislation aimed at helping business, we found a mostly sympathetic audience among the politicians. "Jobs" was the magic byword.

Most of the big, black headlines about job losses had gone to the dreary parade of corporate giants moving their headquarters out of Manhattan—General Foods (one of the earliest to leave), General Electric, Shell, Texaco, Nabisco, Allied Chemical, American Can. Union Carbide had announced its intention to move to Connecticut. I paid a call on William Sneath, Carbide's chairman, to see if his decision might possibly be reversed. Sneath's office, high above Park Avenue, had a huge picture window with a spectacular view looking north over Central Park toward—somewhere up there —Danbury, Connecticut, the site of Carbide's prospective headquarters. "My God!" I said. "You're leaving *this* for that?" He was indeed, and nothing could change his mind.

But while the headlines had gone to the big corporate move-outs, New York's real job loss stemmed from smaller companies that were simply not able to hack it in the city. There are 190,000 business firms in New York, and 90 percent of them employ twenty people or less. All you have to do is walk along any avenue or side street—past the butcher shops and liquor stores and restaurants and grocery stores and hairdressers and discos and pizza parlors and shoe-repair shops and boutiques —to see that the real economic base of the city lies in small business.

Many of these small businesses were plagued by high costs, particularly the high cost of taxes and of energy. We were able to cut some taxes, but we weren't too successful when it came to energy, so essential an ingredient in such industries as printing and plastics. We had endless sessions with Consolidated Edison to see if the "load" couldn't be spread more evenly throughout the day, to ease the pressure on costs, but to little avail. The high costs of labor were another burden— and some unions, particularly in the construction trades, voluntarily cut their hourly-wage rates. Bureaucratic regulation and red tape also contributed to the woes of small business; we tried to cut them both. We set up the Business Action Center, with a "hot line" for small businesses to call in their complaints and get advice. Were the police preventing a metal shop's trucks from parking near its place of business? Was the water department slow in restoring essential service after a pipe break? Companies could call on the hot line, and we would call the city agency concerned—and usually we got fast results. After all, a deputy mayor is acting for the mayor.

Businesses both small and large were demoralized by the seeming neglect and even hostility on the part of government officials to their problems. So I toured all five boroughs, visited bakeries and handbag makers and stationery suppliers, made scores of speeches before local business groups—all to show that the city *cared*.

One of our top-priority schemes was to phase out the state's stock-transfer tax, a particular burden on New York City, where most of the stock-market action takes place. One day a group of us gathered in Abe Beame's office to tell him how important it was for the stock-transfer tax to be removed. I was to open the session with some verbal organ-music about improving the general business climate, about the threatened departure of the American Stock Exchange to New Jersey or Connecticut, about the potential loss of thousands more jobs. Then Sandy Burton, the financial deputy mayor, was to give technical details on the phaseout, and Don Kummerfeld was to explain how the loss of revenues—a whopping $250 million a year—might be recovered. All this was to be played out against approving clucking noises from John Zuccotti, the first deputy mayor, sitting in a corner of Beame's office.

At the end of my disquisition I noticed that a bird, a rather bedraggled starling, was perched *inside* the mayor's window. "Mr. Mayor," I said, "there seems to be a bird in your office." The mayor reached for a phone and requested that the bird be removed. Deputy Mayor Burton, an ample man, then proceeded with his analysis. The bird flew from the window to the top of the door, and glared ravenlike upon us. Then the poor creature—unnoticed by the mayor—fluttered down beneath Beame's table-desk and made a stately progress, on foot, across the mayor's shoes. We all laughed—at least all of us deputy mayors.

"What're you laughin' at?" asked Beame. And when we explained what had just happened under his desk, the mayor laughed, too. "There's something about me and birds," he said in his Brooklyn accent, which doesn't quite pronounce birds "boids." "Last fall I was out campaigning in Brooklyn with Mondale, and there was a whole swarm of birds overhead. Suddenly one of them, you know, *did* something—and it landed right on my head."

A pause for effect. "For the rich," said the mayor in his best Borscht-circuit delivery, "they sing!"

We got back to the matter of the stock-transfer tax. But what will the little guy think? asked the mayor. "You know, to the little guy all these Wall Street people are just a bunch of speculators."

"What will the little guy think," I asked, "if suddenly the American Stock Exchange really does move out of New York, and thousands of Wall Street jobs go with it?"

Within months, with the mayor's full support, the state legislature had voted to phase out the stock-transfer tax—and the American Stock Exchange subsequently decided to stay in New York.

Because of the changed political climate, we economic developers had some other victories. We removed a tax on capital equipment, we cut a tax on commercial rents, we reduced the city's corporate-income tax and "capped" the real-estate tax for a five-year period. One of the most effective devices, just coming into being as I arrived on the scene, was a system of tax incentives for businesses that were expanding by new construction or renovation. Under this program, a number of new hotels and office buildings, worth hundreds of millions of dollars—and creating thousands of new jobs—were launched.

But the key, in my view, remained essentially psychological —and here again I was the beneficiary of some new attitudes among New Yorkers. Because of the financial crisis, the city's business community—along with the rest of the private sector— began to think that if the city went under, chances were that they would, too. And so, suddenly, there was the surprising spectacle of banker David Rockefeller and labor leader Harry van Arsdale putting together something called the Business-Labor Working Group to study the problems of the city's major industries and report on how their troubles might be eased (many of the recommendations were enacted into law). And suddenly you had banker Walter Wriston gathering with

Victor Gotbaum, Jack Bigel, and other representatives of the city's municipal labor unions in a similar effort to find common ground.

Capitalizing on this new sense of community, we formed the Corporate Retention Committee, composed of a dozen or more chief executives and aimed at bringing peer pressure on any of their corporate cohorts who might be thinking of moving their firms out of the city. One such company was Mobil Oil. The word had been around for some time that Mobil might move its whole operation out of New York, taking some three thousand jobs with it. In my first few weeks in office, I went to see Mobil's chairman, Rawleigh Warner, and heard him unload a litany on why it would be a good idea to move —bad commutation, lousy schools, whores and crime and filth around Mobil's Forty-second Street headquarters, difficulty in attracting middle management from the hinterlands to Manhattan, and so on and so forth. It seemed like a lost cause.

When we got the Corporate Retention Committee started, I asked David Rockefeller and Edmund Pratt, chairman of Pfizer, to join me in a second call on Mobil's Warner. I rode uptown with Rockefeller. He is a busy man; he asked to be reminded of what, precisely, our mission was. I told him that we were going to try to persuade Warner to keep all those Mobil jobs in New York.

"Oh yes," said Rockefeller. "Now, it seems to me that my family has had a connection with that company."

Quite right, I said, it used to be Socony Mobil—you know, Standard Oil of New York, and . . .

"Of course!" said David. "My father and grandfather used to have offices in that company!"

By the time we arrived in Warner's office, Rockefeller was booted and spurred and ready to go. "Rawleigh," he started, "it occurred to me on the way uptown that my family has had a longtime connection with Mobil. Now, it seems to me, in the interests of New York City . . ."

Warner unloaded his litany on the commutation, the schools, the whores, the crime, the grime. Even after Pratt had outlined how his own company, Pfizer, had carefully studied the possibility of moving out, and found it made no economic sense whatsoever, Warner seemed untouched. We left feeling defeated. But a few months later, Mobil announced that it not only was staying in New York, it had bought its Forty-second Street building to boot. I called Warner to find out why. What had happened to that long list of complaints? Well, he said a trifle apologetically, "we got a good deal on the building." Sometimes, it seems, what the Greeks called "love of city" can be an affair of the pocketbook.

The new spirit of civic involvement brought a number of good people from the private sector to the city's aid. There was, of course, investment banker Felix Rohatyn, whom I had known since he arrived in New York twenty-five years before, and who became the architect of New York's financial salvation. There was Richard Shinn, president of Metropolitan Life, who supervised important management studies of the city's government. There was Don Kummerfeld, another cool and able investment banker who later succeeded John Zuccotti as first deputy mayor—Zuccotti himself being a brilliant recruit from the law. There was Professor Ray Horton of Columbia University, who shepherded through a number of important studies on the city's economy. And there was Richard Ravitch, a builder who saved the state's Urban Development Corporation after it defaulted on $130 million of debt and who orchestrated New York City's bid to be host for the summer Olympic Games of 1984.

This effort, in which I played a tiny role, was a truly Olympian undertaking. While it was ultimately unsuccessful, the fact that New York, in its time of woe, was even willing to enter the fray provided the kind of upbeat symbol that I believed essential for economic development. It also afforded me a view of a couple of elected officials at their best—and worst. The city had invited members of the Olympic site-selection committee to visit the city over a beautiful August weekend in 1977. We laid on buses and helicopters and boats and even a special Long Island Rail Road train to show them the facilities that New York had to offer, for every sport from archery and swimming and track (Shea Stadium would have to be enlarged) to wrestling and fencing and crew. A lot of us gave up a nice weekend in the country to play hosts, and a highlight of the weekend was to be a Saturday-night dinner given by Governor Hugh Carey at Windows on the World, atop the World Trade Center. Midway through our Saturday tour, word came that Carey would not be able to attend the dinner. But Mayor Beame did—and this on the very day when the headlines were blackest with SEC charges against Beame for alleged irregularities in his management of the city's finances. Abe Beame "worked the room," telling little jokes as he went; he had his dinner, made a gracious little speech, and left. Carey, who had mounted the whole Olympic campaign, never showed.

A few weeks later, when we went to Colorado Springs to make the final pitch for New York before the entire Olympic site-selection committee, Hugh Carey redeemed himself. Using just a few scribbled notes, he delivered a stirring and compelling speech. "The governor persuaded me," said one committee member as he changed his vote. But New York lost to Los Angeles in the end. Given the difficulties and the strain that would have been placed on the city, most of us decided that it was perhaps just as well we lost—although we were glad we had made the run.

In almost every initiative we took to encourage development, we aimed at including the private sector as a partner.

One example was an imaginative program launched by Bankers Trust to train its executives as ambassadors for the city—a program that was adapted by such other companies as American Express, Philip Morris, Hilton Hotels, and Merrill Lynch. "Pretty soon," I said in one speech, "we're going to have thousands of New Yorkers around the world boring people stiff about what a great place this is to live and work." Not long thereafter, "I Love New York" became a nationally known slogan.

To my surprise, I discovered that New York—the world capital of communications—had never had a program to sell itself as a place to do business. We set up the Business Marketing Corporation to promote and advertise the city, named scores of business, labor, and cultural leaders to its board of directors, and persuaded the city to put up $1.5 million for the initial effort.*

What were we able to accomplish in those fourteen months? When a city has fallen as far and as fast as New York had, you can't expect any miracles. But I think we had some successes. I think we educated some politicians about economic realities, and restored some measure of confidence within the business community, and nurtured the rebirth of a vibrant civic spirit in the Big Apple. Recently there have been signs that the city's overall employment picture has improved. In 1978, after all those years of devastating losses, New York actually gained some fifty thousand jobs.

Toward the end of my tenure, I wrote an article for *The New York Times Magazine,* much of which appears in this

---

* I announced formation of the marketing company at a luncheon for businessmen in *Newsweek*'s executive dining room—an affair somewhat marred by a remark by Citicorp's chairman Walter Wriston, widely quoted in the press. "You can't sell a bad product with good PR," said Wriston. Sometimes our tycoons can be, as the British say, too clever by half.

chapter. I was pleased by the response to the article, especially by a letter that came from a Union Carbide employee who had been trying to decide whether or not to move with her company to Danbury. "I very much needed to know," she wrote, "that there are others who think it is worth the effort to remain in New York, and I will reread your article periodically as I prepare my résumés and start job-hunting here."

I had not been able to persuade Carbide to stay, but at least I got to one of its employees.

•XI•
THEY CALL
ME DEAN

Another decade passes, the 1970s end, the high ideals and superheated passions and hateful corruptions of recent years seem of another era. Outside my window at Columbia University's Graduate School of Journalism, the grass is green and the throwing of Frisbees has evolved into a fine art. They call me Dean.

When I left *Newsweek* to join the city government in 1976, there was a big, teary bash. I have to confess that I was pleased to see all those people looking so sad; I felt like Tom Sawyer attending his own funeral. *Newsweek*'s art director, Fred Lowry, gave me a lovely watercolor of our summer place, our remodeled church, which he had painted as a surprise. The cover director, Bob Engle, drew a cartoon of me as Hercules, carrying New York City on my shoulders, with a caption that asked: CAN THE BIG O SAVE THE BIG APPLE? The women of *Newsweek*, who had fought so strenuously for their rights, gave me a suitably sexist scrapbook chronicling their victory. The men and women responsible for laying out the magazine and transmitting eighty thousand words a week to the printing plants dummied up a Periscope page with a lead item titled OZ, WE THANK YOU FOR 21 YEARS.

A lot of nice letters came in—including one from Arnaud de Borchgrave: "You're the best friend I ever had at *Newsweek* —or anywhere in the world for that matter. . . . It has been a very long—and at times very hard—trail but you made it all worthwhile. . . ."

Kay Graham delivered a cozy speech, which she asked me to help her write; it did me no injustice at all. And in that week's issue of *Newsweek* she made a farewell statement which—I swear—I *didn't* help her write: "Oz Elliott is one of the major journalistic figures of this period. He established excellence at the magazine and made *Newsweek* matter. His imprint will endure."

Now, at Columbia, there is the opportunity to leave a mark on a new generation of journalists. We have learned a lot, of late, about our recent past—mostly that things are often not what they appear to be. We now have reason to suspect that the assassination in Dallas that November day in 1963 was not the work of one crazed man, acting alone. We know now that America's central dilemma of race has yet to be resolved— though we seldom confront that dreary fact anymore. We know now that our nation's adventure in Southeast Asia was misconceived, misrepresented, and misread until far too late. We know now how infinitely corruptible American institutions can be—yet how essentially strong they are.

As our information explodes, and our knowledge inches ahead, the craft of journalism becomes ever more demanding. In this age of high technology it is important to know how many millirems of radioactivity a person can be safely exposed to—and how many black families can move into a neighborhood before the whites move out. What is an acceptable number of nuclear warheads—and what a desirable number of women in the executive suite? Where will our energy come from—and where is our national spirit going? Is war avoidable? Will Johnny ever learn how to read?

And what is the function of a School of Journalism? My associate at Columbia, Fred Yu, likes to say: "We don't teach journalism; we teach journalists." I think that is a pretty good distinction. I hope we teach them how to think analytically, how to judge fairly, how to approach the world with compassion and a healthy respect for its complexities. That is why, in my first communication to the Journalism School's Class of 1980, I enumerated some of the qualities that should be found in any journalist of the late twentieth century:

—An open mind, a willingness to learn, and the knowledge that the truth is not always what it seems.

—A belief in the dignity of man, and a compassion for those upon whom the world too often heaps indignities.

—A high regard for the riches of the English language, and a dedication to its proper use.

—An appreciation for the conflicts and complexities of modern life, and an understanding that they often cannot be reconciled.

—An awareness that even the best-motivated persons make mistakes, and a willingness—too seldom found among journalists—to admit your own.

—A capacity for hard work and long, irregular hours.

—An abiding concern for justice.

—A commitment to the truth.

—A sense of humor.

I begin my new job at a time when the press is in conflict as never before—with other American institutions, with the American people, even with itself. Recent court decisions seem to be going against the Fourth Estate, which is to say against those First Amendment rights that belong to all the people. The press has provided protection under the Constitution—

but that protection is really for the people. They have the right to know what is going on in their neighborhoods, in their towns, and in their country. It is their right to know which forces are causing what changes to take place in their lives, and it is the duty of the press to provide that information as best it can. In the present atmosphere of challenge and suspicion, I worry about journalism's ability to perform that duty.

The press served the people reasonably well in covering the wonderful and horrible events of recent years, and I was privileged to run a magazine that played a significant role in that coverage. I learned a lot about what people yearn for—people of all races and both sexes, rich and poor alike. I learned how people can fail, in places high and low—and how they can gloriously succeed. I learned how madness can lead a person to take his own life—or someone else's. And I learned, in a brief stint of public life, something of the imperfections of journalism.

Now I am in a position to pass some of this along. I am glad of that. And I rejoice at the prospect of starting to learn all over again.

INDEX

New York City (*cont.*)
bid to host, 235–36; stock-transfer tax and, 231–33; television-news coverage of, 222–23
New York *Daily News,* 223
New York *Herald Tribune,* 36
New York Journal of Commerce, 178–80
New York Post, The, 225–26
New York Times, The, 156; offshore oil industry story and, 223–25; Pentagon Papers and, 160, 161
New York Times Magazine, The, 237–38
Nhu, Madame, 208
Nieman Fellowship, 119
Nixon, Richard M., 15; Agnew and, 155–57; Cambodian invasion and, 97–99; "Checkers" speech of, 153–73; Pentagon Papers and, 159–61; Watergate scandals and, 163–65, 168–73
Nixon, Tricia, 170, 171
Nolting, Frederick, 90
Norman, Lloyd, 114*n*
North Vietnam, bombing of, 91–92
Norton, Eleanor Holmes, 147
Novak, Robert, 109

O'Dwyer, Paul, 227
Office of Economic Development (OED), 229–30
O'Hara, John, 31

Olympic Games of 1984, New York City's bid to host, 235–36
O'Neil, Paul, 112*n*, 184, 187
"Operation Waikiki," 94
Osborn, Andrew, 87
Osborn, Josefa Neilson, 140–142
Oswald, Lee Harvey, 40–41

Paladino, Ralph, 43
Paradise, Charlie, 4–5
Parker, Maynard, 101–102, 114*n*
Parrish, Maxfield, 34
Paul VI, Pope, 109–10, 211
Peckham, Content, 142
Peer, Elizabeth (Liz), 143, 151
Pelletier, Joan, 99
Pentagon Papers, 159–62, 165
Pepper, Bill, 211, 212
Permissiveness, 58–59
Perry, Mert, 94, 104–106, 123–24
Pleiku, raid on American barracks at (1965), 91
Pratt, Edmund, 234
Proffitt, Nicholas, 103, 114*n*
Progressive, The, 162*n*
Purtell, Joe, 32, 185–87
Pusey, Nathan M., 122–29, 131

Rabb, Harriet, 150
Racquet & Tennis Club, 37
Ravitch, Richard, 235
Researchers, 142, 150, 151
Restaurants, 33–34, 36–37